D0935933

Variation and Change
in Language

Variation and Change in Language

Essays by William Bright

**Selected and Introduced
by Anwar S. Dil**

Stanford University Press, Stanford, California   1976

Language Science and National Development

A Series Sponsored by the
Linguistic Research Group of Pakistan

General Editor: Anwar S. Dil

Stanford University Press
Stanford, California
© 1976 by William Bright
Printed in the United States of America
ISBN 0-8047-0926-2
LC 76-23370

Contents

Acknowledgments   vii

Introduction by Anwar S. Dil   xi

I. ETHNOLINGUISTICS AND SOCIOLINGUISTICS

   1.   Language and Culture (1968)   1

   2.   Toward a Cultural Grammar (1970)   12

   3.   The Dimensions of Sociolinguistics (1966)   24

   4.   Social Dialect and Language History (1960)   32

II. SOUTH ASIA

   5.   Linguistic Change in Some Indian Caste
       Dialects (1960)   39

   6.   Sociolinguistic Variation and Language
       Change (1964)   47

   7.   Language, Social Stratification, and
       Cognitive Orientation (1966)   57

   8.   Phonological Rules in Literary and
       Colloquial Kannada (1970)   65

III. NORTH AMERICA

   9.   Semantic Structures in Northwestern California
       and the Sapir-Whorf Hypothesis (1965)   74

10.   Reduction Rules in Fox Kinship (1966)   89

11.   Linguistic Innovations in Karok (1952)   98

12.   Spanish Words in Patwin (1959)   116

13.   Animals of Acculturation in the California
      Indian Languages (1960)   121

14.   The Linguistic History of the Cupeño (1967)   163

15.   Archaeology and Linguistics in Prehistoric
      Southern California (1969)   189

16.   On Linguistic Unrelatedness (1970)   206

17.   North American Indian Language Contact (1973)   210

18.   Areal Features in North American Indian
      Languages (1976)   228

      Author's Postscript (1976)   269

      Bibliography of William Bright's Works   275

Acknowledgments

The Linguistic Research Group of Pakistan (LRGP) and the General Editor of the Language Science and National Development Series are deeply grateful to Dr. William Bright, Associate Member of the Group, for giving us the privilege of presenting his selected writings as the tenth volume in our series established in 1970 to commemorate the International Education Year.

We are indebted to the editors and publishers of the following publications. The ready permission on the part of the holders of the copyrights, acknowledged in each case, is a proof of the existing international cooperation and goodwill that gives hope for better collaboration among scholars of all nations for international exchange of knowledge.

Language and Culture. International Encyclopedia of the Social Sciences, ed. by David L. Sills (New York: The Macmillan Company & The Free Press, 1968), Vol. 9, pp. 18-22, with permission of Macmillan Publishing Co., Inc. © 1968 by Crowell Collier and Macmillan, Inc.

Toward a Cultural Grammar. Indian Linguistics, Journal of the Linguistic Society of India 29. 20-29 (1970), with permission of the publisher.

The Dimensions of Sociolinguistics. Sociolinguistics, ed. by William Bright (The Hague: Mouton & Co., 1966), pp. 11-15, with permission of the publisher. © 1966 Mouton, The Hague.

Social Dialect and Language History. Current Anthropology 1: 5-6. 424-425 (1960), with permission of The University of Chicago Press.

The Linguistic History of the Cupeño; with Jane Hill. Studies in Southwestern Ethnolinguistics, ed. by Dell Hymes (The Hague: Mouton & Co. , 1967), pp. 351-371, with permission of the publisher. © 1967 Mouton, The Hague.

Archaeology and Linguistics in Prehistoric Southern California; with Marcia Bright. University of Hawaii Working Papers in Linguistics 1:10. 1-26 (1969). Revised by the author for this volume.

On Linguistic Unrelatedness. International Journal of American Linguistics, IJAL/ Native American Text Series 36:4. 288-290 (1970), with permission of The University of Chicago Press.

North American Indian Language Contact. Current Trends in Linguistics, ed. by Thomas A. Sebeok (The Hague: Mouton & Co. , 1973), Vol. 10, North America, pp. 713-726, with permission of the publisher. © 1973 Mouton, The Hague.

Dr. Afia Dil, Lecturer in Linguistics, United States International University, San Diego, and Dr. Nasim Dil, Assistant Professor, Department of Special Education, University of Texas at Austin deserve our gratitude for help in many ways.

Typing of the camera-ready manuscript has been done by Jean McCrady of USIU and Marilyn Cape of San Diego. Jerrold C. Kulm of USIU and Kamran Dil of the Black Mountain Middle School assisted the Editor in library research and several matters of detail. They all deserve a word of appreciation for a job well done.

This volume is dedicated to Susannah Bright,
the author's daughter, with love.

EDITOR'S NOTE

These essays have been reprinted from the originals with only minor changes made in the interest of uniformity of style and appearance. A few changes in wording have been made in consultation with the author. In some cases bibliographical entries and notes have been updated. Footnotes marked by asterisks have been added by the Editor.

Introduction

William Oliver Bright was born in Oxnard, California, on August 13, 1928. He grew up in surroundings where he developed interest in Spanish and native American languages and cultures. He entered the University of California, Berkeley, as a pre-medical student, but soon his interest in linguistics led him to Professors Murray B. Emeneau and Mary R. Haas, who encouraged him to study the languages of California's American Indians. After taking his bachelor's degree in 1949, he began doing fieldwork on the Karok language as a pilot project for the proposed Survey of California Indian Languages. With an interruption for army service during 1952-54, he continued his work on Karok until 1955, when he earned his Ph.D.

Bright spent the next two years in India with a number of American linguists, among them C.A. Ferguson and J. J. Gumperz, training Indian linguists and developing a linguistic research program at the Deccan College, Poona. On his return to the United States he spent a year teaching Hindi and Urdu at the Foreign Service Institute in Washington, D.C., and another year teaching English as a second language at the University of California, Berkeley. In 1959, Professor Harry Hoijer invited him to teach linguistics in the department of anthropology at the University of California, Los Angeles, where he has held a joint appointment as Professor of Linguistics and Anthropology since 1966.

Bright has taught as visiting professor at the universities of Chicago, Colorado, Indiana, and Hawaii. He spent part of 1967 in India as a linguistic consultant to the Central Institute of English at Hyderabad and as a visiting scholar at the University of Delhi. In 1963 he was

invited to serve as editor of abstracts and translations for the International Journal of American Linguistics, and since then he has continued to work for the journal in various capacities. He has served on
the editorial boards of the Handbook of Latin American Studies,
Romance Philology, The Indian Historian, and Language in Society, and
is currently a member of the editorial committee of the Malki Museum
in Banning, California. His most distinguished assignment came in
1966, when the Linguistic Society of America appointed him chairman
of its committee on publications and editor of Language. He has held
this position with notable perspicacity.

In the early 1950's, Bright published a series of interesting
articles based on his field studies of that time, starting with "Linguistic Innovations in Karok" (1952) and ending with The Karok Language,
published in 1957 as the inaugural monograph of the Survey of California Indian Languages. At the time, Karok was spoken by only about
one hundred persons living along the Klamath River in northwestern
California; today there are only about a dozen Karok speakers left.
Soon after the volume was published, Dell Hymes hailed it in American
Anthropologist as providing indispensable and irreplaceable material
for any theory of Amerindian linguistic relationships. Ten years later,
Eric Hamp saluted the book in IJAL as "a mine of suggestive information in a difficult and many-faceted field" and a model for other students of language.

Bright's fieldwork in South India resulted in An Outline of
Colloquial Kannada (1958), sponsored by the Linguistic Society of India
as the first volume in its Monograph Series. The book is a concise and
pioneering structural description of the spoken form of an important
Dravidian language, based on his collection of the actual everyday
speech of educated urban speakers of Kannada. Bright followed it with
a series of important articles on caste dialects, sociolinguistic development and language change, and linguistic aspects of cognitive orientation.

His next monograph, Animals of Acculturation in the Californian Indian Languages (1960), was his first bold attempt at an areal
survey of the historical process of linguistic and cultural contact
through a study of the loanwords for domesticated animals introduced

by the Ibero- and Anglo-Americans in a number of languages in California. By carefully arranging his extensive data according to their
etymologies and the languages in north-to-south order, and by sorting
the process of linguistic contact from the American Indian side along
scales of primary and secondary accommodation, he was able to demonstrate the important role played by the nature and quality of culture
contact in linguistic borrowing. His more recent researches have
centered around the use of linguistic data in reconstructing the socio-
cultural past of the American Indian people. "Areal Features in North
American Indian Languages," which appears for the first time in the
present volume, reports his progress so far in this field.

In 1964, Bright convened a conference whose proceedings,
entitled Sociolinguistics and published in 1966 under his editorship,
have become standard reference material. In his introductory essay,
"The Dimensions of Sociolinguistics," he proposed that the main task
of the sociolinguist is to explore the systematic covariance of linguistic
structure and social structure and their causal relationship in one direction or the other. In particular, Bright has focused his attention on
variation and change in languages in the context of intercultural contact.
To this topic he brings not only a linguist's insight into classical and
modern languages with rich written traditions and an impressive knowledge of the languages of preliterate peoples, but an anthropologist's
involvement with the cultural history and prehistory of the native American people whose heritage is threatened with extinction.

To a superficial viewer, Bright's data-oriented approach may
appear unrewarding. In fact, however, most of his articles report
the results of carefully designed experiments aimed at testing precisely formulated hypotheses, and a number of them effectively validate,
refute, or refine basic theoretical positions. He has demonstrated,
for example, the important role of areal diffusion in the cultural grammar and history of a people, and the need for studying the history of
the interaction of language and culture. Some of his findings —notably
from South India that there is no correlation between the amount of linguistic change manifested in a dialect and the social status of a people
who speak it, and from North America that the diffusion of linguistic
phenomena requires contact under favorable sociocultural conditions —

offer interesting possibilities for the formulation of more enlightened
cultural policies. An outstanding contribution to the humanistic tradition in social sciences, Dr. William Bright's work deserves the interest of thoughtful readers throughout the world.

Anwar S. Dil

United States International University
San Diego, California
August 12, 1976

**Variation and Change
in Language**

Part I. Ethnolinguistics and Sociolinguistics

1 | Language and Culture

The key role of language in all human activities has made it perhaps inevitable that the field of linguistics should represent a mingling of several streams of interest. Modern linguistics has arisen from the philological tradition, concerned basically with the classical and modern written languages, and from the anthropological tradition, which has been concerned largely with preliterate peoples. The anthropologist has long recognized the importance of language, not only as a tool for more effective field work, but as a critical element of the cultural fabric which he studies. Thus we sometimes refer to "anthropological linguistics", which may be defined as the study of previously unknown speech varieties in the context of their cultures; the term contrasts the anthropological approach to language with philological, psychological, or philosophical approaches. Alternatively, we may wish to speak of "linguistic anthropology", focusing attention on language as one element of human culture; the term is analogous to "social anthropology", "economic anthropology", and the like. The older term "ethnolinguistics" may well be used to refer to the same area of interest.

All writers in this field have struggled with the expressions "language and culture" versus "language in culture", both of which are in common use as titles for university courses, scholarly symposia, etc. "Language and culture" seems to imply a dichotomy, which we must then reject in the light of our position that language is part of culture. But if we speak of "language in culture", we then lack a separate name for all the other cultural areas whose relationship to language we wish to study. Perhaps the best solution is to give formal recognition to what has most often been done in practice and to use the word "culture" in two ways, on two different levels of

a semantic hierarchy. Distinguishing these meanings by subscript
numerals, culture$_1$, on the higher level of generality, constitutes
learned patterns of human habitual behavior. Language is included
along with everything else that contrasts with instinctive behavior.
Culture$_2$, on a more specific level, is that part of "culture$_1$" which
is not verbal communication; in this sense, "culture" contrasts with
"language". In most cases, the context of discussion will make it
clear whether we are referring to "culture$_1$" or "culture$_2$", just as
context normally eliminates confusion between "man$_1$" (opposed to
"animal") and "man$_2$" (opposed to "woman").

Taking the view that language is part of culture, linguistic
anthropologists have been concerned with these basic questions: In
what respects does language fit into the general conception of cultural
systems, and in what ways is it distinguished from other components?
What similarities are there between the internal structures of language and of other branches of culture? What role does language
play in the over-all functioning of culture? In what way do language
and culture reflect each other's structure at a given point in time or
influence each other over the span of history? What techniques may
we use to infer linguistic from nonlinguistic behavior, or vice versa,
either in terms of predicting the future or of reconstructing the past?
At this moment, most of these questions still lack definitive answers;
the rapid growth of ethnolinguistics, however, suggests that the near
future will bring, if not answers to all questions, at least a more unified framework for discussion.

The cultural nature of language. Language is assured a position as a branch of culture by its distinctively patterned nature, by
its restriction to the human species, and above all because languages
are learned, not transmitted genetically. In spite of the fact that
race and language frequently have a historical connection — so that
many people who share ancestors also share a common language —
such connections are in no way necessary. The nongenetic transmission of languages is vividly demonstrated by the linguistic "melting
pot" of the United States, in which people of the most diverse racial
backgrounds share common standards of English usage. However,
the fact that individual languages are transmitted culturally, not genetically, does not rule out the possibility that mankind has certain
unique inborn capacities for linguistic behavior. For some purposes,

we may distinguish between <u>language</u>, an inherited set of capabilities, and <u>languages</u>, particular structures which are built on those capabilities by culture.

<u>The distinctiveness of language</u>. Language obviously stands apart from other communication systems used by humans or animals because of the magnitude of its resources. It is especially impressive to consider that every normal child, by the age of four or five, is capable of using the language of his community to produce a literally infinite number of meaningful utterances. We are far from understanding all of the characteristics of language or of the human nervous system which make this possible. Two things, however, are clearly important — man's ability to invent <u>symbols</u> and the <u>duality of patterning</u> in linguistic structure.

If we understand a <u>sign</u> to be anything from which the existence of something else may be inferred, then we may define a symbol as a special kind of sign — one with arbitrary, conventionally assigned meaning. Thus, black clouds are a sign of rain, the relationship being intrinsic; but a particular weather flag, as a conventional sign of rain, is a symbol. By the same token, the word "rain" is a symbol; our use of this particular word is conventional and subject to change. Other animals may learn to respond to many arbitrary signals, including words of human language, but it is uniquely human to have the ability to assign arbitrary meaning to signs, i.e., to <u>invent</u> symbols.

But language goes beyond other symbolic systems, such as those of gestures, in one very specific feature — the duality of patterning. The meaningful symbols of language — such as words and meaningful parts of words, called <u>morphemes</u> — are not indivisible, like a flag or a gesture, but are themselves built up of smaller units. These smaller units are the <u>phonemes</u> or sound units of spoken language, and they are meaningless in themselves. Every language uses a small number of these meaningless units — usually less than fifty — to build up a huge number of meaningful units. It is this two-level structuring which gives language a degree of efficiency that is qualitatively superior to, not merely quantitatively different from, other communication systems.

Similarities between language and culture. The identification of such building blocks of language as the phoneme and the morpheme has given linguistics great prestige among the branches of anthropology; it is sometimes said that linguists are the only social
scientists to have identified the basic units of their subject matter.
The method used in this process of identification is one which moves
from the level of observation to the level of structure. First, raw
data are classified in terms of a universal taxonomic grid; in studying
sound systems, this is the phonetic classification. Then the investigator finds that some phonetic differences, in particular languages,
are not associated with contrastive meaning; e.g., the meaning of
the Spanish día ("day") is the same whether the initial d is pronounced
as an occlusive (completely blocking the flow of air with the tongue
and then releasing it), or as a fricative (letting air issue continuously
between the tongue and the teeth). In every language, however, the
linguist also finds that some phonetic differences are correlated with
differences of meaning; e.g., the difference between occlusive and
fricative, although nonsignificant in Spanish, is contrastive in English,
serving to distinguish "day" from "they". The result of such observations is the replacement of phonetic classifications by phonemic
classifications, unique for each language. The phoneme is defined
simultaneously by the range of noncontrastive sound differences which
it subsumes and by the contrasts which it displays with the other phonemes of the system.

This method of qualitative contrast, first applied in phonological study, has been successfully extended to the identification of morphemes, i.e., grammatical units; and many scholars have speculated
about their applicability to other areas of culture. The terms etic and
emic have been coined (after "phonetic" and "phonemic") to refer to
the observational and structural levels, respectively, which might be
distinguished in such areas as kinship, religion, music, art, and folklore. Such studies are still in their infancy, but they constitute one
of the most interesting frontiers of anthropology, based as they are
on the assumption that each branch of culture, or indeed culture as
a whole, is, like language, an internally cohesive system.

The role of language in culture. Language is not merely one
of several aspects of culture: it is, at the very least, prima inter
pares, in that it makes possible the development, the elaboration,

the transmission, and (particularly in its written form) the accumulation of culture as a whole. One can imagine handicrafts being taught by one generation to the next without the use of language; but social, legal, religious, political, or economic institutions are another matter. It is hard to imagine that a community of deaf-mutes (if they were deprived of such speech surrogates as writing) could carry on human social life.

But how, exactly, does language (or any other symbolic system) relate to experience? It is commonly said that symbols, like signs in general, "stand for" or "mean" something else. The definition of meaning itself clearly cannot be taken for granted. A variety of theoretical models for the concept of meaning, each one valuable for its own ends, has been proposed by philosophers, psychologists, and linguists of various persuasions. The model presented below is not intended to compete with others in defining the "real" nature of meaning, but it may be useful as a framework for ethnolinguistic discussion.

Structural linguists have customarily been extremely cautious in semantic matters, sometimes attempting to exclude them from linguistics altogether. Until very recently, a strictly behaviorist conception of meaning was much in vogue:

> We have defined the meaning of a linguistic form
> as the situation in which the speaker utters it and the
> response which it calls forth in the hearer... The sit-
> uations which prompt people to utter speech include
> every object and happening in their universe. In or-
> der to give a scientifically accurate definition of mean-
> ing for every form of a language, we should have to
> have a scientifically accurate knowledge of everything
> in the speaker's world... We can define the names of
> minerals, for example, in terms of chemistry and
> minerology, as when we say that the ordinary mean-
> ing of the English word salt is "sodium chloride
> (NaCl)", ... but we have no precise way of defining
> words like love or hate, which concern situations
> that have not been accurately classified... (Bloom-
> field [1933] 1951, p. 139)

These statements seem to imply a model of linguistic function with just two parts — on the one hand, the linguistic form, and on the other hand, the associated nonlinguistic events (and, presumably, contextual linguistic events as well). Thus the definition of the word "salt" would be, at least in part, the actual substance NaCl. But Bloomfield seems to ignore the essentially arbitrary association between the word "salt" and the substance NaCl, in that his model has no place for the human individuals or the human cultures which have chosen this particular linguistic form.

A more satisfactory model was provided some two thousand years ago by the Hindu philosopher Patañjali: "Concentrate separately on the word, the meaning, and the object, which are mixed up in common usage" — which a modern commentator explicates with this example — "When we utter the word 'elephant', we find that the word, the meaning and the object are mixed up; the word lives in air, the meaning lives in mind, the elephant lives by itself" (Patañjali, Aphorisms...). It is indeed true that the word "lives in the air", in the sense that it is transmitted as vibrations of air molecules. It is equally true that the actual elephant "lives by itself", i.e., exists independently of all human conventions of nomenclature. The only way that these two isolates are related, then, is through the human mind; and we may define meaning not as a "thing", but rather as the relationship which associates word and object.

This three-part model is more adequate than Bloomfield's but still does not clarify the relation of language and culture. In order to do so, we may expand the model still further. First, a division may be made between the observational, or etic, universe, to which "word" and "object" belong, and the structural, or emic, universe, within the human mind. Second, we may distinguish linguistic behavior from its subject matter or content (though the subject matter may itself, as a special case, be linguistic behavior, as when linguists talk about language). The two dichotomies then intersect as shown in Figure 1.

In this figure, the arrows marked a, b, and c indicate relationships of importance to the ethnolinguist. Arrow a is the relationship which concerns him when he functions purely as a linguist: it may be thought of inductively, in terms of the process by which the

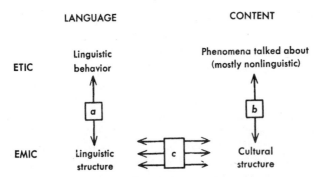

Figure 1. The Relation of Language to Culture

investigator sets up a structure to account for his raw behavioral data, or deductively, as the process by which psychological patterns of linguistic competence give rise to observable linguistic performance. Arrow b is the analogous relationship that is investigated by the ethnographer: the actual objects and events which concern a particular human group are here linked, by induction or by deduction, to subjective patterns of organization. Finally, the set of arrows marked c represents the relationships to which we assign the term "meaning"; this is conceived of not as a direct connection between the utterance "elephant" and the flesh-and-blood Elephas maximus, but rather as a connection mediated by "elephant" as an item of the English lexicon and by "the elephant" as an item in the cultural inventory of English speakers.

There are two types of structural units which are linked by the relationships of meaning. The relevant linguistic units are not phonemes or morphemes, but units of a higher level, which are called lexemes: these are the minimum units which participate in arbitrary relationships of meaning. Thus single morphemes like "green" and "house" are lexemes, but so also is the two-morpheme combination "greenhouse" (as opposed to "green house"), since it arbitrarily designates a particular kind of structure. There is still little agreement about structural units of cultural behavior; insofar as they can be identified, they are often called sememes. To be sure, there is not always a one-to-one correspondence between lexemes and sememes; people sometimes show culturally determined differences in behavior where their language provides no lexemic differentiation. However, the general regularity of lexeme-sememe correspondences reflects the close integration between language and the rest of culture, and it is in this way that language may be regarded as a key to culture as a whole.

   Ethnosemantics. The study of vocabulary as a guide to the way in which members of a culture divide up their universe has received increasing attention, and the relativity of cultural classifications is emphasized with every new empirical study. Thus, where English vocabulary reflects its users' approach to spatial orientation with the four-way classification "north, south, east, west", the Indian languages of northwestern California reflect the functionally similar but incommensurable division "upriver, downriver, toward the river, away from the river". Anthropologists have begun to pay close attention to such lexemic systems, understanding that they reflect an emic view of the culture being studied, a view uncontaminated by the varying etic frameworks of outside observers. Various terms have been used to identify this study, such as "ethnoscience", "folk taxonomy", "structural semantics", and "ethnosemantics".

   A further development in ethnographic semantics is generally known as "componential analysis". This method tries to answer the question, Given a particular set of taxonomic terms used by members of a culture, what are the criteria for applying the individual terms? Taking an example from kinship terminology, if some male collateral kin in generations above ego's are called "uncle" and some are called "cousin", what does one need to know in order to label a particular kinsman correctly? Attempts to answer such questions have resulted in the idea that terms may be conceived of as bundles of simultaneously occurring semantic components. Thus the term "uncle" is applied when the features of "maleness", "ascending generation", and "colineality" are simultaneously present. (A "colineal" in this case is a nonlineal kinsman all of whose ancestors are included in the ancestors of ego.) The term "cousin" is applied in a larger number of cases, but they include those where the features of "maleness", "ascending generation", and "ablineality" are simultaneously present. (An "ablineal" is a consanguineal kinsman who is neither a lineal nor a colineal.) This type of analysis, as applied to kin terms, results in definitions which are both more concise and more exact than the extensional

definitions given in traditional ethnographies. Application of componential analysis to areas other than kinship holds great promise.

   Language and world view. In addition to correspondences
between vocabulary and cultural inventory, a much more controversial type of correlation between language and culture has been proposed. This involves, on one side, whole grammatical systems or
subsystems, and, on the other side, whole philosophies or ways of
life held to be characteristic of particular cultures (though often not
brought to the level of conscious formulation). The interest of anthropologists was drawn to such correlations by Edward Sapir, who not
only recognized a linguistic relativity, covarying with cultural relativity, but also postulated a linguistic determinism operating on culture:

> Human beings do not live in the objective world
> alone, nor alone in the world of social activity as or-
> dinarily understood, but are very much at the mercy
> of the particular language which has become the me-
> dium of expression for their society... The fact of the
> matter is that the "real world" is to a large extent un-
> consciously built up on the language habits of the group.
> No two languages are ever sufficiently similar to be
> considered as representing the same social reality.
> The worlds in which different societies live are dis-
> tinct worlds, not merely the same world with differ-
> ent labels attached.   (Sapir [1910-1944] 1949, p. 162)

   Benjamin Lee Whorf, a student of Sapir, continued the exploration of the matter, although with less emphasis on the tyranny of language over culture. His position has become known as the "Whorfian
hypothesis", which holds that "language patterns [and] cultural norms
...have grown up together, constantly influencing each other. But in
this partnership the nature of the language is the factor that limits
free plasticity and rigidifies channels of development in the more au-
tocratic way" (Whorf [1927-1941] 1956, p. 156). The deterministic
role of language is easy to understand when we consider how much of
culture is transmitted through the linguistic medium. However, the
Whorfian hypothesis is easier to accept intuitively than to prove in a
rigorous way; in particular, no correlations can be traced between

language and world view until specific world views are themselves defined in terms of observable behavior. Whorf shows that Hopi linguistic structure is compatible with a world view involving a peculiar relation between subjective and objective experience; but he tends to assume, rather than to demonstrate, that the Hopi actually hold such a view of the world. Pending the outcome of extensive, strictly controlled, cross-cultural testing of the Whorfian hypothesis, we may limit our acceptance to the following modified formulation: "Insofar as languages differ in the ways they encode objective experience, language users tend to sort out and distinguish experiences differently according to the categories provided by their respective languages. These cognitions will tend to have certain effects on behavior" (Carroll 1963, p. 12).

Language and society. While the studies mentioned above have regarded each language as a unified whole, another type of research has focused attention on the variation that exists within languages or within multilingual speech communities. Such variation, apart from that associated with geographical dialects or with the idiosyncrasies of individuals, is commonly found to be correlated with one or more socially defined factors, such as the social identity of the speaker, the addressee, or the person referred to, and the social context in which communication takes place. Study of the covariance between linguistic diversity and social structure thus constitutes the new field of sociolinguistics. The findings of this field are applicable, from the synchronic viewpoint, to the diagnosis and analysis of social encounters, and, from the diachronic viewpoint, to examination of the ways in which linguistic patterns and social systems each change under the influence of the other.

BIBLIOGRAPHY

The most valuable reference that can be given for linguistic anthropology is Hymes 1964, which contains not only a rich selection of papers in the field but also very extensive bibliographies.

Bloomfield, Leonard (1933) 1951 Language. Rev. ed. New York:
        Holt.
Carroll, John B. 1963 Linguistic Relativity, Contrastive Linguistics,
        and Language Learning. IRAL: International Review of
        Applied Linguistics 1:1-20.

Diebold, A. Richard Jr. 1964 [Review of] Sol Saporta (editor), Psy-
     cholinguistics. Language 40:197–260. → An extensive review
     of the whole field of psycholinguistics, including many mat-
     ters of interest to linguistic anthropology.
Hammel, Eugene A. (editor) 1965 Formal Semantic Analysis.
     American Anthropologist New Series 67, no. 5, part 2
     (Special publication).
Hymes, Dell H. (editor) 1964 Language in Culture and Society: Read-
     er in Linguistics and Anthropology. New York: Harper.
Nida, Eugene A. 1964 Toward a Science of Translating. Leiden
     (Netherlands): Brill. → Chapter 5, "Referential and Emotive
     Meanings", summarizes recent work in ethnosemantics.
Patañjali Aphorisms of Yoga. Translated into English with a com-
     mentary by Shree Purohit Swāmi. London: Faber, 1938.
Romney, A. Kimball; and D'Andrade, Roy Goodwin (editors) 1964
     Transcultural Studies in Cognition. American Anthropologist
     New Series 66, no. 3, part 2 (Special publication). → Con-
     tains contributions by linguists, anthropologists, and psychol-
     ogists to problems of ethnosemantics.
Sapir, Edward A. (1910–1944) 1949 Selected Writings in Language,
     Culture, and Personality. Edited by David G. Mandelbaum.
     Berkeley: Univ. of California Press.
Whorf, Benjamin L. (1927–1941) 1956 Language, Thought and Real-
     ity. Edited by John B. Carroll. Cambridge, Mass.: M.I.T.
     Press.

2 | Toward a Cultural Grammar

The title of this paper requires some explanation. When I speak of a 'cultural grammar' or a 'grammar of culture', I am using the words 'culture' and 'grammar' in somewhat special senses. 'Culture', as anthropologists and ethnolinguists use the term, is often ambiguous: in its broadest sense it includes language, but in a somewhat narrower sense it may exclude and be contrasted with language, and it is the latter sense which I am using here. The word 'grammar' of course, generally refers to a description of a language, of a rather formalized type. I wish, in fact, following Chomsky's notions of generative grammar, to apply the term to a highly explicit and detailed type of description, with predictive power. That is, a grammar should be able to account for an infinite number of sentences which have not actually been spoken, but which would nevertheless be acceptable to native speakers; and the grammar should at the same time rule out sentences which are not potentially acceptable in this way. Such a grammar can be further thought of in two ways: as an explanation of the competence of the native speaker — a psycholinguistic model of what the speaker <u>knows</u> about his own language; or, it can be taken by an outsider as a set of rules or instructions which, once internalized, will enable him to produce acceptable sentences and to attach correct interpretations to sentences which he hears. To be sure, no perfect grammar of this sort has been written; yet it represents a goal which linguists are taking very seriously nowadays, and the extent to which a linguistic description approaches this goal may be taken as a measure of its adequacy. But if such a description is a useful goal for the study of language, why should we not set a similar goal in describing other aspects of human existence? Why, for instance, should we not attempt a musical grammar — i.e., an explicit, detailed, predictive account of the acceptable possibilities

within a particular musical style? If it is possible to extend the notion of 'grammar' in this way, then we may also envision a grammar
for a culture as a whole — a kind of supergrammar, actually, which
would have separate sections for the description of a culture's music,
of its kinship structure, of its religion, of its technology, etc., but
which would also account for the relationships between all these subdivisions.

     Some such goals for ethnographic description have, in fact,
been proposed. In 1957, when Chomsky's work was first published
and when few linguists had yet come to think of a grammar as a characterization of a psychological competence, the anthropologist Ward
Goodenough wrote about the ethnographer's task as follows:

> A society's culture consists of whatever it is one
> has to know or believe in order to operate in a manner
> acceptable to its members...Culture is not a material
> phenomenon; it does not consist of things, people, be-
> havior, or emotions. It is rather an organization of
> these things. It is the forms of things that people have
> in mind, their models for perceiving, relating, and
> otherwise interpreting them...Given such a definition,
> it is obviously impossible to describe a culture proper-
> ly simply by describing behavior or social, economic,
> and ceremonial events and arrangements as observed
> material phenomena. What is required is to construct
> a theory of the conceptual models which they repre-
> sent. We test the adequacy of such a theory by our
> ability to interpret and predict what goes on in a com-
> munity as measured by how its members, our infor-
> mants, do so. A further test is our ability ourselves
> to behave in ways which lead to the kind of responses
> from the community's members which our theory
> would lead us to expect. Thus tested, the theory is a
> valid statement of what you have to know in order to
> operate as a member of the society and is, as such, a
> valid description of its culture.

Similarly, in 1964, Charles Frake wrote:

> Ethnography...is a discipline which seeks to ac-
> count for the behavior of a people by describing the

> socially acquired and shared knowledge, or culture,
> that enables members of the society to behave in ways
> deemed appropriate by their fellows...It is not...the
> ethnographer's task to predict behavior. In this re-
> spect the ethnographer is...akin to the linguist who
> does not attempt to predict what people will say but to
> state rules for constructing utterances which native
> speakers will judge as grammatically appropriate. The
> model of an ethnographic statement is not: 'if a person
> is confronted with stimulus X, he will do Y,' but: 'if a
> person is in situation X, performance Y will be judged
> appropriate by native actors.'

If we may apply the term 'grammar' to the type of ethnographic description envisioned by Goodenough and by Frake, we may say
that the ideal cultural grammar, like the ideal linguistic grammar, is
yet to be written, but that it represents a goal which should be taken
seriously. The questions which have to be considered first, however,
are these: Is there in fact any reason to believe that culture <u>can</u> be
described in a way comparable to linguistic description? Are there
in fact notions used by linguists which can be applied in ethnography?
Or is it rather the case, as some might claim, that cultural anthropology is basically a historical discipline, having few principles in
common with descriptive linguistics?

For many years, lectures have been given and papers have
been written on the topic of 'language and culture' or 'ethnolinguistics',
based on the proposition that language stands in some kind of especially important relationship to culture. As Hymes (1964: 6) has pointed
out, two types of link between language and culture have been emphasized. One, associated especially with Malinowski and other British
anthropologists, stresses the 'interdependence between [language and
culture as] different aspects of the same event or social action'; the
other, associated with Lévi-Strauss and other French scholars, is
concerned more with the 'congruence between [language and culture
as] parallel systems or products of collective psychology'. The existence of such links has been widely accepted, and we can perhaps
see that the two emphases are themselves interrelated. Language
and culture are not acquired by the children of a society as two separate things; the interdependence of language and culture in most

human activities means that each serves as the vehicle in which the other is learned. This in turn implies that the structure of one system will be apprehended at least partly in terms of the structure of the other system. And since language is the medium through which so much of culture is explicitly learned, we cannot be surprised if we find that the structural organization of language is reflected in cultural patterns. Notions which have proved important in linguistic description may then be found also applicable in the description of culture.

Such reasoning has seemed valid to a number of scholars. The apparent successes which the so-called 'structuralist' linguists of the 1940's and '50's had, in their attempt to isolate formal units in the structure of language, led some anthropologists to look to linguistics as a model of rigor, which might inspire similar achievements in ethnography. The distinction made by the linguist between allophone and phoneme, and between allomorph and morpheme, made a considerable impression; and Kenneth Pike's distinction between 'emic' units, defined as validated by differential native response, as opposed to the purely observational level of 'etic' phenomena, attracted particular attention. And yet, in spite of some expectations, the mechanical application of 'structuralist' linguistic methodology has not enabled anyone to identify precise cultural analogs to the phoneme and the morpheme. Indeed, attempts along these lines have often produced disappointing results, in which two causal factors may well have played a part. On the one hand, some attempts have been based on rather insecure command of linguistics, 'structuralist' or otherwise. Secondly, some researchers have been unaware of the revolution in descriptive linguistics which has been effected in the last decade by the transformationalists. As part of these recent developments, the whole basis of 'structuralist' methodology, and the concepts of the phoneme and the morpheme, have been called into question. But the arguments of the transformationalists have not always reached the attention of anthropologists who are concerned with the application of linguistic methods. Some of the resulting research has elicited a deservedly adverse reaction, such as was recently expressed by Berreman (1966) in an article entitled 'Anemic and emetic analyses in social anthropology'.

At the same time, there have been some productive applications of linguistic notions in cultural anthropology, and some real

progress toward the ideal of a cultural grammar. In the remainder
of this paper, I would like to review some of this work, and indicate
the lines of research which may be most productive in the future. [1]

One of the most impressive and sustained influences of linguistic thinking upon the study of culture is to be found in the work of
Lévi-Strauss (e.g., 1945), who has specifically acknowledged his
debt to the linguists Trubetzkoy and Jakobson. It must be admitted
that Lévi-Strauss may sometimes have misunderstood his linguistic
models, or extended their application in ways which few linguists
could approve. There are, nevertheless, important analogies between linguistic structure and cultural structure which Lévi-Strauss
has brought to the fore. One of these is the insistence that the units
of a system are defined by the relationships between them, and that
these relationships are more fundamental than the units themselves.
The basic phonological units of a language like English are not the
phonemes /p/, /b/, /m/, etc., but rather the relationships of contrast in voice, occlusion, and nasality which underlie the phonemes.
And thus, in Lévi-Strauss' view of social structure, what is basic is
not any unit such as the family, but rather the relationships of con-
sanguinity, marriage, and descent, in terms of which the family itself must be defined. Beyond this, another emphasis of Lévi-Strauss
is especially related to current linguistic discussion — namely, his
concern with universals. Universal features in language have been a
subject of fluctuating interest among linguists: their existence has,
by turns, been taken for granted, categorically denied, and only recently subjected to serious study. In the meantime, Lévi-Strauss
has consistently sought to identify universals in culture such as the
incest tabu, the self-perpetrating nature of kinship, and the law that
men exchange women rather than vice versa. It is clear that such
universals, in language or in culture respectively, must constitute
the very foundation of our ideal linguistic or cultural grammars.

A somewhat more recent application of linguistic method in
ethnography, which has become increasingly prominent since 1961,
is the work in ethnoscience or folk taxonomy, pioneered by Conklin
(1962) and Frake (1962). This is based on the view, current among
anthropologists for some time, that different cultures embody different ways of classifying or organizing the infinite diversity of the physical world. Furthermore, the stock of words in a language commonly

bears a close relationship to the classificatory system used by its speakers, so that it constitutes a kind of inventory of their culture. From this, the idea has developed that the ethnographer's job is essentially the description of a semantic system, one which is manifested in his informants' vocabulary. In this task, as in linguistic description, the principal effort must be to discover the informants' own system — the inherent system of the culture — rather than to impose the investigator's own conceptions. The possibilities of this approach have produced considerable interest and enthusiasm, as reflected for instance in Sturtevant's statement (1964: 100) that 'A culture itself amounts to the sum of a given society's folk classifications, all of that society's ethnoscience, its particular ways of classifying its material and social universe'. In this light, ethnography becomes synonymous with descriptive semantics.

        This approach, in spite of being hailed by some as 'the new ethnography', has still fallen somewhat short of revolutionizing the field. For one thing, there are a number of publications which offer partial ethnotaxonomic descriptions — e.g., of beer-making among the Subanun, in the Philippines (Frake 1964), or of firewood as used by the Tzeltal, in Mexico (Metzger & Williams 1966) — but most of these are incidental to discussions of methodology, and no one has published a detailed study of any major cultural subdivision, such as would enable an uncommitted researcher to evaluate the entire ethnotaxonomic approach. Beyond this, certain theoretical criticisms can also be made. Thus, a basic notion in ethnoscience is that of the contrast set — a set of coördinate categories such as dog, cat, horse, cow, etc. The contrast set is formally defined by Sturtevant (1964: 108) as 'a class of mutually exclusive segregates' — that is, terminological categories — 'which occur in the same culturally relevant environment'. But cultural relevance is exactly what the ethnographer is struggling to identify; Sturtevant's definition thus begs the question as to how the field worker may proceed in order to identify specific contrast sets. Similarly, in several of the published papers on Tzeltal folk taxonomy, we find that great emphasis is placed on the discovery of semantic classes by the technique of substitution in frames: one sets up a frame such as 'A blank is an animal', and then ascertains what words, such as dog, cat, horse, cow, are mutually substitutable within that frame. But how does one know what is a suitable frame to begin with? All of this seems to be inspired by the

techniques of 'structuralist' linguistics, with its emphasis on discovery procedures which are now widely seen as inadequate: a noun is
defined, in part, as something that can follow an adjective; but an
adjective is something that can precede a noun, and a vicious circle
results. The remedy for such problems is, perhaps, to recognize
that the researcher, whether he is attempting to describe a semantic
system or a system of linguistic form, must attempt to account not
merely for a body of co-occurrence patterns, but for a psychological
competence possessed by the members of a society. There may be
no automatic procedure for reaching this goal; and the researcher
may rely on trial-and-error, on divine inspiration, or on his own empathy with the cognitive processes of his informants. The only way
to measure the adequacy of his discovery procedures is by his result,
and by its power to predict socially acceptable behavior, linguistic
or non-linguistic.

A final criticism that may be directed at much work in ethnoscience is its excessive preoccupation with one particular kind of
semantic relationship — that of the taxonomic hierarchy. Such hier-
archies, exemplified in English, for instance, by the statement that
'A terrier is a type of dog, which is a type of mammal, which is a
type of vertebrate, which is a type of animal', are probably important in every culture of the world, but there are many other kinds of
semantic relationship which are equally important. A study of hier-
archies can only tell us that the butcher, the baker, and the candle-
stick maker are coördinate terms under the category of occupations,
but it cannot tell us how they are related, respectively, to meat, to
bread, and to candlesticks. The study of the broader spectrum of
ethnosemantic relationships has been opened by Frake 1964, but much
yet remains to be done. [2]

Another type of research, generally known as componential
analysis, has raised a somewhat different type of semantic question.
Whereas folk taxonomy will say simply that dog and cat are members
of the same contrast set mammal, the componential analyst will ask:
What is the essential difference between a dog and a cat? What are
the culturally recognized attributes of these animals which allow members of a given society to say, 'This is a dog, but that is a cat'? Or,
to put the problem in more general terms: What are the essential
definitions, the necessary and sufficient conditions for the use of each

concept which a given society employs? Up to the present time, this approach has been applied principally in the area of kinship. We can say, for instance, that the essential definition of the English term uncle (where the word includes grand-uncles, etc.) is that a kinsman must be male, must be of ascending generation, and must be a 'co-lineal', to use Goodenough's term (in Wallace & Atkins 1960:61) — that is, all of his ancestors must be included in the ancestors of ego. But my grandfather's brother's son does not fall under this definition, since his maternal ancestors are not included in my ancestors; he is therefore categorized not as an uncle but as a cousin, where this word (in its broadest sense) is defined as a person, of either sex and of any generation, who is neither lineal nor colineal, but rather, in Goodenough's terminology, 'ablineal'. The sets of three necessary attributes which I have just given for the terms uncle and cousin may be called semantic components, and each such bundle of components comprises a componential definition.. An obvious linguistic analog is the definition of phonemes in terms of simultaneous phonological components: /p/ can be defined as a bundle of bilabiality, occlusion, and voicelessness; /b/ agrees in bilabiality and occlusion but differs in voicedness; /m/ adds a component of nasality, etc.

This type of analysis has been shown to have considerable advantages in explicitness and economy over the more traditional type of kinship analysis. There have, however, been a number of criticisms leveled against it, many of which have raised the issue of so-called 'structural validity' versus 'psychological validity'. A set of componential statements may be capable of distinguishing a set of kinship terms unambiguously, one from another, and may then be said to have structural validity. But such an analysis may not account for all the behavioral data involving those kinship terms — that is, it may not completely account for what the native knows about his own use of the terms; it could then be said to lack psychological validity. Thus, one might protest the componential distinction between uncle and cousin given above, on the grounds that a member of English-speaking society does not, after all, reckon kinship in terms of 'colineal' vs. 'ablineal' kin — indeed, most of us have some difficulty in getting these concepts through our heads. One might argue instead that we distinguish between uncle and cousin by referring them back to more basic kinship terms: if a man is the brother of my parent, or other direct ancestor, then he is some type of cousin to me. The need for such relational rather than componential definitions becomes even more obvious in certain other cases. For instance, the alternative componential analyses of English kinship terminology published by Goodenough 1965 and Schneider 1965 could be made much simpler and less contradictory if they were reformulated in a combination of the componential and relational approaches. Burling 1963 has described a kinship term which is used by the Garo, of Assam, in such a way as to form an endless network; if Mr. A is in kinship relation X to me, then everyone who is X to Mr. A is also X to me, and so ad infinitum. It is clear that such a recursive notion cannot be given a simple componential definition.

The most useful type of relational definition which has so far been offered for kinship terms is the 'equivalence rule' of Lounsbury (e.g., 1964). Such a rule may be formulated either as a rule of extension or as its converse, a rule of reduction; thus certain societies have a rule that the term for father may be extended to include father's brother — or, conversely, that the concept of father's brother is reduced to that of father for terminological purposes. Such rules then have wider implications: if father's brother is called father, then we will expect father's father's brother to be called father's father, father's brother's son to be called father's son (i.e., brother), etc. Although this type of semantic rule has so far been formulated principally for kinship terms, it would seem to offer important possibilities in other areas, wherever we wish to characterize the native's awareness that some meanings of a word are more <u>basic</u> than others. For instance, where an English word like <u>father</u> has two meanings, 'male parent' and 'Christian priest', English speakers may well feel that the first meaning is in some way more basic than the second, and the researcher can formulate a rule of extension to account for this fact.

All of these approaches to the task of writing a cultural grammar may be thought of as types of ethnosemantic research, attempts to describe cultural patterns as semantic systems. Unfortunately, ethnosemantics has aroused not only widespread interest, but also a good deal of hostility. Thus Berreman 1966 quotes an unnamed colleague who sums up the whole movement as 'an attempt to understand the mood and temper of man through empty words: vacuous, sterile, inconclusive, programmatic, hyper-professionalized, and

the product of apolitical, asexual, amoral, asocial anthropology'. It
should be clear that I do not share this opinion. I do feel, however,
that ethnosemanticists have sometimes been too narrow in their outlook, emphasizing such particular semantic relationships as that of
hierarchy and that of the componential definition, and neglecting the
many other types of link which operate in cultures. Semantics has
for many years been a topic of study for philosophers, psychologists,
and literary scholars; the would-be cultural grammarian must learn
from these other disciplines, and must be prepared to recognize many
types of semantic relationships which have no analog in the syntax or
phonology of purely linguistic grammars. If the ethnographer will
keep his mind open to all such possibilities, the cultural grammar
can become not merely an ideal, but a reality.

NOTES

An earlier version of this paper was delivered as a public lecture at
Delhi University in December, 1967.
[1] A valuable collection of ethnosemantic research papers,
most of them previously published, has now been compiled by Tyler
(1969).
[2] Such relationships have been explored in some recent publications, e.g. Casagrande & Hale 1967, Perchonock & Werner 1969.
As yet, however, there has been little formalization or cross-cultural
comparison.

REFERENCES

Berreman, Gerald, 1966. Anemic and emetic analyses in social an-
        thropology. American Anthropologist 68.346-54.
Burling, Robbins, 1963. Garo kinship terms and the analysis of mean-
        ing. Ethnology 2.70-85.
Casagrande, J.B., and Hale, K. L., 1967. Semantic relationships in
        Papago folk definitions. In: Hymes, Dell (ed.), Studies in
        Southwestern Ethnolinguistics. The Hague: Mouton, pp. 165-
        93.
Chomsky, Noam, 1957. Syntactic structure. The Hague: Mouton.
Conklin, Harold, 1962. Lexicographical treatment of folk taxonomies.
        In: Householder, F.W., and Saporta, Sol (ed.), Problems in
        lexicography. Indiana University Research Center in

Anthropology, Folklore and Linguistics, publication 21.
Bloomington, Ind. Pp. 119-41. Reprinted in Tyler 1969: 41-
59.

Frake, Charles O., 1962. The ethnographic study of cognitive systems. Anthropology and human behavior, ed. by T. Gladwin
and W. Sturtevant, pp. 72-93. Washington, D.C.: Anthropological Society of Washington. (Reprinted in Tyler 1969: 28-
41.)

_____, 1964. Notes on queries in ethnography. In: Romney and
D'Andrade 1964: 132-45. (Reprinted in Tyler 1969: 123-36.)

Goodenough, Ward, 1957. Cultural anthropology and linguistics.
Georgetown University monograph series in languages and
linguistics, 9.167-73. (Reprinted in Hymes 1964: 36-9.)

_____, 1965. Yankee kinship terminology: a problem in componen-
tial analysis. In: Hammel 1965: 259-87. (Reprinted in Tyler
1969: 255-88.)

Hammel, Eugene (ed.), 1965. Formal semantic analysis. American
Anthropologist 67:5, part 2 (special publication). Menasha,
Wisc.: American Anthropological Association.

Hymes, Dell (ed.), 1964. Language in culture and society. New York:
Harper and Row.

Lévi-Strauss, Claude, 1945. L'analyse structurale en linguistique et
anthropologie. Word 1.1-21. (Later published as Anthropologie structurale, chap. 2 [Paris, Plon, 1958]. English translations in Structural Anthropology, pp. 31-54 [New York,
Basic Books, 1963], and in Hymes 1964: 40-51.)

Lounsbury, Floyd, 1964. A formal account of the Crow- and Omaha-
type kinship terminologies. Explorations in cultural anthropology, ed. by W. Goodenough, 351-93. New York: McGraw-
Hill. (Reprinted in Tyler 1969: 212-55.)

Metzger, Duane, and Williams, Gerald, 1966. Procedures and results
in the study of native categories: Tzeltal firewood. American
Anthropologist 68.389-407.

Perchonock, Norma, and Werner, Oswald, 1969. Navaho systems of
classification: some implications for ethnoscience. Ethnology 8.229-42.

Romney, A.K., and D'Andrade, R.G. (ed.), 1964. Transcultural
studies in cognition. American Anthropologist 66:3, part 2
(special publication). Menasha, Wisc.: American Anthropological Association.

Schneider, David M., 1965. American kin terms and terms for kins-
  men: a critique of Goodenough's componential analysis of
  Yankee kinship terminology. In: Hammel 1965: 288-308.
  (Reprinted in Tyler 1969: 288-311.)
Sturtevant, William, 1964. Studies in ethnoscience. In: Romney and
  D'Andrade 1964: 99-131.
Tyler, Stephen A. (ed.), 1969. Cognitive anthropology. New York:
  Holt, Rinehart and Winston.
Wallace, Anthony F.C., and Atkins, John, 1960. The meaning of
  kinship terms. American Anthropologist 62.58-80. (Re-
  printed in Tyler 1969: 345-69.)

3 | The Dimensions of Sociolinguistics

The term 'sociolinguistics' is a fairly new one. [1] Like its elder sisters, 'ethnolinguistics' and 'psycholinguistics', it is not easy to define with precision; indeed, these three terms tend to overlap somewhat in their subject matter, and to a certain extent reflect differences in the interests and approaches of investigators rather than differences in material. It is certainly correct to say that sociolinguistic studies, like those carried out under the name of 'sociology of language', deal with the relationships between language and society. But such a statement is excessively vague. If we attempt to be more exact, we may note that sociolinguistics differs from some earlier interests in language–society relationships in that, following modern views in linguistics proper, it considers language as well as society to be a structure, rather than merely a collection of items. The sociolinguist's task is then to show the systematic covariance of linguistic structure and social structure — and perhaps even to show a causal relationship in one direction or the other.

However, although sociolinguists derive much of their approach from structural linguistics, at the same time they break sharply with one linguistic trend. This is the approach which treated languages as completely uniform, homogeneous or monolithic in their structure; in this view, now coming to be recognized as a pernicious one, differences in speech habits found within a community were swept under the rug as 'free variation'. One of the major tasks of sociolinguistics is to show.that such variation or diversity is not in fact 'free', but is correlated with systematic social differences. In this and in still larger ways, linguistic diversity is precisely the subject matter of sociolinguistics.

To be sure, such a characterization still falls short of suggesting the broad range of sociolinguistic studies which is possible —
and which is, indeed, exemplified in this volume.* We may perhaps
come closer to describing this range by trying to identify the dimensions of sociolinguistics — the separate lines of interest which run
through the field. Wherever two or more of these dimensions intersect, we may expect to find a subject of sociolinguistic study.[2] In
the following paragraphs, seven such dimensions are discussed.

Viewing diversity as a key concept of the field, it is reasonable that a most important set of dimensions should be related to the
conditioning of linguistic diversity. This term refers to the various
socially defined factors with which linguistic diversity is found to be
correlated. The number of such factors may differ from one case to
another, but three of them seem to account for most reported cases
of diversity: the dimensions of sender, receiver, and setting (cf.
Hymes 1962).

1) The social identity of the sender or speaker is illustrated
most clearly by cases of 'class dialects', where speech differences
are correlated with social stratification — such differences perhaps
reaching their extreme form in the caste dialects of India. The same
dimension is relevant in cases of difference between men's and women's speech (Furfey 1944).

2) The social identity of the receiver or person spoken to is
relevant wherever special vocabularies of respect are used in addressing superiors, as has often been reported from the Orient (e.g.
Martin 1964) and from Oceania (Garvin and Riesenberg 1952). Another special style of speech conditioned by this factor is 'baby talk' as
used in English and many other languages — where this term refers,
not essentially to the way that babies talk, but to the way that adults
talk to babies (Ferguson 1964). Still other types of speech determined
by the identity of the receiver are the special styles used by the
Nootka in addressing children, dwarfs, hunchbacks, one-eyed people,
and uncircumcised males (Sapir 1915). In many cases, a special style
used in speaking to a person is also used in speaking about him; but

---

*Sociolinguistics, Proceedings of the UCLA Sociolinguistics
Conference, 1964. Edited by William Bright. The Hague: Mouton &
Co., 1966.

the identity of the person spoken about is rarely, if ever, correlated with an independent dimension of linguistic variation.

3) The third conditioning dimension, that of setting, comprehends all possibly relevant elements in the context of communication other than the identities of the individuals involved. This is exemplified by the special linguistic usage of Apaches when on the warpath (Opler and Hoijer 1940), or by the differences between formal and informal style which are determined by social setting in most (perhaps all) languages. Where sharp differences in form and function exist between formal and informal style, we speak of a situation of diglossia; this is found in the Arabic-speaking countries, in modern Greece, Haiti, German-speaking Switzerland, and in most of South India (Ferguson 1959).

It should be understood, of course, that the three dimensions which have been listed are by no means mutually exclusive, but commonly intersect to condition a particular type of sociolinguistic behavior. Thus the so-called male and female speech of the Yana involved considerations of both sender and receiver: 'male speech' was used whenever a man was either the sender or the receiver, while 'female speech' was used only between women (Sapir 1929). The complex linguistic etiquette of Javanese involves the factors of sender, receiver, and setting. It should also be understood that each of these dimensions may have to be broken down into smaller ones in particular cases. For example, usage determined by the identity of the sender or receiver may involve a complex interaction of such factors as age, social rank, and closeness of kin ties, as is illustrated by Friedrich's paper in this volume.*

4) Other dimensions of sociolinguistics are based not so much on the actual diversity of linguistic behavior, but rather on the scope and aims of the investigator. Thus, as in other fields, sociolinguistic research can be synchronic or diachronic. In the realm of the caste dialects of India, we can point to studies of both types: that of Gumperz (1958) focusses primarily on the present-day differences and functions of caste dialect in a Hindi-speaking village; that of Bright and Ramanujan (1964) tries to find historical causes for the differences between caste dialects of South India.

---

*Sociolinguistics, ed. by William Bright (1966), pp. 214-59.

5) A dimension introduced to the discussions of the UCLA Conference by Hoenigswald's paper was that of the difference between how people use languages and what they believe about the linguistic behavior of themselves and others. The latter topic, aptly labelled 'folk-linguistics', is of frequent concern to the sociolinguist. In many parts of the world, for example, the native view tends to confuse 'high vs. low' speech, in the sense of formal vs. informal, with 'high vs. low' as referring to the social status of the sender. In such cases, the investigator must not be deceived into accepting the folk-view as corresponding to actual linguistic behavior; at the same time, he should realize that the folk-view is itself a part of a sociolinguistic situation, and worthy of study in its own right.

6) Another dimension is that of the extent of diversity. This term should not be understood as referring to purely geographical measures, nor to simple linguistic measures, such as the number of shared words. Rather it refers to the difference between parts of a single society or nation as opposed to the difference between separate societies or nations, and to the difference between varieties of a single language as against the difference between separate languages. Specifically, three classifications seem to be useful under this heading of extent. One, here labelled multidialectal, includes the cases where socially conditioned varieties of a single language are used within a single society or nation; examples are the contrast between 'U' and 'non-U' speech in Great Britain, or between formal and informal usage in the Tamil-speaking society of South India. A second classification, the multilingual type, includes cases where several different languages are used within a single society or nation. This category refers in particular to the problems of multilingual nations, such as Belgium, Ghana, India, Canada, and Paraguay — to take examples from five different continents. The third classification is multisocietal, including studies of separate languages spoken in separate societies. The aim here is to find correlations between differences in language and differences in social structure, following the lead of the Whorfian hypothesis, which postulates correlations between linguistic structures and the associated non-linguistic cultures. Thus Whorf might have proposed — although he did not — correlations between Hopi grammar and Hopi social organization, to be contrasted with correlations between English or SAE grammar and SAE social organization. An actual study of this kind is Fischer's paper in this

volume, * in which the Trukese and Ponapean languages and societies
are contrasted.

7) A final dimension to be recognized here is that of <u>applica-
tion</u> — the broader implications which are inherent in descriptions of
sociolinguistic diversity. Again, three categories may be recognized,
corresponding to the interests of three types of investigator.

The first application, reflecting the interest of the sociolo-
gist, involves the use of sociolinguistic data as a diagnostic index of
<u>social structure</u> in general, or of particular social phenomena. Thus,
the recognition of a three-way division of caste dialects in South India, plus a two-way distinction of formality, may be correlated with
other kinds of data to yield a description of the socially defined differences between people and the socially defined differences of setting
which are significant for South Indians. Furthermore, once the socially relevant classifications of people and situations have been recognized in this way, the investigator can use linguistic criteria in order to classify particular individuals and situations: a man who speaks
in such-and-such a way reveals himself as a Brahmin; an occasion on
which such-and-such language is used is recognized as a formal occasion.

The second type of application reflects the interest of the <u>his-
torical</u> linguist. The questions posed here are: Do languages change
in different ways under different social circumstances? Do different social dialects of the same language change at different rates or
in different ways? How does the history of a language reflect the interaction of social dialects? The study of these questions can be un-
dertaken either by the examination of historical records, where available, or — better still — by studying the currently ongoing processes
of linguistic change, as Labov has done on Martha's Vineyard and in
New York (1963, 1964).

The third type of application is that made by the <u>language
planner</u> — the linguist, educator, legislator or administrator who
must work with official policies regarding language use. Thus, giv-
en an organized society in which a diversity of dialects or languages

---

*Sociolinguistics, ed. by William Bright (1966), pp. 168-87.

are current, the language planner must consider such questions as:
What varieties are to be given recognition as 'official' or 'national'
languages? What varieties are to be sanctioned for use in official
publications, in officially encouraged literary work, in educational institutions of various levels, in courts of law? What should the official attitudes be toward varieties not sanctioned for any of these situations? To what extent should political subdivisions of a nation correspond to linguistic subdivisions? How should writing systems be
developed or standardized? The most complex problems of language
planning, perhaps, are those faced by the recently independent nations
of Africa and Asia, and the diverse policies being followed by these
nations provide current illustrations of the types of difficulties which
arise.

The papers and discussions presented in this volume* reflect the above dimensions, intersecting in a variety of combinations.
Clearly, all the possible combinations have not been exhausted; many
new lines of research remain to be developed, along with the collection of new data on problems already raised. But the prospect is very
bright for all of the possibilities to be explored. Sociolinguistics has
recently been the topic not only of the UCLA Conference, but also of
a symposium in San Francisco in 1963 published under the editorship
of Gumperz and Hymes (1964). It seems likely that sociolinguistics is
entering an era of rapid development; we may expect that linguistics,
sociology, and anthropology will all show the effects.

NOTES

[1]An early use is that of Currie 1952. The Third Edition of
Webster's New International Dictionary (1961) does not list the word.
[2]This approach is modelled after the method of componential
analysis current in phonology and semantic analysis, used in specific
sociolinguistic contexts by Brown and Gilman (1960) and by Friedrich
in the present volume*; cf. also Ervin-Tripp 1964.

---

*Sociolinguistics, ed. by William Bright (1966).

REFERENCES

Bright, William, and A. K. Ramanujan, "Sociolinguistic variation and language change", Proceedings of the 9th International Congress of Linguists (The Hague, 1964), pp. 1107-13. [In this volume, pp. 47-58.]

Brown, Roger, and A. Gilman, "The pronouns of power and solidarity", in Style in Language, ed. by Thomas A. Sebeok (New York and Cambridge, Mass., 1960), pp. 253-76.

Currie, Haver C., "A projection of socio-linguistics: the relationship of speech to social status", Southern Speech Journal, 18 (1952), 28-37.

Ervin-Tripp, Susan, "An analysis of the interaction of language, topic, and listener", in Gumperz and Hymes (1964), 86-102.

Ferguson, Charles A., "Diglossia", Word, 15 (1959), 325-40.

_____, "Baby talk in six languages", in Gumperz and Hymes (1964), 103-14.

Furfey, Paul H., "Men's and women's language", American Catholic Sociological Review, 5 (1944), 218-23.

Garvin, Paul L., and S. Riesenberg, "Respect behavior on Ponape: an ethnolinguistic study", American Anthropologist, 54 (1952), 201-20.

Gumperz, John J., "Dialect differences and social stratification in a North Indian village", American Anthropologist, 60 (1958), 668-82.

Gumperz, John J., and Dell Hymes, "The ethnography of communication", American Anthropologist Special Publication (= Vol. 66, no. 6, pt. 2) (Menasha, Wisc., 1964).

Hymes, Dell H., "The ethnography of speaking", Anthropology and Human Behavior, ed. by Thomas Gladwin and W. C. Sturtevant (Washington, D. C., Anthropological Society of Washington, 1962), pp. 15-53.

Labov, William, "The social motivation of a sound change", Word, 19 (1963), 273-309.

_____, "Phonological correlates of social stratification", in Gumperz and Hymes (1964), 164-76.

Martin, Samuel, "Speech levels in Japan and Korea", Language in Culture and Society, ed. by Dell Hymes (New York, 1964), pp. 407-12.

Opler, Morris E. , and Harry Hoijer, "The raid and war-path lan-
        guage of the Chiricahua Apache", American Anthropologist,
        42 (1940), 617-34.
Sapir, Edward, "Abnormal types of speech in Nootka" (1915). Re-
        printed in Selected Writings of Edward Sapir, ed. by David G.
        Mandelbaum (Berkeley, 1949), pp. 179-96.
_____ , "Male and female forms of speech in Yana" (1929). Reprint-
        ed in Selected Writings of Edward Sapir, ed. by David G.
        Mandelbaum (Berkeley, 1949), pp. 206-12.

4 | Social Dialect and Language History

Within any recognizable speech community, variations are
normally found on all levels of linguistic structure — phonological,
grammatical, and lexical. Some of these variations are correlated
with geographical location: there are systematic differences, for instance, between the English of London and the English of New York.
This type of linguistic variation has been studied in detail by dialectologists. Other types of linguistic variation, however, have received
less attention. Some of this variation may be said to depend on the
identity of the person spoken to or spoken about; the classical instances are those in Nootka, where separate linguistic forms are
used in speaking to or about children, fat people, dwarfed people,
hunchbacks, etc. (Sapir 1915). Other variations are correlated with
the identity of the speaker. These include cases of difference between
men's and women's speech, e.g. in Koasati (Haas 1944). More typically, linguistic variation is correlated with the social status of the
speaker; this may be termed a variety of sociolinguistic variation.
An instance which has recently received considerable attention is
that involving "U" (upper-class) and "non-U" (middle-class) speech
in England; it is claimed that the difference in speech has now become virtually the only overt mark of difference between these two
classes (Ross 1954: 20-23). This type of variation thus provides a
potential diagnostic index to social status, though sociologists have
exploited this potential very little so far.

It should be noted that some cases of linguistic variation are
correlated simultaneously with the identity of the person spoken to
and the identity of the person speaking. Thus "female speech" in
Yana was used not only by women, but also by men in speaking to women; "male speech" was used only by men speaking to men (Sapir

1929). In the sociolinguistic area, linguistic variation often reflects
the relation between the status of the speaker and the status of the
person addressed, rather than the absolute status of either; an example is Vietnamese (Emeneau 1950:206-09).

   Still other cases of linguistic variation are correlated not
primarily with the identity of persons, but with other factors in the
social and cultural context. For instance, a special type of speech
was used by the Chiricahua Apache when on the war-path (Opler and
Hoijer 1940). A type of variation which is familiar in most societies
is correlated with the difference between formal and informal situations — "formality" and "informality" being defined, of course, in
terms of each particular society. Thus, as most Americans can confirm, pronunciations like huntin' are found more commonly in informal situations, while pronunciations like hunting are more common
in formal situations (Fischer 1958:50). Variations such as this one
in English are, to be sure, usually correlated with other factors besides that of formality. In some languages, however, the styles of
speech used in formal vs. informal situations are highly standardized
and strictly differentiated. Ferguson (1959) has applied the term diglossia to this type of linguistic variation, and has described it in the
Arabic, Swiss German, Haitian French, and modern Greek language
communities. We may consider this another type of sociolinguistic
variation, correlated with the varying social context within which an
individual communicates. Here too, the linguistic differences provide a potential means for definition and recognition of social situations.

   The Indian subcontinent is an exceptionally good field for the
study of both types of sociolinguistic variation, and a volume describing such phenomena in several South Asian languages has been issued
(Ferguson and Gumperz 1960). First of all, the Indian caste system
makes for easy recognition of the social levels with which linguistic
variation is correlated. Thus, in the Dharwar District of Mysore
State, "there appear to be three styles of conversational Kannada
which correspond to the three main cleavages in the social system...
the Brahmin, the non-Brahmin, and the Harijan ['untouchable']"
(McCormack 1960). Secondly, several of the languages of South Asia
show a clear difference between formal style (usually equated with
the "literary language") and informal or colloquial style. Thus, in
Kannada, overlying the dialect differences which correspond to caste

and to geography, there is a single formal style which all educated
people use in certain situations — in lecturing, in dramatic perfor-
mances, and in all written composition. See Table 1 for a few comparisons between the formal style, on the one hand, and two colloquial
dialects, the Brahmin speech and the middle-caste speech of the Bangalore area, on the other hand.

It seems likely that distinct caste dialects have existed in
India for a long period, always remaining similar enough to preserve
mutual intelligibility. Yet both the Brahmin and non-Brahmin dialects
of modern Kannada show historical changes from the Old Kannada and
Medieval Kannada languages. In some respects the two dialects show
different changes, but they agree in many changes, as in the loss of
medial vowels. To explain the cases of identical change in the two
dialects, we may consider three hypotheses: (1) the Brahmin dialect
inaugurated the changes, and the non-Brahmin dialect followed suit;
(2) the non-Brahmin dialect was the innovator, and the Brahmin followed suit; (3) the two dialects independently developed in the same
directions. Putting the possibilities in the form of a more general
question, we may ask: In the over-all history of a language, are
changes initiated predominantly by the higher social strata or by the
lower?

It has been suggested that phonetic change, and perhaps linguistic change in general, are initiated by the upper strata, in order
to "maintain a prestige-marking difference" from the lower strata
(Joos 1952: 229). The lower classes are said to narrow the gap again
by imitating their social superiors, who are then forced to innovate
once more. Thus language change is explained as a "protracted pursuit of an elite by an envious mass, and consequent 'flight' of the
elite" (Fischer 1958: 52). For a test of this hypothesis, we may consider the Kannada evidence. It can be shown that the Brahmin dialect
does indeed innovate more as regards vocabulary change (Bright 1960).
Thus in the middle-caste dialect, "curry" is yesru, from Old Kannada esar (attested from the 13th century); but the Brahmin form is
huḷi, originally meaning "sour, a sour substance", and used to mean
"curry" only in recent times. Much vocabulary change involves borrowings from Sanskrit or English, and the Brahmin dialect here often
introduces foreign sounds along with the foreign words. Thus the
Brahmin dialect introduces / z/ in words like ḍazan from English

"dozen", where non-Brahmins say dajan. On the other hand, the non-
Brahmin dialect shows more sound-change within native vocabulary:
cf. non-Brahmin ālu "milk", Brahmin hālu (Medieval hāl, Old Kannada pāl); non-Brahmin gombe "doll", Brahmin bombe (Old Kannada
bombe). In the realm of grammar, the non-Brahmin dialect again
seems to have innovated more, showing for example a locative suffix
-āgi as against Brahmin and Old Kannada -alli. In general, the Brahmin dialect seems to show great innovation on the more conscious
levels of linguistic change — those of borrowing and semantic extension — while the non-Brahmin dialect shows greater innovation in the
less conscious types of change — those involving phonemic and morphological replacements.

       Some evidence is available of a similar pattern in the caste
dialects of Tamil. For instance, Old Tamil had a retroflex fricative
which may be transcribed /ž/; this is preserved in Brahmin dialects,
but merges with /y/, /ḷ/, /l/ or zero in most non-Brahmin dialects.
Thus Brahmin kīže "down" corresponds to kīye and kīle in several
middle-caste dialects, and to kī in a Pariah dialect (Bloch 1910:5-7;
and my own observations). On the other hand, Brahmin dialects often innovate by adopting loan words, where non-Brahmin dialects preserve native Tamil vocabulary: "water" is Brahmin tīrtham or jalam
(both from Sanskrit), where most non-Brahmin dialects use tanni
(from older tan-nīr "cold water"; Bloch 1910:22). Fuller material
on Tamil dialects (e.g. Zvelebil 1959) should make the picture much
clearer.

TABLE 1

	Formal	Brahmin Colloquial	Non-Brahmin Colloquial
"name"	hesaru	hesru	yesru
"man"	manušya	manšya	mansa
"friend"	snēhita	snēyta	sinēyta
"excuse me"	kšamisu	kšemsu	čemsu
"for doing"	māḍuvudakke	māḍokke	māḍakke
"doesn't do"	māḍuvudilla	māḍolla	māḍalla
"to a wedding"	maduvege	madvege	maduvke
"in a cart"	banḍiyalli	banḍīli	banḍyāgi

Both in Kannada and in Tamil, it is understandable that Brahmins' familiarity with foreign languages and their more active intellectual life should favor innovation on what I have called the more conscious level. It is less apparent, however, why the Brahmin dialect should be more conservative than others in the less conscious types of change. A possible hypothesis is that literacy, most common among Brahmins, has acted as a brake on change in their dialect — that the "frozen" phonology and grammar of the literary language have served to retard change in Brahmin speech. A possible test of this hypothesis lies in a consideration of the Tulu society of South India, on the coast west of the Kannada-speaking area. Brahmin and non-Brahmin dialects exist in Tulu, as in other South Indian languages; but there is no established writing system for any form of Tulu, and literacy among the Tulu people exists only for their second languages — Sanskrit, Kannada, and English. Material on the Tulu caste dialects is scanty, but suggestive: the Brahmin and non-Brahmin dialects show phonemic change in approximately equal degree (Bright 1960). When further Tulu data become available, they may give strong support to the hypothesis that although "conscious" linguistic change comes largely from higher social strata, "unconscious" change is natural in all strata where the literacy factor does not intervene.

Finally, we should consider the possible role of social dialects in the process of sound change itself. It has recently been suggested that the locus of phonemic change may be not within individual dialects, but in the process of large-scale borrowing from one dialect to another. "No speaker of English can easily see himself giving up the contrast between, say, clip and lip ... Yet that is more or less what happened to knight and night...a few centuries ago." It is hypothesized that some members of the English-speaking community may have pronounced knight with, let us say, an unreleased /k/; other speakers, attempting to imitate "the source dialect of their high-prestige neighbors", misheard the /kn/ as /n/ and initiated the new pronunciation, homonymous with night (Hoenigswald 1960: 55). This hypothesis can be applied to the Kannada material: When Old Kannada pāl "milk" became Medieval Kannada hāl, the initial /h/ presumably at first retained the voicelessness of its prototype. In modern Kannada, however, the /h/ of Brahmin hālu is at least partly voiced. It is possible that this subphonemic change, occurring in the Brahmin dialect, was misapprehended by non-Brahmins; so that attempting to

imitate hālu with voiced /h/, they said ālu instead. Such an explanation would change the picture previously presented of Brahmin and
non-Brahmin roles in linguistic innovation: The upper class would
now appear to originate sound change on the phonetic level; the lower
class, imitating this inaccurately, produces change on the phonemic
level.

Needless to say, we cannot now be certain that such a process
operated in any particular historical change. What is possible and
highly desirable is that social dialects and their interactions in contemporary societies should be studied in minute detail, with hypotheses like the above in mind. South Asia appears to provide an exceptionally rich field for this type of sociolinguistic investigation.

REFERENCES

Bloch, Jules. 1910. Castes et dialectes en Tamoul. Mémoires de la
        Société de Linguistique de Paris 16: 1-30.
Bright, William. 1960. "Linguistic change in some South Indian caste
        dialects" in Linguistic Diversity in South Asia (Ed. C. A.
        Ferguson and J. J. Gumperz). [In this volume, pp. 39-46.]
Emeneau, M. B. 1950. Language and non-linguistic patterns. Lan-
        guage 26: 199-209.
Ferguson, Charles A. 1959. Diglossia. Word 15: 325-40.
Ferguson, Charles A., and John J. Gumperz (Eds.). 1960. Linguis-
        tic Diversity in South Asia. Supplement to International Jour-
        nal of American Linguistics 26.
Fischer, John L. 1958. Social influences in the choice of a linguistic
        variant. Word 14: 47-56.
Haas, Mary R. 1944. Men's and women's speech in Koasati. Language
        20: 142-49.
Hoenigswald, Henry M. 1960. Language change and linguistic recon-
        struction. Chicago: University of Chicago Press.
Joos, Martin. 1952. The medieval sibilants. Language 28: 222-31.
        (Reprinted in Readings in Linguistics [Ed. , M. Joos], 372-
        78. 1957. Washington: American Council of Learned Socie-
        ties.)
McCormack, William. 1960. "Social styles in Dharwar Kannada", in
        Linguistic Diversity in South Asia (Ed. C. A. Ferguson and
        J. J. Gumperz).

Opler, Morris Edward, and Harry Hoijer. 1940. The raid and war-
     path language of the Chiricahua Apache. American Anthropol-
     ogist n. s. 42: 617–34.
Ross, Alan S. C. 1954. Linguistic class indicators in present–day
     English. Neuphilologische Mitteilungen 55: 20–56.
Sapir, Edward. 1915. Abnormal types of speech in Nootka. Geological
     Survey of Canada Memoir 62, Anthropological Series no. 5.
     (Reprinted in Selected Writings [Ed. David Mandelbaum] 179–
     96. 1949. Berkeley: University of California Press.)
_____. 1929. "Male and female forms of speech in Yana", in Donum
     Natalicium Schrijnen (Ed. St. W. J. Teeuwen) 79–85. Nij-
     megen–Utrecht: N. v. Dekker & van de Vegt. (Reprinted in
     Selected Writings [Ed. David Mandelbaum] 206–12. 1949.
     Berkeley: University of California Press.)
Zvelebil, Kamil. 1959. Dialects of Tamil I, II. Archiv Orientální 27:
     272–317, 572–603.

Part II. South Asia

5 | Linguistic Change in Some Indian Caste Dialects

Introductory

Dialect differences in the languages of India may be thought of in a three-dimensional framework: in addition to the horizontal distribution of geographical dialects, as is found throughout the world, India offers exceptionally clear cases of dialects which are spoken in a single spot, but which may be arranged in a vertical scale correlated with social class. These are the caste dialects, such as those of a North Indian village which have recently been described by Gumperz.[1] In the study of such dialects, the following question may be raised: Is there a correlation between the amount of linguistic change manifested in a dialect and the social status of the people who speak it? In other terms, in what caste dialects are the more archaic features to be found? Investigation of this question may require separate consideration of various parts of the language: that is, phonemic change, grammatical change, and lexical change may not all operate at the same speed in a given dialect.

This paper does not attempt to answer the question completely, but merely to contribute toward an answer, primarily by comparing data recorded from two Kannada dialects of Bangalore District, Mysore State, South India. One is a Brahmin dialect, as spoken by a young woman born and raised in the city of Bangalore. The other is of the agricultural Okkaliga community, as spoken by a young man from a village a few miles outside the city. Both informants have college educations.[2] The transcriptions are in terms of the following phonemes: /p t ṭ c k b d ḍ j g f s s š z m n ṇ ŋ v l ḷ y r h i ī e ē æ ɨ a ā u ū o ō ɔ/.[3] No attempt is made here to describe all existing differences between the two dialects in question; the differences which are described are those best attested in the data.

1. Phonological Differences

The phonemic systems of the two dialects display the following differences:

1) The Brahmin dialect (hereafter abbreviated as B.) has the phonemes /f z ō/ in loanwords from English; in the Okkaliga dialect (O.) these are replaced by /p j ā/ respectively. E.g.: B. k̲ō̲f̲i̲, O. k̲ā̲p̲i̲ 'coffee'; B. d̲azan, O. d̲ajan 'dozen'.

2) B. /c/, when intervocalic, sometimes corresponds to O. /s/: B. s̲a̲m̲ā̲c̲ā̲r̲a̲, O. s̲a̲m̲ā̲s̲ā̲r̲a̲ 'news', from Skt. s̲a̲m̲ā̲c̲ā̲r̲a̲-. The other cases noted are also loanwords. The data suggests that O. lacks contrast between /c/ and /s/, at least in medial position. This is reminiscent of the situation in Tamil, where affricate and fricative are members of one phoneme;[4] the situation was probably the same in Primitive Dravidian.[5]

3) B. /š/, occurring mainly in loanwords from Sanskrit, often corresponds to O. /s/: B. š̲ā̲n̲t̲i̲, O. s̲ā̲n̲t̲i̲ 'peace'; B. d̲ē̲š̲a̲, O. d̲ē̲s̲a̲ 'country'; B. k̲a̲š̲t̲a̲, O. k̲a̲s̲t̲a̲ 'difficulty'. (The B. forms are identical with the Sanskrit stems in each case.) The lack of contrast between /s/ and /š/ is also a characteristic of Tamil, and presumably of Primitive Dravidian.

4) B. /h/ usually corresponds to O. zero: B. h̲ā̲k̲u̲, O. ā̲k̲u̲ 'put'. After pause, B. /he hē ho hō/ correspond to O. /ye yē va vō/ respectively. This is in conformity with morphophonemic changes also operative in B., by which onglides are added to mid vowels after pause, and /vo/ is further replaced by /va/. E.g.: B. h̲e̲s̲r̲u̲, O. y̲e̲s̲r̲u̲ 'name'; B. h̲o̲g̲e̲, O. v̲a̲g̲e̲ 'smoke'; B. h̲ō̲g̲u̲, O. v̲ō̲g̲u̲ 'go'. In all these cases, the B. forms represent the earlier stage of development, reflecting PDr. forms with initial *p: cf. OKa. p̲e̲s̲a̲r̲, Ta. p̲e̲y̲a̲r̲, Te. p̲ē̲r̲u̲ 'name'; OKa. p̲o̲g̲e̲, Ta. p̲u̲k̲a̲i̲, Te. p̲o̲g̲e̲ 'smoke'; OKa. p̲ō̲g̲u̲, Ta. p̲ō̲k̲u̲, Te. p̲ō̲v̲u̲ 'go'.

5) Aspirated stops of B. correspond to unaspirated ones in O. The examples are principally loanwords: B. b̲h̲ū̲m̲i̲, O. b̲ū̲m̲i̲ 'land' (Skt. b̲h̲ū̲m̲i̲-).

6) Syllable-initial consonant clusters, occurring in loan words in B., are rare in O. Thus sequences of sibilant plus oral sonorant in B. correspond to /s/ alone in O.: B. <u>svāmi</u>, O. <u>sāmi</u> 'sir' (Skt. <u>svāmin-</u>); B. <u>manšya</u>, O. <u>mansa</u> 'man' (Skt. <u>manušya-</u>). B. /s/ plus nasal sometimes corresponds to O. /si/ plus nasal: B. <u>snēyta</u>, O. <u>sinēyta</u> 'friend' (Skt. <u>snehita-</u>). B. /kš/ corresponds to O. /c/: B. <u>kšemsu</u>, O. <u>cemsu</u> 'excuse me' (from Skt. √<u>kšam</u> 'to pardon'.)

7) B. /ē/ often corresponds to O. /yā/ when a mid or low vowel occurs in the next syllable: B. <u>pēte</u>, O. <u>pyāte</u> 'town'. In these cases the pronunciation with /ē/ is older: cf. Ta. <u>pēttai</u>, Marathi <u>peth</u>.

8) B. /o/ often corresponds to O. /a/, as in the second morpheme of B. <u>mal-koll-ōṇa</u>, O. <u>mal-kaḷ-ani</u> 'let's go to bed'. This element, having reflexive meaning in Ka., is cognate with Ta. <u>koḷ</u> 'receive', Te. <u>konu</u> 'take'. Cf. also B. <u>barokke</u>, O. <u>barakke</u> 'for coming'; B. <u>āgolla</u>, O. <u>āgalla</u> 'doesn't become'. Both of these are contracted from forms such as the literary equivalents <u>bar-uvu-da-kke</u> and <u>āg-uvu-d-illa</u> respectively.

9) B. /ɨ/ in the sequence /rɨ/ , occurring in loans from Sanskrit, usually corresponds to O. /u/: B. <u>srɨŋgāra</u>, O. <u>suŋgāra</u> 'beauty' (Skt. <u>śrŋgāra-</u>).

The foregoing correspondences may be summarized as follows: Insofar as it fails to accept new phonemic contrasts occurring in loan words, the O. dialect is the more archaic of the two. It is innovating, however, in its loss of earlier /h/, and in the changes of /ē/ to /yā/ and /o/ to /a/.

2. Grammatical Differences

Grammatical differences between the two dialects include the following:

1) The dative suffix of B. has the allomorphs -<u>kke</u> after /a/ and -<u>Age</u> elsewhere. (<u>A</u> is a morphophoneme commonly actualized as zero after consonants; a vowel plus <u>A</u>, however, becomes immune to the syncope which otherwise affects short vowels.) This corresponds to O. -<u>ke</u> after nouns of all types: B. <u>ūta-kke</u>, O. <u>ūt-ke</u> (with

syncope) 'to dinner'; B. <u>madve-ge</u>, O. <u>maduv-ke</u> 'to a wedding'; B.
<u>mārket-ge</u>, O. <u>mārket-ke</u> 'to the market'. O. also has the variant
-<u>kya</u>: B. <u>pēte-ge</u>, O. <u>pyāt-kya</u> 'to town'. Historically, B. -<u>kke</u> and
-<u>Age</u> may be traced to OKa. -<u>kke</u> and -<u>ige</u> respectively. OKa. also
has the form -<u>ke</u>, however;[6] this has been lost in B. , but generalized
in O. to the point of replacing other allomorphs.

2) Locative formations in B. contain an element -<u>alli</u>, corresponding to O. -<u>āgi</u>: B. <u>bandy-alli</u> (also contracted to <u>bandīli</u>), O.
<u>bandy-āgi</u> 'in a cart'. The B form may be identified with the adverb
<u>alli</u> 'there'; the O. form is of uncertain origin, though homonymous
with <u>āgi</u> 'having become', from <u>āgu</u> 'become'. Formations in -<u>alli</u>
are attested in OKa. , along with several other types lacking in the
modern dialects;[7] those in -<u>āgi</u> are apparently innovations.

3) The first person plural imperative suffix is B. -<u>ōna</u>, O.
-<u>āni</u>, -<u>ani</u>, -<u>ana</u>. E.g.: B. <u>hōg-ōna</u>, O. <u>vōg-āni</u> 'let's go'; B. <u>mugs-</u>
<u>ōna</u>, O. <u>mugs-ani</u> 'let's finish'; B. <u>kūt-koll-ōna</u>, O. <u>kūt-koll-āna</u>
'let's sit down'. Cf. OKa. -<u>uvam</u>, MKa. -<u>uva</u>, modern written Ka.
-<u>uva</u>, -<u>uvana</u>, -<u>uvana</u>, -<u>ōna</u>.[8] If, as is claimed by Kittel, /n/ is earlier than /ṇ/ in this suffix, then the O. forms are archaic in retaining
it. The vowels of the O. forms, however, appear to be innovations.

4) Certain verb stems show different allomorphy in the two
dialects: <u>āgu</u> 'become', but B. <u>āg-ta</u>, O. <u>ā-ta</u> 'becoming'; B. <u>hōgu</u>,
O. <u>vōgu</u> 'go', but B. <u>hōg-ta</u>, O. <u>vō-ta</u> 'going'; <u>bā</u> 'come', but B. <u>bar-</u>
<u>ta</u>, O. <u>bat-ta</u> 'coming'. The O. forms are unattested in older Kan-
nada. A different case, however, is B. <u>kū-tu</u>, O. <u>kun-tu</u> 'having sat'
(from a stem occurring only in these forms); both of these date from
the medieval period, being attested from 1398 and 1585 respectively.[9]

5) The verb <u>iru</u> 'be' has a set of forms in B. which lack a
tense suffix; corresponding to the third person forms of these, O.
uses pronouns plus the emphatic morph -<u>e</u>. E.g.: B. <u>iddāne</u>, O.
<u>avn-e</u> 'he is' (<u>avnu</u> 'he'); B. <u>iddāre</u>, O. <u>avr-e</u> 'they are' (<u>avru</u> 'they');
B. <u>ide</u>, O. <u>ad-e</u> 'it is' (<u>adu</u> 'it'). All of these are modern formations:
of the O. forms, however, only the neuter <u>ad-e</u> is found in the modern written language.[10] The other O. forms may represent an analogical extension on this model.

The foregoing grammatical correspondence thus show the B. dialect to be generally more archaic.

3. Lexical Differences

Finally, the following cases typify the differences of vocabulary between the two dialects (OKa. and other Dravidian forms are from Kittel's dictionary):

1) In some cases, where there is only a slight phonemic difference between B. and O. forms, the B. form is known to be the earlier one; e.g.:

B. hordu, O. voldu 'start out'; cf. OKa. pora, pera 'out', Ta. pir 'outer', Malayalam pur 'outside', Te. per 'foreign'.
B. baglu, O. baklu 'door'; cf. OKa. bagil.
B. bombe, O. gombe 'doll'; cf. OKa. bombe, Ta. pommai, Te. bomme.
B. matte, O. mante 'again'; cf. OKa. matte, Ta. marrai.

2) In other cases, the O. form is known to be earlier; there is not necessarily any similarity between the two forms. E.g.:

B. prayāna, O. payna 'journey'. The B. form is a recent copy of Skt.; the O. form is from OKa. payana, which in turn is from Skt. prayāna- or prayana-.
B. bahla, O. balu 'much, very'. Cf. MKa. bahala, from Skt. bahala; but OKa. bal 'strength, greatness', Ta. val, Te. balu.
B. togo, O. teko 'take'; cf. OKa. tekkoll-.
B. hēge, O. yenge 'how'; cf. MKa. hēge, but OKa. uṅge.
B. huli, O. yesru 'curry'; cf. OKa. esar.
B. ūta mādu, O. unnu 'eat a meal'; cf. OKa. un, Ta. un.

3) In the remaining cases, the relative age of the forms is not clear. E.g.:

B. sumne, O. sumke 'quiet'; cf. OKa. summane and summage, both attested in the same work.
B. yeštu, O. yēsu 'how much', both attested in the same MKa. work.

B. _sarti_, O. _sāri_ 'time, turn'. Both are attested only in modern times. The B. form may be from Skt. _sarat_ 'going'; with the O. form, cf. Malayalam _sāri_.

B. _solpa_, O. _rav-asṭu_ 'a little', both modern. The B. form is from Skt. _svalpa_; the O. form is literally 'as much as (_asṭu_) a grain (_rave_)', cf. Te. _rav-aste_.

B. _snāna māḍu_, O. _nīr āk-kō_ 'bathe', both modern. B. is literally 'to make a bath', with Skt. _snāna-_ 'bath'; O. is literally 'to put water on oneself'.

B. _sinima_, O. _bayskōpu_ 'movies', from English _cinema_ and _bioscope_ respectively; the former may be the more recent borrowing.

4. Conclusions

Generalizing from the above comparisons, we may draw the following conclusions: O. accepts foreign words and foreign phonemic patterns less rapidly than does B. Its vocabulary is thus more archaic, and its phonemic system is likewise archaic in that it lacks certain contrasts which B. has taken over from Sanskrit and other languages. B., on the other hand, is more resistant to phonemic changes of native sounds, and to grammatical change.

Reasons for B.'s receptiveness to importations from other languages are not hard to find: the Brahmins have traditionally been conversant with Sanskrit, and more recently with English. The prestige attached to both these languages has increased the likelihood for bilingual speakers to introduce words from them into Kannada. It is not quite as easy to account for the conservative tendency of B. as regards phonemic and grammatical change. A conditioning factor may be the greater literacy of the Brahmin community; that is, the permanence of the written word may retard change in the spoken language.

In this connection, data from Tulu, another Dravidian language of South India, deserves examination. Although separate dialects of Tulu are spoken by Brahmins and by non-Brahmins or Shudras, neither dialect is commonly written. We may therefore hypothesize that the B. dialect of Tulu will show no greater retardation of phonetic change than the S. (Shudra) dialect. The Tulu data available[11] shows, first of all, some correspondences in which the B. forms are more archaic:

B. initial vowel corresponds to S. zero in a number of cases where PDr. has the initial vowel: B. imbolu, S. mōlu 'this woman' (Ta. ival, Ka. ivalu); B. edaŋguɩ, S. danguɩ 'left (hand)' (Ta. itai, Ka. yeda); B. uṇpu, S. nuppu 'food' (cf. Ta. uṇ, Ka. uṇnu 'to eat').

B. /s/ corresponds to S. /t/ in some cases where PDr. has *c: B. sik-, S. tik- 'be obtained' (Ta. cikku, Ka. sikku); in retaining sibilant quality, B. here appears more archaic.

B. /j/ corresponds to S. /d/ where PDr. has *ñ[12] in B. jeñji, S. deñji 'crab' (Ta. ñantu, ñentu, Ka. yēdi). B. appears more archaic, in that it retains palatal quality.

There are, however, other correspondences in which S. has the more archaic forms:

B. initial /ē/ corresponds to S. /yā/ in some cases where PDr. has *ia:[13] B. ēnuɩ, S. yānuɩ 'I' (Ta. yāṇ, OKa. ān); B. ēruɩ, S. yāruɩ 'who' (Ta. yār, ār, Ka. yāru).

B. /s/ corresponds to S. /t/, where PDr. has *t, in B. sōj-, S. tōj- 'appear' (Ta. tōnru, Ka. tōru).[14]

In another correspondence, both dialects innovate, and neither can be considered the more archaic: B. /l/ corresponds to S. /r/ where PDr. has *r:[15] B. bāḻæ, S. bāræ 'plantain' (Ta. vāṟai, OKa. bāṟe, modern bāḻe); B. kōḻi, S. kōri 'hen' (Ta. kōṟi, OKa. kōṟi, modern kōḻi); B. būḻ-, S. būr- 'fall' (Ta. viṟ-, OKa. būṟ-, modern bīḻu).

On the basis of the limited data, we may therefore conclude that the difference between B. and S. dialects of Tulu, as regards rate of phonetic change, is less marked than that between the B. and O. dialects of Kannada. A further study of Tulu should be especially rewarding in the investigation of Indian caste dialects.

NOTES

[1] John J. Gumperz, Dialect differences and social stratification in a North Indian village, American Anthropologist 60. 668-82 (1958).

[2] The Brahmin idiolect presented here is that of my chief in-

formant in an intensive study of the Bangalore Brahmin speech, and
may be taken as typical. The Okkaliga dialect, on the other hand,
was studied only briefly. The data obtained is not 'pure' Okkaliga
speech; that is, the informant's idiolect has been influenced by the
prestige of the Brahmin dialect. Even so, the salient features of Okkaliga speech show up clearly enough in the data recorded from him.

[3] The phonemic system of Kannada is described in detail in
my monograph, An outline of colloquial Kannada (Poona, 1958).

[4] Murray Fowler, The segmental phonemes of Sanskritized
Tamil, Language 30. 360-67 (1954).

[5] T. Burrow, Dravidian Studies VI, Bulletin of the School of
Oriental and African Studies (University of London) 12. 132-47 (1947).
Primitive Dravidian is hereafter abbreviated PDr.; so also Ka. for
Kannada, OKa. for Old Kannada, MKa. for Medieval Kannada, Ta.
for Tamil, Te. for Telugu, Skt. for Sanskrit.

[6] A. N. Narasimhia, A grammar of the oldest Kanarese in-
scriptions 141-46 (Mysore, 1941).

[7] Narasimhia, Grammar, 151-54.

[8] F. Kittel, A grammar of the Kannada language 148-51 (Mangalore, 1903). The symbol ṃ stands for the Kannada sonne, pronounced (in this position) as /m/ in modern Kannada.

[9] F. Kittel, Kannada-English Dictionary 441, 457 (Mangalore,
1894).

[10] Kittel, Grammar, 133-34.

[11] From L. V. Ramaswami Aiyar, Materials for a sketch of
Tulu phonology, Indian linguistics 6. 385-439. The author's phonetic
symbols are altered to agree with the transcription used above for
Kannada.

[12] According to T. Burrow, Dravidian Studies V, BSOAS, 11.
595-616 (1946), esp. 605.

[13] Burrow, Dravidian Studies V, 599.

[14] The complicated history of Tulu initial /t c s d j/ is dealt
with by Ramaswami Aiyar, Tulu initial affricates and sibilants,
Quarterly journal of the Mythic Society (Bangalore) 22. 259-73 (1932).
However, the author does not clearly distinguish the various Tulu dialects represented in his material. Thus, the stem meaning 'to be en-
tangled' is given as cikk-, tikk-, śikk-, and sikk-, only the first being distinguished as 'rare sub-dialectal'.

[15] Information on the history of *ṛ, and on its modern pronunciation, is given in Bh. Krishnamurti, Proto-Dravidian *ẓ, Indian linguistics 19. 259-93 (= Turner jubilee volume I, 1958).

6 | Sociolinguistic Variation and Language Change

In Collaboration with A. K. Ramanujan

1. Introduction

It seems probable that no language is as monolithic as our descriptive grammars sometimes suggest; wherever sufficient data are available, we find diversity within languages on all levels — phonological, grammatical, and lexical. Such diversity can be studied along three synchronic dimensions — geographical, social, and stylistic. The geographical dimension is, of course, the main one which has occupied the attention of dialectologists and which has been presented in dialect atlases. Other types of variation within languages, however, have received less attention. What is here termed the social dimension of linguistic variation is correlated with the socially established identity of the speaker and/or the person addressed or mentioned. Examples are the special linguistic forms used in Nootka to speak to or about children, fat people, dwarfs, hunchbacks, etc. (Sapir, 1915); cases of separate men's and women's speech, as in Koasati (Haas, 1944); and the cases, familiar from our own society, where speech differences are correlated with the speaker's social status. The term "sociolinguistic variation" may be applied to cases such as these, and in addition to those where linguistic variation is correlated not with the identity of persons, but with other factors in the social context. These are the factors we have called stylistic. Linguistic styles determined by such factors range from the special war-path speech of the Chiricahua Apache (Opler and Hoijer, 1940) to the written styles appropriate to particular literary contexts in societies like our own. Included here also are differences between formal and informal styles of speaking. Although these occur, perhaps, in most languages of the world, some speech communities such as those of Arabic and Modern Greek show such a marked difference between formal and informal style as to produce a kind of bidialectism which Ferguson (1959) has named <u>diglossia</u>.

The study of all these varieties of sociolinguistic variation has proved especially fruitful in the South Asian area (India, Pakistan, Ceylon), and a volume recently published (Ferguson and Gumperz, 1960) has dealt with several aspects of the subject. On the one hand, clear-cut social dialects are found to be associated with the caste system of Hindu society, and these "caste dialects" constitute one important field for investigation. On the other hand, many Indian languages have formal and informal styles which are differentiated to the point of diglossia. However, since most published works on South Asian languages concentrate on high-caste dialects or formal style, adequate data on differences of caste dialect and on diglossia, as well as on relationships between the two phenomena, are still lacking.

In the Dravidian languages of South India, we find sociolinguistic factors organized into at least two contrasting patterns. In Tamil and Kanarese (and probably also in Telugu and Malayalam), there are classic cases of diglossia. The formal or literary style is used by educated persons in writing and in public address; it varies only slightly with the social class or place of origin of the person using it. Contrasting with this is an informal or colloquial style, showing much greater internal diversity. Differences correlated with the regional and caste background come to the fore in this informal style, although the speech of the educated may be somewhat more uniform than that of the uneducated. An entirely different pattern is found in the Tulu speech community, occupying a small area on the western coast of South India, and probably also in the area of the Kodagu or Coorg language, farther inland. Here we find Hindu societies comparable to those in the rest of South India, but lacking a tradition of written literature in the native tongue. The social functions which are elsewhere served by a formal style of the local languages are here served by the formal variety of Kanarese. Tulu is, to be sure, sometimes written in Kanarese script for informal purposes, but the language is not the customary medium either for education or for a literary tradition. Dialect divisions corresponding to regional differences and caste differences do occur in Tulu, however, just as in the informal styles of Kanarese or Tamil.

The question then arises: What processes have operated to bring about the differences that exist between modern caste dialects ? If forms of the present-day dialects are compared with earlier forms of Dravidian speech, it is apparent that some modern forms represent retentions of earlier ones, while others represent innovations. It has been claimed that linguistic innovation in general comes from the lower social levels; thus a recent paper speaks of "la langue populaire, riche en innovations, qui a pour elle le grand nombre, et la langue des classes aisées, qui est plus conservatrice" (Schogt, 1961, 91). On the other hand, it has also been argued that phonetic change, and perhaps linguistic change in general, are initiated by the upper social strata, in order to "maintain a prestige-marking difference" from the lower strata (Joos, 1952, 229). The lower class is said to narrow the gap again by imitation, forcing the upper class to innovate still more. Thus language change is viewed as a "protracted pursuit of an elite by an envious mass, and consequent 'flight' of the elite" (Fischer, 1958, 52). The information available on Indian caste dialects can be used to test such views. Two years ago, an investigation of material from Kanarese, and to a lesser extent from Tulu (Bright, 1960a, 1960b) reached the following conclusions: 1) It is inadequate to operate simply in terms of "change"; changes must be classified as phonological, grammatical, or lexical, and as involving loan materials or native materials. 2) In a comparison of a Brahmin dialect of Kanarese with a middle-caste Non-Brahmin dialect (the abbreviations B and NB will be used hereafter), the B dialect showed innovation on the more conscious levels of phonological and lexical borrowing and of semantic change, while the NB dialect showed changes on the less conscious levels of native phonology and morphology. 3) However, in a similar study of Tulu, B and NB dialects showed phonological change in similar degrees; the data then at hand were insufficient for the study of other types of change in Tulu.

In an effort to account for the difference between the Kanarese case and the Tulu case, it was hypothesized that it might be due to the existence of a separate formal style in Kanarese, especially as actualized in the written language. That is, the greater literacy of Kanarese Brahmins was seen as a force counteracting tendencies to change in their dialect — the "frozen" phonology and grammar of the literary language serving to retard the unconscious processes of change to which speech is normally subject. Tulu Brahmin speech,

on the other hand, having no written Tulu tradition to affect it, has
been subject to changes of the same type that have operated in the NB
dialects of Tulu. In more general terms, it is suggested that literacy,
wherever it is present in human societies, acts as a brake on processes of linguistic change. This suggestion has recently been supported
by a study of Latin legal terminology over a 2000-year period. This
study finds an unusually high retention rate in legal vocabulary, and
concludes that "since these materials have been selected within an
area where total literacy is a primary and integral necessity in the
communicative process, it seems reasonable to conclude that it is to
be reckoned with in language change through time and may be expected to retard the rate of vocabulary change" (Zengel, 1962, 138-39).

It is clear that further study of South Asian caste dialects is
desirable in order to establish more clearly the role of literacy in
linguistic change. To this end, we have now examined data on caste
dialects of Tamil, a language with an exceptionally long literary tradition; at the same time, an expanded body of Tulu data has been
taken into consideration. The following sections present our findings
on these two language communities.

2. Tamil

The majority of publications on Tamil deal exclusively with
the formal style of the language, as manifested in the writing system.
Colloquial Tamil, in its various geographical and social dialects, has
received attention in publications of Vinson (1895), Matthews (1942),
and Jothimutthu (1956); but these works suffer from lack of organization, and they fail to give clear geographical and social identifications
of their data. More systematic discussions have been presented by
Bloch (1910), Shanmugam Pillai (1960), Zvelebil (1959, 1960, 1961),
and the present authors (1962). The work done to date, however, has
barely scratched the surface of the subject, and generalizations about
Tamil dialectology are still risky.

With these qualifications in mind, we have nevertheless attempted to find general features distinguishing B from NB dialects of
Tamil, and to ascertain which social group plays the innovating role
in each case. B data have been obtained from Ayyangar and Ayyar
informants; NB data have been obtained from members of Vellala,

Nadar, Chettiar, and Christian communities. The historical perspective is provided by considering the Literary Tamil form (which is usually, though not always, historically prior to the colloquial form), the cognates in other Dravidian languages (by reference to Burrow and Emeneau, 1961), and the forms which loanwords have in their source languages. The comparisons made are divided into those involving 1) vocabulary, 2) phonology, and 3) morphology; syntactic comparisons are yet to be carried out. [1]

    2.1. Caste differences in Ta. vocabulary may be classified into two types. In the first type, one caste has a loanword and the other has a native word, e.g. B jaḷõ "water" (Skt. jala-), tīrtõ "drinking water" (Skt. tīrtha-), tanni "water not for drinking" (native), as aginst NB tanni "water in general". In most of the cases noted, it is B which has innovated by introducing the loanword; a contrary case occurs, however, in B āmbaḍeyā "husband", NB puruṣẽ (Skt. puruṣa-). In a second type of vocabulary, both castes have native terms, e.g. B tūṅgu, NB oraṅgu "sleep". The B form also has the meaning "hang" (intransitive), which is apparently the original sense; cf. the corresponding transitive tūkku "lift", and Ka. tūgu "weigh". The NB form reflects LTa. uraṅku and other Dravidian forms meaning "sleep". Here B has innovated through semantic shift where NB has not; our sample contains no cases of the opposite possibility. There are, however, cases where the two dialects differ without evidence that one has innovated more than the other, e.g. B alambu, NB kaḻuvu "wash", both apparently descended without change of meaning from PDr. stems.

    2.2. Phonological comparisons of B and NB again may be classified into two types. The first type is that of loanwords, in which B frequently preserves non-native phonology, while NB assimilates them to the native pattern, e.g. B svāmi, NB sāmi, cāmi (Skt. svāmin-). At the same time, B is prone to hypercorrections in loan words, such as jīni "sugar" (NB cīni, from Hindi cīni), and krāfu "haircut" (NB krāppu, from English "crop"), where the foreign sounds /j/ and /f/ are erroneously introduced. The second type of phonological comparison involves native words, where the differences found between caste dialects are most clearly typified by the cases where B has /ṟ/ while NB has /ṛ/ inconsistently varying with /y/ (in northern areas) or /ḷ/ (in southern areas); e.g. B vāṟeppaṟõ "banana" as against NB forms like vāṟeppaḷŏ, vāḷepparŏ, and vāḷeppaḷŏ. The overall picture thus shows B as innovator in the introduction of foreign phonemes, sometimes in etymologically unpredictable places. NB, on the other hand, innovates in native material, although the result (at least for educated speakers) is often free variation between older and newer forms, rather than complete replacement of the older.

2.3. Morphological differences between B and NB mostly involve varying shapes of morphemes, not all of which can be explained by the regular phonemic correspondences. An example is B -du, NB -ccu "it" (subject of verb), as in B vandudu, NB vanduccu "it came" (LTa. vantatu). In this case it appears that the NB form represents an analogic extension of the ending found in both B and NB pōccu "it went", āccu "it became" (LTa. pōyiṟṟu, āyiṟṟu). In this, as in other examples, NB plays the innovating role. In some other examples, to be sure, B and NB seem to have innovated equally, but in different directions, as when the present tense marker (LTa. -kiṟ) becomes -h in some NB dialects, but -r in B; e.g. B paṉṟã, NB paṇṇuhã "he does" (LTa. paṇṇukirāṉ). But no clear case has been noted in which B has innovated while NB remains conservative.

2.4. The examination of Tamil materials which has been carried out so far shows a situation similar to that previously noted for Kanarese. Neither dialect has a monopoly of innovations in any part of the structure, and yet tendencies are discernible: on the part of B, toward greater use of foreign vocabulary, foreign phonology, and semantic shifts; on the part of NB, toward shifts in native phonology and in morphology.

3. Tulu

Published data on Tulu are found in Brigel (1872), Ramaswamy Aiyar (1932a, 1932b, 1936), and Krishnamurti (1958). These sources do not, unfortunately, distinguish regional dialects, so that there is difficulty in separating regional variations from social variations. This problem has been solved in part by checking with three Tulu speakers.

3.1. The comparisons between B and NB dialects of Tulu can be classified as were those of Tamil. Thus we have: 1) vocabulary

differences involving loan words, such as B puruṣe "husband" (Skt.
puruṣa-), NB kaṇḍane (cognate with Ta. kaṇṭaṇ, Ka. gaṇḍa); 2) vocabulary differences involving native words, such as B jōvu, jēvu
"girl", NB poṇṇu. The B form means "child" in some NB dialects,
and can be compared with Parji cēpal, Ollari sēpal "boy"; the NB
form is cognate with Ta. peṇ "woman, girl". A semantic shift is ev-
ident in the B usage. In both these types of correspondence only the
B dialect is found to innovate, either by loans from Sanskrit, Hindi,
or Kannada, or by semantic shifts of native terms.

　　3.2. Phonological correspondences are also of two types.
1) Some cases involve loan phonology, as when B aspirated stop corresponds to NB unaspirated stop. Some of these cases are loans from
Indo-Aryan, e.g. B gandha, NB ganda "fragrance" (Skt. gandha-).
In other cases, however, B forms with aspiration may be traced to
PDr., which had no distinctive aspiration: e.g. B chāḷi, NB caḷi
"cold" (cf. Ta. caḷi). The B aspiration in such cases presumably
originates as a hypercorrect pronunciation. 2) Other cases involve
native phonology, such as B /s/ , NB /t/ from PDr. *c, as in B
sikk-, NB tikk- "be obtained" (cf. Ta. cikku). The B form may be
regarded as the more conservative, especially since Pdr. *c probably included sibilant allophones (as in many modern Ta. dialects).
Five other sound correspondences have been noted in which NB shows
greater innovation. But we also have a smaller number of cases
where the opposite is true, such as the correspondence of B /ē/ to
NB /yā/ where PDr. appears to have had *yā, as in B ēnuu, NB
yānuu "I" (cf. Ta. yaṇ). It thus appears that both B and NB have innovated in phonology, with the NB dialect showing the greater number of innovations. The B dialect, however, shows one special kind
of innovation, the introduction of the foreign element of aspiration.

　　3.3. Morphological correspondences between B and NB Tulu
are more difficult to deal with historically, since we have no writing
system to reflect older forms, and no full reconstruction of PDr.
morphology has yet been made. Certain correspondences do yield to
investigation, however, such as the one between B -no, NB -da, Genitive suffix with "rational" nouns; thus we find B āṇuu-no, NB āṇuu-da
"of the boy" (cf. Ta. āḷ-iṇ, with cognate stem). With "irrational"
nouns Tulu has B -nte, NB -da; apparently NB has generalized the
dental suffix so as to apply to all types of noun. On the other hand,

we find a correspondence between B -i, NB -a, Present Participle marker, as in B barpi, NB barpa "coming"; the NB form agrees with other Dravidian languages, as in Ta. varu-kinr-a, Ka. bar-uv-a "coming".

3.4. In the morphological comparisons, as in the phonological ones, both B and NB are found to innovate. In summary, the Tulu evidence shows the Brahmins as chief innovators in the more conscious varieties of change — semantic shift, lexical borrowing, and phonological borrowing. In the less conscious processes of phonological and morphological change involving native materials, both B and NB dialects innovate.

4. Conclusion

We feel that the evidence so far examined supports the hypothesis that upper and lower class dialects innovate independently of one another, and in two ways, here labelled conscious and unconscious. Of these types of change, the more conscious variety is regularly the mark of the upper class dialect. The less conscious changes apparently may affect both upper and lower dialects, as seen in the Tulu case; but in Kanarese and Tamil, where there is widespread literacy among Brahmins, the formal written style seems to have retarded the less conscious processes of innovation. A study of the Kodagu language, which like Tulu lacks a literary tradition, would be extremely valuable for the further testing of this hypothesis.

The importance of sociolinguistic factors in language history has recently been pointed up by Hoenigswald (1960: 55) and by Schogt (1961). We feel that further investigation of social dialects in the South Asian context can contribute much to understanding the mechanisms of linguistic change.

NOTE

[1] Abbreviations used below are Ta. for Tamil, LTa. for Literary Tamil, Ka. for Kanarese, PDr. for Proto-Dravidian, and Skt. for Sanskrit.

BIBLIOGRAPHY

Bloch, Jules, "Castes et dialectes en Tamoul", Mémoires de la So-
      ciété de Linguistique, 16 (Paris, 1910), 1-30.
Brigel, J., A grammar of the Tulu language (Mangalore, 1872).
Bright, William, "Linguistic change in some South Indian caste dia-
      lects", in Ferguson and Gumperz (1960), pp. 19-26. (a) [In
      this volume, pp. 39-46.]
_____. "Social dialect and language history", Current Anthropology,
      1 (1960), 424-25. (b) [In this volume, pp. 32-38.]
_____, and A. K. Ramanujan, A study of Tamil dialects. Commit-
      tee on South Asian Studies, University of Chicago (mimeo-
      graphed), 1962.
Burrow, T., and M. B. Emeneau, A Dravidian etymological diction-
      ary (Oxford, 1961).
Ferguson, Charles A., "Diglossia", Word, 15 (1959), 325-40.
_____, and John J. Gumperz, Linguistic diversity in South Asia
      (= Indiana University Research Center in Anthropology, Folk-
      lore, and Linguistics, Publication no. 13) (Bloomington,
      1960).
Fischer, John L., "Social influences in the choice of a linguistic var-
      iant", Word, 14 (1958), 47-56.
Haas, Mary R., "Men's and women's speech in Koasati", Language,
      20 (1944), 142-49.
Hoenigswald, Henry, Language change and linguistic reconstruction
      (Chicago, 1960).
Joos, Martin, "The medieval sibilants", Language, 28 (1952), 222-31.
Jothimutthu, P., A guide to Tamil by the direct method (Madras, 1956).
Krishnamurti, Bh., "Proto-Dravidian *ẓ", Indian Linguistics, 19
      (1958), 259-93.
Matthews, Gordon, "The vulgar pronunciation of Tamil", Bulletin of
      the School of Oriental Studies, 10 (London, 1942), 992-97.
Opler, Morris, and Harry Hoijer, "The raid and war-path language
      of the Chiricahua Apache", American Anthropologist, 42
      (1940), 617-34.
Ramaswamy Aiyar, L. V., "Tulu prose texts in two dialects", Bulle-
      tin of the School of Oriental Studies, 6 (London, 1932), 897-
      931. (a)
_____. "Tulu initial affricates and sibilants", Quarterly Journal of
      the Mythic Society, 22 (Bangalore, 1932), 259-73. (b)

————, "Materials for a sketch of Tulu phonology", Indian Linguistics, 6 (1936), 385–439.

Sapir, Edward, Abnormal types of speech in Nootka (= Geological Survey of Canada, Memoir 62, Anthropological Series, no. 5) (Ottawa, 1915).

Schogt, H. G. , "La notion de loi dans la phonétique historique", Lingua, 10 (1961), 79–92.

Shanmugam Pillai, M. , "Tamil — literary and colloquial", in Ferguson and Gumperz (1960), pp. 27–42.

Vinson, Julien, "Les variations phonétiques de la prononciation populaire tamoule", Centenaire de l'Ecole des Langues Orientales Vivantes (Paris, 1895), pp. 115–26.

Zengel, Marjorie S. , "Literacy as a factor in language change", American Anthropologist, 64 (1962), 132–39.

Zvelebil, Kamil, "Dialects of Tamil, I–II", Archiv Orientální, 27 (1959), 272–317, 572–603.

————, "Dialects of Tamil, III", Archiv Orientální, 28 (1960), 414–56.

————, "Some features of Dindigul Tamil", Te. Po. Mī. Maṇiviṟā Malar (T. P. Meenakshisundaram Commemoration Volume) (Coimbatore, 1961), pp. 424–46.

7 | Language, Social Stratification, and Cognitive Orientation

Sociolinguistics is a thriving infant, but an infant neverthe-less. Thus, the literature is still meager in the subfield dealing with the linguistic correlates of social stratification. Ten years ago it was noted that of two review articles on social stratification, "neither lists any study dealing with language as a status-related factor;"[1] and the same comment holds for a similar review article published only last year.[2] In fact, it is only very recently that any combination of socio-logical and linguistic sophistication has been brought to bear on the subject. Thus, on the level of linguistic structure or langue, we still have no thorough phonological, grammatical, and semantic compari-son of even a single pair of class dialects; and on the level of linguis-tic behavior or parole, we still have no "ethnography of speaking" (to use Hymes' term) for even the simplest kind of community.[3] Lacking such basic bodies of data, discussion in sociolinguistics must often suggest rather than claim.

Among the more interesting suggestions that have been made are those which point to a relationship within social strata between language and cognitive orientation, using this term to cover such mat-ters as world view, value systems, and other matters of psychologi-cal outlook. Here we are dealing with what has been called the con-cept of linguistic relativity, associated with the name of Benjamin Lee Whorf, but in an extended sense. Whorf was concerned with correla-tions between world view and linguistic structure; but as has been pointed out by Hymes,[4] we may apply Whorf's concepts also to lan-guage behavior, i.e. to the different ways that language is used in var-ious societies. Furthermore, although Whorf's comparisons involved widely differing linguistic communities, such as that of the Hopi ver-sus "Standard Average European", we may equally well undertake

comparisons between parts of a single community, such as those parts
which are characterized by differing linguistic structures and/ or
differing patterns of linguistic behavior.

The relations between language, social stratification, and
cognitive orientation have been studied most deeply in a series of publications by Bernstein. In these papers, a distinction is made between a "restricted code", speech which uses relatively limited linguistic resources and is consequently predictable to a high degree, as
against an "elaborated code", which allows a larger number of structural options and shows a correspondingly low level of predictability.
In terms of social-psychological correlates, the restricted code is
"status oriented": it "elicits and progressively strengthens a relatively undifferentiated adherence to the normative arrangements of a
local structure" and "promotes the transmission of social rather than
individual symbols".[5] The elaborated code, on the other hand, is
"person rather than status oriented".[6] Bernstein finds that (in the
British context of his work) "a restricted code is available to all members of society"; the middle class learns, in addition, an elaborated
code, but "sections of the lower class population" have access only
to the restricted code.[7] This difference in code use is said both to
reflect and to perpetuate the social-psychological differences between
the middle class and the working class.

It is clear that the differences between Bernstein's restricted and elaborated codes are matters of language behavior rather than
of language structure: both codes draw on the same grammar, but the
elaborated code, for instance, uses a higher percentage of subordinate
clauses. The question then remains open as to whether the notion of
linguistic relativity may apply to differences of linguistic structure
between class dialects.

Some of our most detailed and useful data on social dialect
comes from India; indeed, we may say that much of the current interest in sociolinguistics derives directly from work on Indian languages. Dialect differences specifically correlated with the caste
system of India have been reported widely; the general picture is of
a dichotomy between Touchable and Untouchable usage in North India,
as against a three-way division in South India between Brahmin, Non-
Brahmin, and Untouchable dialects.[8] It should be made clear that

caste dialects are independent of the dichotomy between formal and informal styles. It may be true that the higher castes have the opportunity to receive an education more often and thereby to become proficient in the formal style. But formal usage is quite a separate system from high-caste informal usage; it is used in a substantially uniform way by all educated people, whatever their caste background may be.

Descriptions of Indian caste dialects, like other sociolinguistic studies, have usually been organized along another dimension, which corresponds to the divisions of language structure recognized by descriptive linguists. The features usually noted under this heading are phonological, grammatical, and lexical. Under the phonological rubric we may be told, for example, that the Brahmin Kanarese initial /h/ corresponds to Non-Brahmin zero in examples like Brahmin hālu, Non-Brahmin ālu "milk". Under grammar it is explained that Brahmin Kanarese has the locative morpheme -alli corresponding to Non-Brahmin -agi. Under lexicon such differences as Brahmin sinima, Non-Brahmin bayskōpu "movies" are noted.[9]

Most published data of this kind refer mainly to differences of phonological shape between semantically equivalent utterances. That is, both Brahmin and Non-Brahmin dialects have morphemes meaning "milk, locative, movies"; these morphemes have the differing phonemic shapes hālu versus ālu, -alli versus -agi, and sinima versus bayskōpu respectively. These differences may be accounted for historically in a variety of ways involving considerations such as regular sound change, borrowing, or analogical change. But the fact remains that such comparisons do not point to any differences in structure between the two caste dialects compared. The dialects have the same grammatical units, but in different phonological shapes. If we use the term morphophonemics to refer to the part of linguistic description which accounts for the phonological shapes of grammatical elements, then we may say that the type of description of caste dialects which has been illustrated above is altogether a matter of morphophonemic comparison.

Some publications, to be sure, have also pointed out that one dialect has a different inventory of basic elements from that of another. Under phonology, for instance, it can be stated that the difference between Kanarese Brahmin hālu, Non-Brahmin ālu "milk" reflects the fact that the Brahmin dialect has an /h/ phoneme while the Non-Brahmin dialect does not; furthermore, the Brahmin phonemes /f z š/ are also lacking in the Non-Brahmin dialect. Under the heading of grammar, however, it becomes harder to find reports of structural differences. And under the lexical heading, we again find only scant report of differences deeper than those of the morphophonemic level.

The suggestion which I would like to make is that caste dialects may differ not only in various ways that are phonologically definable, but also in important ways which are reflected in differences of grammar and vocabulary which basically derive from different semantic structures. That is, caste dialects, like separate languages (but probably to a lesser degree), may reflect different ways of classifying nonlinguistic phonenmena, be they subjective or objective.

The scarcity of data on these differences probably results from several factors. For one thing, semantic differences are less obvious to the investigator than are the other types of difference which have been mentioned. In addition, semantic structure has only recently become a favored area of research for descriptive linguists. Even so, the published data on Indian social dialects provide adequate evidence that difference in semantic structures is in fact present. The following are illustrative of the data to be found:

1) In the Tamil of the Iyengar (Brahmin) and Mudaliyar (Non-Brahmin) castes, as reported by Ramanujan,[10] the semantic area of male affinal kin is subdivided in two different ways:

	Brahmin	Non-Brahmin
son-in-law ⎱	*maaple* ⎤	*marumahā*
younger sister's husband ⎰		
elder sister's husband	*attimbeer* ⎬	*maccāā*
wife's brother	*maccinā* ⎦	

This particular semantic difference is, of course, correlated with differences in marriage practices.

2) The same caste dialects of Tamil also show different classifications in the semantic area of food and water. Thus we find the following:

	Brahmin	*Non-Brahmin*
holy water	*perumaal tiirtõ*	*tiirtõ*
drinking water	*tiirtõ* ⎫	
water in general	*jalõ* ⎬	*tanni*
nondrinkable water	*tanni* ⎭	

Note here that the fact that <u>tiirtõ</u> means "drinking water" to Brahmins and "holy water" to Non-Brahmins means only that the two dialects overlap in their morphophonemic actualizations. The more important fact is that the Brahmin dialect uses <u>tiirtõ</u> in making a four-way distinction, while the Non-Brahmin dialect uses it in a two-way distinction.

   3) Still in the Iyengar and Mudaliyar dialects of Tamil, Brahmin usage shows connotational distinctions of meaning between certain terms which are used interchangeably in the Non-Brahmin dialect. Thus:

	Brahmin	*Non-Brahmin*
food (neutral)	*saadõ* ⎫	*Sooru,* "food" (∼ *saadõ* as free variant)
food (pejorative)	*sooru* ⎭	
eat (neutral)	*saapdu* ⎫	*tinnu,* "eat" (∼ *saapdu* as free variant)
eat (pejorative)	*tinnu* ⎭	

   4) In the Kanarese of Dharwar, Brahmins address mother and elder sister with the same forms, while Non-Brahmins (Lingayats) make a distinction. There is a similar pattern in addressing father and elder brother. [11]

   5) Also in Dharwar, Brahmins use a single morpheme -<u>u</u> of general-purpose address; Lingayats distinguish -<u>apa</u>, used to men, from -<u>be</u>, used to women; and untouchables add special elements for addressing a son-in-law and for addressing affinal kin.

   6) Again in Dharwar, Brahmins and Lingayats distinguish two cases of the noun which can be called accusative and dative, but the Untouchable dialect shows merger of the two cases into one.

   7) According to Ramaswami Aiyar, [12] the Brahmin dialect of Tulu has a single third person honorific pronoun <u>arī</u>, where the Non-Brahmin dialect retains a distinction (paralleled elsewhere in both

dialects) between ā̲r̲ī̲, "he (honorific) there", and m̲ē̲r̲ī̲ ,"he (honorific) here".[13]

8) In Brahmin Tulu, there are distinctions of gender, number, and person in negative tenses of the verb; Non-Brahmin Tulu lacks these distinctions in negative forms.[14]

Such differences in semantic structure may be supposed to have counterparts in other structures. It seems possible, in spite of the scarcity of data, to suggest that semantic differences between caste dialects may reflect differences in cognitive orientation from one caste to another.[15] Thus it has been suggested by various scholars that Brahmins are more concerned than other castes with verbalization, or with hierarchical classification of phonemena, or with differentiation as opposed to generalization of experience. Such hypotheses as these might derive support from the kind of data presented above. What is needed, then, is a "social dialectology" which will apply a structural approach not only to linguistic form,[16] but also to meaning. If field workers will give greater attention to semantic structures, and if more data on the subject are made available, then it may be possible to fit semantic diversity into a larger understanding of how caste functions in India, and of how social stratification functions throughout the world.

NOTES

Material from this paper was presented at the Conference on Social Structure and Social Change in India, held at the University of Chicago in 1965. I am indebted to Punya Sloka Ray for helpful comment.

[1]George N. Putnam and Edna M. O'Hern, The Status Significance of an Isolated Urban Dialect (Language Dissertations number 53, Supplement to Language, volume 31, number 4), Baltimore: Linguistic Society of America, 1956.

[2]Raymond J. Murphy, "Some Recent Trends in Stratification Theory and Research", Annals of the American Academy of Political and Social Science, 356 (1964), 142-167.

[3]Dell Hymes, "The Ethnography of Speaking", in Thomas Gladwin and William Sturtevant, editors, Anthropology and Human Behavior, Washington: Anthropological Society of Washington, 1962.

[4] Dell Hymes, "Two Types of Linguistic Relativity", in William Bright, editor, Sociolinguistics, The Hague: Mouton, 1966.

[5] Basil Bernstein, "Elaborated and Restricted Codes: Their Social Origins and Some Consequences", in John J. Gumperz and Dell Hymes, editors, The Ethnography of Communication, Special Publication, American Anthropologist, 66 (December, 1964), p. 66. Studies with similar aims and results, but with less careful methodology, are Leonard Schatzman and Anselm Strauss, "Social Class and Modes of Communication", American Journal of Sociology, 60 (January, 1955), and Ernest A. T. Barth, "The Language Behavior of Negroes and Whites", Pacific Sociological Review, 4 (Fall, 1961), 69-72.

[6] Bernstein, op. cit., p. 63.

[7] Ibid., p. 60.

[8] Paul Friedrich (personal communication) suggests that a four-way division of Malayalam social dialects exists in Kerala, between Brahmins, Nayars, other touchable castes, and Untouchables.

[9] William Bright, "Linguistic Change in Some Indian Caste Dialects", in Charles A. Ferguson and John J. Gumperz, editors, Linguistic Diversity in South Asia (Research Center in Anthropology, Folklore, and Linguistics, publication number 13; Supplement to International Journal of American Linguistics, volume 26, number 3), Bloomington: Indiana University, 1960, pp. 19-26. [In this volume, pp. 39-46.]

[10] A. K. Ramanujan, "The Structure of Variation: A Study in Caste Dialects", in Milton Singer and Bernard S. Cohn, editors, Structure and Change in Indian Society (Viking Fund publications in anthropology, 47), Chicago: Aldine, 1968, pp. 461-74. Examples under (2) and (3) are also from this source.

[11] Examples in (4), (5), and (6) are from William McCormack, "Social Dialects in Dharwar Kannada", in Ferguson and Gumperz, editors, op. cit., pp. 79-91. It is McCormack's data that elicited the comment in Paul Friedrich's review, Language, 37 (January-March, 1961), p. 167, that "the comparative componential analysis of the kinship terms in two contiguous caste dialects is perhaps of greater theoretical significance than the relatively banal issue of language as 'an index of social status'." However, such comparative componential analyses from caste dialects remain to be worked out. M. Shanmugam Pillai, "Caste Isoglosses in Kinship Terms", Anthropological Linguistics, 7:3 (1965), 59-66, compares kin terms from 13 castes in a Tamil community; but his interest is in the terms peculiar to

single castes, and he does not give the complete data which would permit a semantic analysis.

[12] L. V. Ramaswami Aiyar, "Tulu Prose Texts in Two Dialects", <u>Bulletin of the School of Oriental Studies</u> (University of London), 6 (1932), pp. 896–931.

[13] <u>Ibid.</u>, p. 903.

[14] <u>Ibid.</u>, p. 905.

[15] Cf. the comment by Friedrich, <u>op. cit.</u>, p. 164, that "conservatism in phonemics and grammar... might be the linguistic aspect of the deeply internalized values of caste status among the Brahmins."

[16] Cf. Uriel Weinreich, "Is a Structural Dialectology Possible?", <u>Word</u>, 10 (August–December, 1954), 388–400.

8 | Phonological Rules in Literary and Colloquial Kannada

It has been recognized for some time that the languages of India present several cases of the phenomenon which Ferguson has called diglossia:[1] the co-existence of two styles of speech having a common origin but only a limited degree of mutual intelligibility, and functionally specialized in terms of a literary vs. colloquial dichotomy.[2] Such diglossia has been described for Bengali and Tamil[3], as well as for the language under discussion in the present paper: Kannada (Kanarese), the Dravidian language of Mysore State in South India. The older reference grammars of the language are based on literary style alone; but in recent years several varieties of colloquial Kannada have been described, the most detailed treatments being my own description of Bangalore usage, Hiremath's of Dharwar, and Upadhyaya's of four more localities (Gulbarga, Bellary, Kumta, and Nanjangud).[4] However, all of these works are essentially on the model of neo-Bloomfieldian, taxonomic grammar, and there is little attempt to show the relationship of the colloquial dialects described either to the corresponding literary style or to historical origins. Thus particular interest attaches to a recent work by H. Manappa Nayak, originally written as an Indiana University dissertation, and now published under the title Kannada, Literary and Colloquial: a study of two styles.[5] Nayak's book not only has greater sociolinguistic sophistication than the other works cited, but even (in one brief section) promises to follow "the technique of Transformational-Generative grammars" (p. 69).[6]

Unfortunately, Nayak's study does not live up to its promise. What it provides is, essentially, a list of surface-structure correspondences between literary and colloquial Kannada, without explanation in terms of deeper-level structures, of cross-dialectal comparison, or historical background. Like the other works I have cited, it

fails to account for the following facts: (1) For the most part, literary Kannada is an archaism, a stage which the language reached some
centuries ago, when it became "frozen" by social convention. The
colloquial dialects, which are spoken as everyone's first language,
continued to change, while the literary style was preserved for the
use of an educated minority. But the result was that modern literary
Kannada represents, to a large extent, an earlier historical stage of
the modern colloquial dialects. (2) As a result, the morphophonemically basic forms of the colloquial dialects are to a large extent identical with literary Kannada — just as the morphophonemically basic
forms of French are much closer to Latin than the actual pronunciation of modern French.[7] (3) Similarly, the synchronic morphophonemic rules of colloquial Kannada reflect, to a large extent, the processes of historical sound change which characterize the modern colloquial dialects. All of this is to say that Nayak, in making an artifi-
cial barrier between synchrony and diachrony, has cut himself off
from a historical perspective,[8] one which would make it possible to
explain, not merely to classify, his data.

    In the present paper I attempt to formulate some phonologi-
cal rules which will have both diachronic and synchronic validity for
Kannada. Lexicon, grammar, and phonological alternations peculiar
to particular morphemes are not dealt with here; nor is there any attempt to account for all dialects of colloquial Kannada, since we have
adequate data on relatively few. Rules will be stated in an informal
way, without reference to possible distinctive-feature analyses; but
the order of their application is significant. The rules are intended
to operate on Kannada morphemes in a phonological transcription
which is "morphophonemically basic" in neo-Bloomfieldian terminology, or "systematic-phonemic" in Chomskyan terms; the output of
the rules should be phonetic symbols reflecting the pronunciation of
literary and colloquial Kannada.

    (1) First of all, it must be specified that a large number of
Sanskrit loanwords are used in Kannada, and that compounds of such
elements obey Sanskrit sandhi rules: e.g. deva "god" + ālaya "place"
→ devālaya "temple". Nayak has listed some of these as his morphophonemic rules 11-12 for both styles (p. 71) and rules 2-3 for the literary style (p. 73); the whole list may be found in, e.g., Emeneau
and van Nooten.[9]

(2) Some words of Sanskrit origin, however, undergo differ-
erent changes when they are used outside of Sanskrit compounds.
Specifically, final a̱ regularly becomes e̱: cf. bhāsā- "language", com-
pounded as bhāsā-śāstra "linguistics", but otherwise occurring as
bhāṣe. Feminine proper names obey this rule only for some speakers:
sītā may or may not become sīte. Some loans from modern Indo-Aryan, by contrast, normally preserve final a̱, e.g., rajā "holiday"

(3) The Sanskrit syllabic ṛ is replaced by ri or ru, as in ṛtu
→ ritu ~ rutu "season" (OCK p. 2, §1.3.2).

(4) A number of morphophonemic changes affect the consonant clusters which result when verb stems are combined with the
past-tense suffix -d ~ -t (Nayak p. 70, rules 3-4; p. 73, rule 4).
Many of these changes apply quite irregularly to one or two stems;
e.g. kol- "kill", kon-d-a "he killed", but gel- "win", ged-d-a "he
won". A list of the major types appears in OCK, pp. 22-3. Similar
rules apply in the other South Dravidian languages, and thus seem
likely to have considerable historical depth.

(5) After ṇ, d becomes ḍ, e.g. in kaṇ- "see" + -d "past":
kaṇ-ḍ-a "he saw" (OCK p. 17, §2.11.1; Nayak, p. 73, rule 21).

(6) A long vowel becomes short before two consonants, as
in the example just above, and similarly in bīl- "fall", past *bīd-d-a
→ bidda "he fell" (OCK p. 16, §2.7; Nayak p. 70, rule 5).

(7) Several other sound changes are peculiar to particular
combinations of morphemes: cf. hāvu "snake" with heb-bāvu "big
snake, i.e. python". (More examples appear in OCK p. 18, §2.11.6;
and in Nayak p. 71, rules 7-8, 13-15).

(8) Many Kannada morphemes, in their basic phonological
shape, end in consonants; when these are followed by pause, or by a
word boundary plus consonant, the "enunciative vowel" must be inserted: i after y, as in nāy- "dog" → nāyi, and u elsewhere, as in
māḍ- "do" → māḍu. An exception involves recent loans with final resonants: ḍazan "dozen", huṣār "be careful!" (OCK, p. 13, §2.2).

(9) In the basic forms of native Kannada stems the only contrastive geminate consonants are the voiced stops and the resonants

(m n̪ n̩ l̪ l̩ v y, but not r̩); examples are habe "stream" vs. habba
"festival", hul̩i "sour" vs. bal̩l̩i "vine", rave "grits" vs. tovve "dhall".
Other consonants are predictably long after the first vowel of a word,
except in Sanskrit loans; thus we have large numbers of words like
kappe "frog", but̩t̩i "basket", hakki "bird", as compared with a few
Sanskrit words like kapi "monkey". Furthermore, monosyllabic
stems ending in any consonant will show gemination, as well as the
added enunciative vowel, when produced in isolation: tap- "wrong" →
tappu, kay- "hand" → kayyi, kol- "kill" → kollu. This operates even
in English loans, producing geminates unknown in native words: bas-
"bus" → bassu, bras̩- "brush" → bras̩s̩u.

(10) In certain cases where vowels come into contact, a
semivowel is inserted between them: v if the first vowel is a or u, y
if it is e or i. Examples are magu "child", maguv-ina "of a child";
kud̩i "drink", kud̩iy-uva "drinking" (OCK p. 17, §2.9; Nayak p. 70,
rule 2).

The operation of the above rules will result in a transcription which corresponds rather closely to literary Kannada orthography,
and which in fact amounts to a taxonomic-phonemic notation for the
literary style. This transcription is further subject only to phonetic
rules which apply to both literary and colloquial styles, and which will
be given below.

Rules which now follow operate on the output of those above,
and produce forms in the colloquial style. Basic reference is made
to the urban colloquial standard of Bangalore (Ba.), and secondarily
to Nayak's data from Shimoga (Shi.) and Hiremath's from Dharwar
(Dh.).

(11) The sequences iyV and eyV, resulting from rule 10,
contract to single long vowels, in a number of ways. In Shimoga, iya
→ ē, as in hud̩ugi-aru "girls" → hud̩giyaru → hud̩gēru; and eya → ǣ,
e.g. mane-alli "at home" → maneyalli → manǣlli (Nayak p. 72, rules
7-8); in Bangalore, the usual results would be ī and ē respectively
(hud̩gīru, manēlli). In both dialects, iyu becomes ī, e.g. bari
"write", bari-ut(t)-āne "he writes" → bariyutāne → barītāne. Sequences of the type iyV and eyV are also replaced by long vowels when
word-final, in both dialects: e.g., mane "house", nom. mane-u →

maneyu → manē; gen. mane-a → maneya → manē, homonymous with
the nominative. [10]

(12) The sequences avV and uvV, also resulting from rule
11, contract to ā and ū respectively, in forms like mara "tree", nom.
mara-u → maravu → marā; guru "preceptor", gen. guru-a → guruva →
gurū.

(13) The most striking characteristic of the colloquial dialects is that short vowels tend to be reduced in prominence and lost
when they are not in word-initial syllables; e.g., hancisidaru "they
distributed" → hancsdru. This loss also affects word-final short vowels in certain syllabic environments: avanige koḍu "give it to him"
may become reduced as far as avng koḍu (cf. OCK p. 14-5, §§2.3,
2.4; Nayak p. 70, rule 1, and pp. 71-2, rule 1). It should be noted
that certain short vowels which one would expect to be lost are in fact
retained, e.g., the medial a's of prakaṭa "issue" and duradṛṣṭa "bad
luck". The fact that Sanskrit prefixal morphemes are involved in such
examples suggests that these examples should be regarded as containing junctures in their underlying forms: pra + kaṭa, dur + a + dṛṣṭa.
The rule for vowel loss will then apply only to vowels in the environment after VC_n, but not after $+C_n$ (where C_n = one or more consonants).

(14) After vowel loss has taken place, resulting consonant
clusters may be simplified, as by degemination: a geminate consonant becomes single when next to a single consonant, e.g. ibb-aru
"two people" → ibbru → ibru (OCK p. 15, §2.5; Nayak p. 71, rule 2).

(15) Similarly, a homorganic cluster of nasal plus stop, coming to precede another consonant, loses its stop: nambida "he believed" → nambda → namda (OCK, p. 15, §2.5). This rule creates a
contrast, in the surface phonetics, between [ŋ] and the other nasals,
as in hengasu "woman" → hengsu → heŋsu; but the taxonomic phonemic
analyses of both my book and Nayak's are misleading in suggesting
that ŋ is on a par with the other nasal phonemes.

(16) Certain other consonant clusters show assimilation.
Laterals assimilate to the position of a preceding retroflex or dental:
kēḷ-ali "let him ask" → kēḷḷi; [11] idd-alu "she was" → idḷu → idlu (OCK
pp. 17-18, §2.11.1; Nayak, p. 72, rules 6 and 11).

(17) In many dialects, an assimilatory change affects vowels in the first syllables of stems, whereby long and short e̲ and o̲ have lower allophones [æ] and [ɔ] when a non-high vowel occurs in the next syllable. This development is only sporadically found in Bangalore, but is attested by Nayak's Shimoga data such as g̲æ̲re "line", n̲o̲re "foam" (pp. 44-5). In such cases, the lower vowel quality is, of course, not contrastive. Some dialects also have two qualities of short a̲: [ə] when a high vowel is in the next syllable, [a] elsewhere.

(18) Stem-final e̲ becomes i̲ — in Bangalore and Shimoga, mainly in verbs; elsewhere, e.g. in Dharwar, in nouns as well. Thus kare̲ "to call" → Ba. kari̲, becoming homonymous with Ba. kari̲ "to fry". In Shimoga, however, there is a further implication: bere̲ "to mix", which became b̲æ̲re by the previous rule, now becomes b̲æ̲ri, and the [æ] becomes contrastive in terms of surface phonetics. Similarly, ode̲ "to kick" → o̲de → o̲di. In some dialects the same process also brings [ə] into surface contrast with [a]: Dh. kari̲ "to fry" → k̲ə̲ri, vs. kare̲ "to call" → kari̲. [12] From the data available, no dialect shows any morphophonemic alternations [e ~ ɛ], [o ~ ɔ], or [ə ~ a] to reflect the historical relationship; on the contrary, they tend to generalize a particular vowel throughout a paradigm. Thus tar̲- "bring" comes to have [ə] not only before high vowels, as in tar-ut(t)-ane̲ "he brings" → t̲ə̲rtān̲e, but everywhere else as well, e.g. t̲ə̲nde "I brought" — contrasting with tande̲ "father" (OCK p. 3, §1.3.5; Nayak p. 45). It appears that, for dialects such as Shimoga and Dharwar, ɛ̲ ɔ̲ ə̲ must be recognized as new additions to the systematic-phonemic repertory.

(19) A variety of other phonological rules, of less importance, could be mentioned. E.g., after a lateral, a homorganic d̲ is inserted before r̲: kaḷḷa-ru̲ "thieves" → kaḷru̲ → kaḷdru̲ (OCK p. 18, §2.11.4; Nayak p. 72, rule 13). For other rules, more idiosyncratic to particular dialects, the reader may refer to the sources which have been cited.

(20) The application of rules such as the above will yield broad-phonetic transcriptions for the various colloquial dialects, comparable to the taxonomic-phonemic notations used in my book and Nayak's. Finally, a set of phonetic rules (corresponding to the description in OCK, pp. 1-5) will account for additional details. Only a

few such rules may be noted here: (a) The contrast between short
and long vowels is neutralized to half-length when word-final; (b)
long vowels in the medial syllables of words are also reduced in
length; (c) front vowels /i e/ and back vowels /u o/, whether short
or long, tend to have a semivocalic onglide after word boundary, especially when pause or a vowel precedes (OCK p. 15, §2.6).

The above does not pretend to be a full-fledged phonology of
any single variety of Kannada, much less of any range of dialects. It
is intended rather as a sketch, to suggest what such a fuller description might be like, taking into account that literary and colloquial
Kannada are, after all, related to each other in several ways. For
one thing, many people have a command of both styles, and even il-
literates are able to understand a good deal of literary Kannada, in
dramas or sermons; it seems doubtful that speakers draw on completely separate grammars in order to handle the two styles. Furthermore, the literary style represents, to a great extent, a historical source of the colloquial dialects. Finally, its phonology is largely identifiable with the morphophonemic bases of the colloquial dialects; this being the case, it is hardly surprising that even uneducated
speakers have a fair passive understanding of the literary language:
its phonological structure is already part of their linguistic competence. [13]

NOTES

[1] C. A. Ferguson, "Diglossia", Word 15.325-40 (1959).
[2] Ferguson uses the terms high and low; but I prefer to avoid
these because of possible confusion with a different sociolinguistic
dimension, that of higher vs. lower social class. The terms literary
and colloquial are in wide use, but the former term suggests an exclusive association with writing, which is misleading: we might rather
refer to formal styles (which are regularly used in speaking, e.g.,
from the lecture platform) vs. informal styles (which are increasingly entering literary use).
[3] E. C. Dimock, Jr., "Literary and colloquial Bengali in
modern Bengali prose", Linguistic Diversity in South Asia (edited by
C. A. Ferguson and J. J. Gumperz), pp. 43-58 (Bloomington, 1960);
Suhas Chatterjee, A Study of the Relationship Between Written and

Colloquial Bengali (doctoral dissertation, Harvard Seminary Foundation, 1962); M. Shanmugam Pillai, "Tamil — literary and colloquial",
Linguistic Diversity in South Asia, pp. 27-42; M. Shanmugam Pillai,
"Merger of colloquial and literary Tamil", Anthropological Linguistics
7: 4. 98-103 (1965).

[4]William Bright, An Outline of Colloquial Kannada (Poona,
1958; hereafter OCK); R. C. Hiremath, The Structure of Kannada
(Dharwar, 1961); U. P. Upadhyaya, A Comparative Study of Four
Kannada Dialects (doctoral thesis, Deccan College, Poona, 1968).

[5]Mysore, Rao and Raghavan Publishers, 1967. Nayak compares literary Kannada with his native colloquial dialect of Shimoga
district — although he admits that he has largely replaced the latter
by a "standard colloquial style... almost similar to the one described
by Bright..." (p. 34). It might have been preferable to use the bet-
ter-known urban colloquial standard as the basis for his comparison.
A severely negative review of Nayak's book has been published by
D. N. Shankar Bhat, Linguistic Survey Bulletin no. 8, pp. 21-26
(Poona, Deccan College, 1968).

[6]Nayak makes this mysterious statement (ibid.): "The rules
are numbered serially. They do not strictly indicate the order of
rules, which is an important criterion in Transformational-Generative
grammars. "

[7]It is of course possible for the morphophonemic basic forms
of a colloquial dialect to be quite distinct from the literary equivalents.
E. g. , Nayak (p. 38) lists /f s ś z/ as occurring only in his literary
style; thus he presumably has basic dēśa "country" in literary style,
but basic desa in colloquial style. In other cases, historical change
has reshaped the basic form of the colloquial style; e. g. , as shown
in section 18 below, Shimoga dialect has basic ode "to kick" in literary style, but basic ɔdi in colloquial.

[8]He even states (p. 14) that "[linguistic] variation is not
necessarily a historical product. "

[9]M. B. Emeneau and B. Van Nooten, Sanskrit Sandhi and
Exercises, 2nd rev. ed. (Berkeley, 1968).

[10]By a later rule, the contrast between short and long vowels
is neutralized, in word-final position, to half-length; but morphophonemically long vowels can be recognized by their immunity to the
rules of vowel loss. It may be noted that the literary language allows
nominative and genitive case forms in their contracted as well as
their full forms, but spelled with final short vowels, as mane, etc.

(Harold Spencer, A Kanarese Grammar, revised by W. Preston [Mysore, 1950], p. 55.) Nayak's treatment of these data is especially confusing, since he tries to account for the long vowels in noun forms by means of a morpheme A (p. 72, rule 14, and p. 77), which he borrows, without explanation, from my 1958 grammar. But if we describe colloquial Kannada in relation to the literary language, the "real" vowels a and u can be used instead. Nayak's description of the long vowels in verb forms is even more unfortunate. At one place (p. 72, rule 4), he treats barītane "he writes" in terms of a rule which seems to say that the second vowel of a stem becomes long before any affix, which is clearly untrue. Elsewhere (pp. 39, 50), he describes the basic long vowel in Shi. battīni (Ba. bartīni) "I come" in terms of an ad-hoc juncture (which he ignores in his later discussion of verb morphology).

[11]Note that, although our earlier rule (6) eliminated sequences of long vowel before geminate consonant, vowel loss produces such sequences anew, as in the present case.

[12]Cf. W. Bright, "Dravidian metaphony", Language 42.311-22 (1966), esp. p. 317.

[13]My thanks go to M. B. Emeneau and to M. V. Nadkarni for their constructive criticism of this paper.

Part III. North America

9 | Semantic Structures in Northwestern California and the Sapir-Whorf Hypothesis

In Collaboration with Jane O. Bright

The Indian tribes of northwestern California constitute a well recognized culture area, first defined by A. L. Kroeber. The groups which best typify the northwestern California culture are the Yurok, the Karok, and the Hupa; slightly peripheral are the Smith River Indians (Tolowa), the Wiyot, and the Chilula. The nonlinguistic culture of the area is quite homogeneous, so that Kroeber felt justified in stating (1925: 5) that "The Yurok shared this civilization in identical form with their neighbors, the Hupa and Karok. The adjacent Tolowa, Wiyot and Chilula adhere to the same culture in every essential trait." Linguistically, however, the area is probably as heterogeneous as any of comparable size in the world. Yurok and Wiyot are related to the Algonkian languages of eastern and central North America; but despite their geographical proximity, it is far from clear that they are more closely related to each other than either is to Algonkian (Teeter 1964: 189). Karok is Hokan, but only remotely related to its nearest Hokan neighbors, Shasta and Chimariko. Hupa and Smith River are both Athabascan, but the division of Pacific Coast Athabascan languages into two groups falls between them, so that the closest relatives of Hupa extend southward into Central California, while Smith River has its closest kin in southwestern Oregon.

The paradoxical combination of cultural unity with linguistic diversity in other areas has been commented on by anthropologists — notably in the Southwestern United States, where Pueblo groups with similar cultures speak diverse languages. The northwestern California case was cited by Sapir (1921: 214) as illustrating his point that "language and culture are not intrinsically related." He noted that speakers of the clearly unified Athabascan language family adapted themselves, evidently with considerable speed, to four very different culture areas of North America. "The Hupa Indians," he wrote, "are very typical of the culture area to which they belong. Culturally identical with them are the neighboring Yurok and Karok. There is the liveliest tribal intercourse between the Hupa, Yurok, and Karok, so much so that all three generally attend an important religious ceremony given by any one of them. It is difficult to say what elements in their combined culture belong in origin to this tribe or that, so much at one are they in communal action, feeling and thought. But their languages are not merely alien to each other; they belong to three of the major American linguistic groups..."[1]

Compare this with Sapir's more famous statement, the basis of the Sapir-Whorf (or Whorfian) hypothesis (1929: 209):

> Human beings do not live in the objective world alone, nor alone in the world of social activity as ordinarily understood, but are very much at the mercy of the particular language which has become the medium of expression for their society.... The fact of the matter is that the "real world" is to a large extent unconsciously built up on the language habits of the group. No two languages are ever sufficiently similar to be considered as representing the same social reality. The worlds in which different societies live are distinct worlds, not merely the same world with different labels attached.

When this statement, the basis of the Sapir-Whorf or Whorfian hypothesis, is compared to the previous quotation, a certain discrepancy is apparent. If the Sapir-Whorf hypothesis is maintained, then the Yurok, for example, are seen as being "at the mercy of" their Algonkian-like linguistic heritage; the Smith River and Karok are similarly dominated by Athabascan and Hokan structures, respectively. Given this linguistic diversity, how can these tribes be "culturally identical"? Or is it possible that they do after all share "the same world with different labels attached", contrary to our expectations derived from Sapir and Whorf?

Perhaps we can answer part of this question by suggesting that the languages are more similar than their diverse genetic backgrounds indicate. This is reasonable in terms of Whorf's specific

recognition (1941: 91) that linguistic structures and other cultural patterns "have grown up together, constantly influencing each other."
The mutual assimilation of languages under the influence of a broader
cultural unity is, of course, observable in many parts of the world,
and we can expect to find the same phenomenon in northwestern California. Loan words between languages in the area are few: we know
of only ten between Yurok and Karok, and fewer between Yurok and
Smith River. But there are a number of grammatical similarities between Yurok and Karok (cf. W. Bright 1959: 103): possessive and locative inflection of nouns, but plurality only for a limited group of them;
inflection of verb forms for pronominal object as well as subject; the
use of nominalized verb forms as heads of equational sentences; the
redundant marking of plurality in verbs by an extended stem; and the
use of preverbal particles to mark tense and aspect. Smith River
shares a number of these features: nouns are sometimes inflected
for possession and location, but never for plurality; verbs are inflected for pronominal object as well as subject; and verbal prefixes
are used to mark tense and aspect. Impressionistically, we may say
that Yurok shows more structural similarities with Karok than with
Smith River, although the three languages still show many more differences than similarities. The similarities may be accidental; this
could be proved only if they were reconstructable in the grammatical
systems of Proto-Algonkian, Proto-Hokan, and Proto-Athabascan.
Some of the similarities appear to be due to diffusion. If this is true,
we may reason that the uniformity of culture has tempered language
diversity in the area to the point where the reverse effect — the diversification of culture patterns under the influence of linguistic differences — is partly inhibited.

The apparent incompatibility of cultural identity and linguistic diversity is also mitigated by the possibility that the linguistic diversity of the area may have conditioned certain nonlinguistic differences between the Yurok and their neighbors — differences in cognitive habits, perhaps, which have not received adequate attention from
ethnographers. This amounts to testing the Sapir-Whorf hypothesis
itself; if full data on the northwestern California tribes revealed no
cultural differences correlative with linguistic differences, then we
would be strongly influenced to abandon the view of Sapir and Whorf.
The difficulty in making the test, however, is that available ethnographic data emphasize only the uniformity of the area. After some

brief remarks on the Karok, Kroeber states (1925: 108): "Data are
scarcely available for a fuller sketch of Karok culture. Nor is such
an account necessary in the present connection. In at least ninety-
five institutions out of every hundred, all that has been said of the
Yurok or is on record concerning the Hupa applies identically to the
Karok." Cultural diversity in the area was described mostly in terms
of unsystematized data: "Hupa alone has a first-fruits feast for the
acorn crop" (Kroeber and Gifford 1949: 4). The few general statements available about differences between tribes are vague and hard
to apply — for example, the comment of a Karok informant that the
Hupa are lazier than the other tribes in the area. Furthermore, aboriginal cultures are now nearly extinct, making it difficult to gather
new data on intertribal differences.

A topic on which some data are still collectable, however, is
the taxonomy applied by the Indians to the physical world around them.
This taxonomic system survives precisely because of its close correspondence to the vocabulary of the aboriginal languages, which have
lasted longer than other aspects of native life.[2] Such folk taxonomies
should be examined in the light of Sapir's statement that "the worlds
in which different societies live are distinct worlds, not merely the
same world with different labels attached."

An example of such a taxonomy is spatial orientation: the
inland Yurok and the Karok, living on either side of the Klamath
River, oriented themselves not to the apparent motion of the sun,
which Europeans use to define the terms "north, south, east, west",
but to the direction of river flow. This is reflected in the Yurok and
Karok terms for cardinal directions, words translatable as "upriver,
downriver, towards the river, away from the river". The morphemes
used by these languages for a given meaning have no similarity in
their phonemic shape (cf. Yurok wonew, Karok maruk "away from
the river"): it is rather that both languages reflect the same concep-
tual structure.

More complex systems are to be found in what we may call
the ethnobiotaxonomy of these northwestern California tribes — the
folk classification of their plant and animal world. Stimulated by the
recent work by Conklin (1962a) and Frake (1962) in this area of "ethnoscience", we tried to discover the principles underlying the coastal

Yurok and Smith River classifications of their biosphere.[3] Following
suggestions made by Metzger (1963), questioning was conducted as
much as possible in the Indian language, and features of taxonomic
structure were approached repeatedly from a number of different an-
gles. A typical series might be: (a) a wild strawberry is shown to an
informant, with the question (in the Indian language), "What's this?"
(b) Several kinds of berries are shown, with the question, "What are
these?" (c) The questioner asks, "Is a strawberry a berry?" (d) A
deliberately foolish question is asked, such as, "Is a strawberry a
tree?" (e) Receiving a negative answer to the previous question, the
investigator asks, "What is a strawberry then?" The informants preferred were those who knew least English, to keep the Indian view as
pure as possible. Informants were encouraged to comment as they
went along; tape-recorded interviews were later transcribed, and
translated with the help of informants who spoke good English.

Various difficulties were encountered: informants displayed,
at one time or another, lapse of memory, contamination by white
man's categories, and lack of attention. The most knowledgeable informant was a Yurok, Mrs. Alice Spott Taylor, aged 95 years. She
was the sister of Robert Spott, Kroeber's informant for many years.
Mrs. Taylor was the most "Indian" informant who could be found, but
her very "Indianness" was sometimes troublesome, as when her answers refer less to taxonomy than to mythology. Witness the following exchange:

> Q. nunepuy hes wiʔ kʼi loʔcoʔm "Is a toad a fish?"[4]
> A. paaʔ, nimiʔ nunepuy kʼi loʔcoʔm "No, a toad isn't a fish."
> Q. tiʔ ni šo· wiʔ kʼi loʔcoʔm "What is a toad?"
> A. loʔcoʔm kʷel wencoks wiʔ "A toad is a woman."

This is, of course, a myth reference, and is reminiscent of
Kroeber's statement: "In trying to obtain ordinary ethnographic data
on Yurok, I have had to listen time and again to myths which I had already heard, before I could come to the contemporary facts; and
sometimes these had to be elicited by prodding" (Spott and Kroeber
1942: 214). Many misleading answers were clarified by the cross-
checking built into the routine of questioning, and by consulting several informants. To be sure, there are discrepancies between informants, but these are probably inherent in any taxonomy. English

speakers do not agree, for instance, on whether avocados and tomatoes are fruits or vegetables; California Indians may surely be allowed
a similar lack of unanimity.[5]

One fact emergent from a study of the Yurok and Smith River
taxonomic systems is that they are less hierarchically organized than
our own. We nearly exhaust the universe of living things with multi-
leveled hierarchical classifications such as "plant, bush, berry bush,
gooseberry bush" or "animal, insect, louse, body louse." The Indians, by contrast, have relatively few generic terms, and many terms
which do not fall into any hierarchy. The generic terms noted, with
rough English equivalents, are as follows: Yurok has ho·re?mos
"quadruped mammal", nunepuy "fish", leyes "snake", c'uc'iš "bird,
especially small bird", tepo· "fir tree, tree", ka·p'eł "bush", ?ɹ·-
wɹh "grass", ci·šep "flower", and nɹhpɹy "berry". Smith River has
fewer terms: t'aayəš "snake", tš'eeyáš "duck, bird", tš'aamé? "fir
tree, conifer", tšéeneh "bush, nonconiferous tree", xəmšən "grass",
tš'abáayuh "flower", and deetšíh "berry". The terms available from
Karok (although they were not collected with taxonomic structures in
mind) are comparable in number to those of Smith River: ?ápsu·n
"snake", ?ačvi·v "bird", ?íppaha "tree", píriš "bush, grass",
?iəríha "flower", and ?uxra·h "berry". We note a considerable
core of agreement in these three systems.

In this framework, a term like Yurok wɹ·gɹ "body louse"
cannot be subsumed in larger classes "louse" or "insect", since none
exist; nor is the classification ho·re?mos, sometimes translated
"animal", conceded to apply to it. The answer to the question ti? ni
šo· wi? k'i wɹ·gɹ "What is a body louse?" is simply wɹ·gɹ wi? "It's
a body louse." Furthermore, Yurok informants asked to identify a
plant or animal for which they know no name, often say that it is "like
such-and-such," rather than assigning it to a class: thus several
flowering bushes were described as sahsip segon "like wild lilac", although they bore little resemblance to the wild lilac, from a white
man's point of view. (A similar response was reported by David
French [1960] for the Sahaptin Indians in Oregon.) Where generic
terms exist, they may also refer to a specific member of the class.
This parallels the use of English "man" to refer both to human beings
as a class and to adult males as a subdivision of that class; but the
phenomenon is commoner in the Indian languages. Thus Yurok tepo·

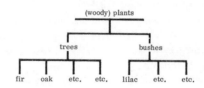

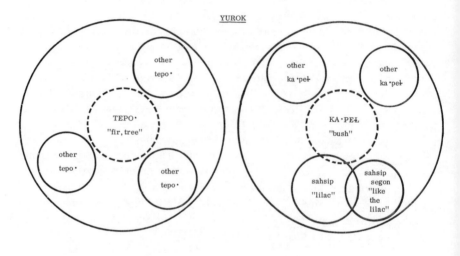

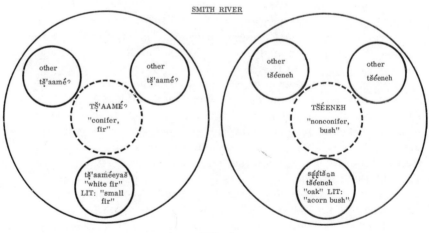

FIG. 1

refers to "fir tree" or "tree" in general; Smith River t̠š'eey̠a̠š is
"duck" in particular or "bird" in general.

　　　We see, then, that a hierarchical model, which shows only
the relationship of domination ("A dominates B" = "B is an A"), cannot account adequately for the Indian taxonomies. In a hierarchy, an
item either is or is not a member of the class named by the next higher node. But there is no way of indicating, in a hierarchical tree, the
situation where a specific term like Yurok tepo· "fir, tree" or Smith
River t̠š'aamé? "fir, conifer" can also be used as a generic term,
thus including other trees which resemble the fir by being coniferous.
In addition, there is no way of indicating when an item is classified in
a certain way because it is "like" another item which is more central
to the focus of the domain in question. Therefore, although our European hierarchic taxonomies can be represented for the most part by
a branching tree (see the English chart in Fig. 1), the aboriginal taxonomies of northwestern California can be represented more faithful-
ly by a kind of "sphere of influence" model. Figure 1 compares a
section of the taxonomies for "(woody) plants", first giving the English hierarchical taxonomy for the items in question, and then sphere
of influence diagrams for parts of the Yurok and the Smith River systems. These charts are designed to point out the few differences between the two Indian systems as contrasted to the English. An example of a term also standing for the generic label of its class is found
in Y1 where tepo· is the tree par excellence, namely the fir tree; and
also in SR1 and SR2 where woody plants are t̠š'aamé? if they are con-
ifers like the fir or t̠šéeneh if they are bushy and nonconiferous like
the oak — the focus of its domain. Y2 illustrates the classification of
numerous bushes which are ka·peł because they are like sahsip, the
lilac, although there is no morpheme for them in the language. Our
sphere of influence model, a type not referred to by Conklin or Frake,
is then only partly hierarchical. [6]

　　　At this point we may raise the question: do semantic structures, such as these biotaxonomies, belong to language or do they belong to nonlinguistic culture? (The term "culture" alone is used hereafter in the sense of "everything in culture except language".) Both
points of view have been held widely. On the one hand, many linguists
have applied the term "lexical structure" to taxonomies such as these,
and have included this structure, along with phonology and grammar,

as the three main parts of descriptive linguistics. On the other hand,
structural semanticists such as Frake have proposed their techniques
as specifically ethnographic. We would like to consider semantic
structure as a part of culture; the model we have in mind is shown in
Figure 2. There is here a very close correspondence between certain
linguistic items — those morphemes and constructions of morphemes
which we call lexemes — on the one side, and certain units of nonlinguistic behavior on the other side. Following Goodenough (1956: 208),
the latter can be called sememes. Thus the English morpheme and
lexeme "uncle" corresponds to a particular point in nonlinguistic behavior patterns, namely the sememe which we may define as the role
of an "uncle" in our culture. Although normally these correspondences are one-to-one, there are exceptions: thus Goodenough's analysis
of Trukese kinship has to recognize several "zero lexemes" — points
in the semantic pattern with no corresponding morphemic material.
The general regularity of these relations, however, leads to differences of opinion as to whether semantic structure is part of language or
part of culture.[7]

If we accept the view that semantic structure is part of nonlinguistic culture, we may attempt to confirm this from the particular

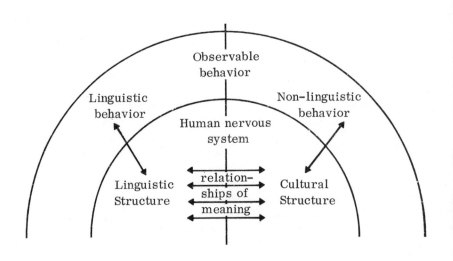

FIG. 2

case of northwestern California taxonomy. Specifically: Do the biotaxonomies of the Yurok, the Smith River, and the Karok reflect the
diversity of their languages, or the relative uniformity of their culture? As we have seen, Yurok has nine taxonomic terms, Smith River seven, and Karok six, but most of these correspond to specific
Yurok terms. All three tribes are alike in their lack of classifications corresponding to English terms such as "insect, worm, shellfish, lizard, plant, fern, weed." It appears that the biotaxonomies
of these tribes are much more similar than are their languages. They
show, in fact, the kind of near-uniformity which characterizes the
nonlinguistic culture of the area. We may take this as support for
our choice of assigning semantic structure to culture rather than to
language. In addition, we may say that the Sapir-Whorf hypothesis
is not strongly applicable to our data; Yurok, Smith River, and Karok
speakers do not appear to live in such "distinct worlds" after all, at
least as far as their views of the northwestern California biosphere
are concerned.

Since we are looking for subtle differences in the cultures of
these tribes, we cannot neglect the fact that the Yurok stand out from
the others by having a somewhat more complex biotaxonomy, containing more generic terms, as well as some classifications based on the
"is like a" relationship. Perhaps this is not surprising, since the
Yurok are generally conceded to represent the climax or culmination
of the northwestern California culture area. We are now, however,
sharpening our focus, replacing the broad notion of "cultural climax"
by the specific one of "greater elaboration of generic terms in biotaxonomy". Pursuing our interest in the Sapir-Whorf hypothesis, we
may ask if there is anything in the Yurok, as opposed to the Smith
River, language, which corresponds to this greater taxonomic com-
plexity. No correspondences with specific grammatical features
have suggested themselves, but certain broad traits of Yurok and
Smith River grammar may be contrasted usefully. (Our approach is
comparable to the overview of Chinook grammar made by Hymes
[1961].) Yurok syntax is characterized by loose order, creating many
ambiguities to be resolved by context, and has little cross-referenc-
ing through the morphology. Smith River, on the other hand, has
rigid syntactic ordering, with extensive morphological cross-refer-
encing. In morphology, Yurok has few obligatory categories: verbs
have suffixes for person and number, but tense and aspect are indicated by particles; nouns have possessive prefixes indicating person

but not number. Smith River morphology, by contrast, shows many
obligatory categories: verb forms have up to 11 prefix positions,
marking person, number, tense, and aspect; nouns have possessive
prefixes which indicate both person and number.

At first glance, there seems to be a paradoxical inverse relation between the two cultures. In Yurok, a relatively complex taxonomy is associated with a loose grammatical structure, whereas in
Smith River a less complex taxonomy goes with a very rigid grammar.
But it is possible to resolve the paradox: the Yurok have more generic classifications, which means that they have more choice when they
refer to plants and animals. Thus the Yurok fisherman can refer to
his catch either as ckʷoɬ "steelhead" or, generically, as nunepuy
"fish". This is consistent with the high degree of choice afforded in
Yurok grammar, with its nearly-free word order and its optional
morphological categories. The Smith River taxonomic system offers
less choice: a steelhead is called tɕslih and nothing else — just as in
Smith River grammar the basic sentence order is Indirect Object,
Direct Object, Subject, Verb, and none other. Here the lack of choice
in the linguistic structure corresponds to the constraint imposed by
the taxonomic structure. (As for Karok, the grammar is intermediate
in rigidity between Yurok and Smith River, but both taxonomy and
grammar seem to approximate the Smith River more than the Yurok
situation.) The Yurok "is like a" relationship also may be correlated
with the greater freedom already noted in Yurok grammar. For
Smith River, woody plants are either tš'aamé? or tšéeneh; there is
a choice only of these two generic terms or of specific lexemes. In
Yurok, classification does not fall into such strict lines: an item may
be included in the ka·p'eɬ "bush" domain if it is merely like another
member of that class. This is an example of a sememe with no lexemic correspondent — Goodenough's "empty lexeme".

We may now make a specific hypothesis about language-and-
culture relationships in northwestern California: namely, a principle
of choice inherent in Yurok linguistic structure has conditioned a similar degree of choice in biotaxonomy, manifested by a greater richness of generic terms; whereas the relative absence of choice in
Smith River and Karok grammar has conditioned a corresponding pov-
erty in taxonomy. This statement, like most of the applications of
the Whorfian point of view, is probably not provable in itself. It may

have a value, however, if taken together with other hypotheses point-
ing in the same direction, providing that each is based on solid data.
The very effort to develop such hypotheses will stimulate the collection
of valuable information which otherwise could be overlooked.[8]

SUMMARY

Northwestern California offers a case of aboriginal groups
living in nearly identical cultures but speaking languages which differ
considerably in structure. This situation can be used as a sort of
test of the Sapir-Whorf hypothesis, especially of Sapir's claim that
groups speaking diverse languages necessarily classify phenomena
into "distinct worlds". The extreme genetic differences between the
northwestern California languages are tempered somewhat by a few
rather striking linguistic similarities — perhaps an indication of mutual linguistic influence. On the other hand, the cultures may not be
as identical as has been thought. This possibility can be investigated
more thoroughly by study of the semantic structures of the tribes concerned, in particular of their folk classifications of the biosphere.
Study of three tribes shows that folk taxonomies are not necessarily
hierarchical; they are better represented by a "spheres of influence"
model than by a "family tree" model. The final question posed is:
Are these taxonomies relatively similar to each other, like the cultures of the area; or are they diverse, like the linguistic structures?
We find them quite similar, contrary to prediction from the Sapir-
Whorf hypothesis. However, the greater choice in the Yurok taxonomic system can be correlated with the relatively greater choice allowed within Yurok grammar — a conclusion which supports Sapir and
Whorf.

NOTES

This paper is based on field work with the Smith River and Yurok
conducted in the summer of 1963 under a grant from the Penrose Fund
of the American Philosophical Society. We express our gratitude in
particular for the coöperation of Amelia Brown and Alice Spott Taylor,
highly knowledgeable representatives of the Smith River and Yurok
cultures respectively; for the assistance of Minnie Macomber and
Florence Shaughnessy in interpreting Yurok data; for the initial inspiration for this paper, provided by Philip L. Newman; and for the

valuable suggestions of Dell H. Hymes and Albert Anderson. Additional thanks are due Hymes for presenting this paper at the Stanford Conference, which we were not able to attend, and to the other members of the Conference for their constructive criticism.

[1] The Smith River Indians also were close to the focal point of northwestern California culture: they intermarried with the Yurok, joined with them in warfare, and enjoyed the prestige of being regarded by the Yurok as rich.

[2] We here assume that taxonomic systems are best regarded not as part of language itself, but as part of nonlinguistic culture, albeit a part having especially close relations with language. This view is developed more fully below.

[3] The coastal Yurok and Smith River peoples lived in almost identical natural environments. The Smith River villages were located primarily upcoast and downcoast from the mouth of the Smith River itself. Farther south, the Yurok clustered around the mouth of the Klamath River. Both groups had settlements some miles up their respective rivers — one of the largest Yurok villages was far inland, adjacent to Karok territory.

[4] Yurok forms are cited in the phonemic system of Robins (1958); Karok forms are as in W. Bright (1957); Smith River forms are as in J. Bright (1964).

[5] In discussing this paper, Floyd Lounsbury made the point that disagreements among English speakers as to avocados and tomatoes may be due not to any inherent loose ends in our taxonomy, but rather to a cross-cutting of two taxonomic systems, one concerned with plant products, the other with prepared foods. In any case, we agree with other participants in the discussion at Stanford who suggested (1) that we cannot exclude the possibility that probabilistic considerations are involved in some folk-taxonomic systems, and (2) that some cultures recognize some classes defined not by their boundaries, but by their centers. Such center-oriented classes are well-known in folk-taxonomies of color, and we believe they are also relevant to the northwest California classification of plants and animals.

[6] A center-oriented classification, such as proposed here, can be converted into a hierarchical classification by putting a single term on several hierarchical levels, as Frake (1961: 119) has done: English "man" (vs. "animal") dominates "man" (vs. "woman"), which dominates "man" (vs. "boy"), which dominates "man" (vs. "unmanly male"). We feel, however, that the investigator who follows this

procedure runs the risk of imposing a scientific taxonomy, or some other systems which he knows, upon the folk-taxonomic data that he is studying. Where members of a culture use a single term to classify objects at different levels of generalization, it may be that the very concept of levels and of hierarchy is irrelevant to their semantic structure.

[7] We here regard linguistic structure as comprising those patterns which account for verbal behavior and certain types of response to verbal behavior. We regard semantic structure as nonlinguistic insofar as it may operate independently: thus one may sort out the produce of a garden plot in terms of culturally-defined categories such as "fruit" and "vegetables", without any verbal behavior being involved.

[8] We feel that the recent statement by Robbins Burling (1964a: 26) that "Whorf's ideas have fallen into disrepute" is exaggerated. As evidence we may cite recent publications, all sympathetic to the Whorfian hypothesis, by Hymes (1961), Fishman (1960), Kluckhohn (1961), and Mathiot (1962). Carroll (1964:12) offers a statement of what we may call the neo-Whorfian position: "Insofar as languages differ in the ways they encode objective experience, language users tend to sort out and distinguish experiences differently according to the categories provided by their respective languages. These cognitions will tend to have certain effects on behavior."

REFERENCES

Bright, Jane O., 1964, The phonology of Smith River Athabascan (Tolowa). International Journal of American Linguistics 30:101-107.

Bright, William, 1957, The Karok language. University of California Publications in Linguistics 13.

————, 1959, Review of R.H. Robins, The Yurok language. Language 35:100-104.

Burling, Robbins, 1964, Cognition and componential analysis: God's truth or hocuspocus? American Anthropologist 66:20-28.

Carroll, John B., 1964, Linguistic relativity, contrastive linguistics, and language learning. International Review of Applied Linguistics in Language Teaching 1:1-20.

Conklin, Harold C., 1962, Comment (on the ethnographic study of
    cognitive systems, by C. O. Frake). In T. Gladwin and
    W. C. Sturtevant, eds., Anthropology and human behavior.
    Washington, Anthropological Society of Washington.
Fishman, Joshua, 1960, A systematization of the Whorfian hypothesis.
    Behavioral Science 5: 323-339.
Frake, Charles O., 1961, The diagnosis of disease among the
    Subanun of Mindanao. American Anthropologist 63: 113-132.
_____, 1962, The ethnographic study of cognitive systems. In
    T. Gladwin and W. C. Sturtevant, eds., Anthropology and
    human behavior. Washington, Anthropological Society of
    Washington.
Goodenough, Ward H., 1956, Componential analysis and the study of
    meaning. Language 32: 195-216.
Hymes, Dell H., 1961, On typology of cognitive styles in language.
    Anthropological Linguistics 3: 1. 22-54.
Kluckhohn, Clyde, 1961, Notes on some anthropological aspects of
    communication. American Anthropologist 63: 895-910.
Kroeber, A. L., 1925, Handbook of the Indians of California. Bureau
    of American Ethnology Bulletin 78. Washington, The Smith-
    sonian Institution.
Kroeber, A. L., and E. W. Gifford, 1949, World renewal, a cult
    system of native northwest California. University of Cali-
    fornia Anthropological Records 13: 1-156.
Mathiot, Madeleine, 1962, Noun classes and folk taxonomy in Papago.
    American Anthropologist 64: 340-350.
Metzger, Duane, 1963, Asking questions and questioning answers in
    ethnography. Paper presented at the Spring Meeting of the
    Southwestern Anthropological Association, Riverside,
    California.
Robins, R. H., 1958, The Yurok language. University of California
    Publications in Linguistics 15.
Sapir, Edward, 1921, Language: an introduction to the study of
    speech. New York, Harcourt, Brace.
Teeter, Karl, 1964, Wiyot and Yurok. In W. Bright, ed., Studies in
    California Linguistics. University of California Publications
    in Linguistics 34.
Whorf, Benjamin L., 1941, The relation of habitual thought and be-
    havior to language. In L. Spier and others, Language,
    culture and personality. Menasha, Wisconsin, Banta.

10 | Reduction Rules in Fox Kinship

In Collaboration with Jan Minnick

With persuasive elegance, Floyd Lounsbury has shown (1962) how kinship systems can be formally described as consisting of two things: a set of basic terms, typically denoting ego's close relatives, and a set of rules which account for extensions of usage of those terms. Dealing with Crow and Omaha terminologies, he has proposed that three types of rules are sufficient: a skewing rule which equates kin types of different generations, a merging rule which equates siblings of the same sex, and a half-sibling rule (proposed as a universal of kinship systems) which equates one's parent's child with one's sibling. In his specific discussion of the Omaha-type kinship system of the Fox Indians, based on data from Tax (1937), he shows that the skewing and merging rules take the following forms. The skewing rule specifies that father's sister, as a link to some other relative, is equivalent to sister (formulaically, FS...→ S...).[1] This implies as a corollary that similar equivalences exist between the reciprocals of the stated types, i.e., that a female linking relative's brother's child is equivalent to that linking kinswoman's sibling (in formulas, ...♀ Bs → ...♀ B, and ...♀ Bd → ...♀ S; note that S = sister, s = son). The merging rule states that a sibling of the same sex as ego, as a link, is equivalent to ego himself (♂ B...→ ♂ ..., ♀ S...→ ♀ ...). The corollary states the equivalence of the reciprocals: a linking relative's sibling of his own sex is equivalent to that linking relative (...♂ B → ...♂, ... ♀ S → ...♀). These rules of reduction, along with the half-sibling rule, account for the terminological equivalence of, for instance, MMSss with MB (Lounsbury 1964: 361):

MMSss → MMss	(by the merging rule)
→ MBs	(by the half-sibling rule)
→ MB	(by the skewing rule corollary)

It seems to us that Lounsbury has developed an exceptionally explicit and economical framework for formal analysis of kinship terms. With regard to his analysis of the Fox system, however, we must disagree with him on two points. Following his demonstration of the reductions to MB, he states (p. 362), "In similar fashion and by use of the same rules, all of the extensions of the other [Fox] kin terms reduce to the primary meanings of their respective terminological classes." Further, he notes that "the rules stated above are an unordered set. This statement can be made, and no hierarchical order of preference given to the rules, because of the fact that when applied as reduction rules no conflict is ever possible...." In working through the full data on Fox, however, as given by Tax (1937: 249ff.), we come to these conclusions: (1) two additional rules must be added to the ones formulated by Lounsbury, though they fall within his general categories of rules; and (2) the addition of these rules requires an added formal device — either the introduction of boundary markers, or statements of priority among rules — if conflicting reductions are to be avoided.

To begin with, Tax reports that all siblings of one's grandparents are called "grandparents"; the basic kin types denoted by the term are FF, MF ("grandfather", nehmehco), and FM, MM ("grandmother", no·hgomehsA). Of the possible kin types concerned, those involving a grandfather's brother or a grandmother's sister are readily accounted for by Lounsbury's rules: FFB → FF by the corollary of the merging rule, and similarly MMS → MM. But a grandmother's brother or a grandfather's sister cannot be treated similarly: types like FMB and FFS are not affected by any of the rules that have been stated. It appears, then, that an additional rule is needed, specifying that a linking relative's mother's brother or father's sister is equivalent to that linking relative's father or mother respectively (... MB → ... F, ... FS → ... M). By this rule, FMB → FF and FFS → FM.

Note that whereas Lounsbury's merging rule equates siblings of the same sex, our new rule equates those of opposite sex (and in a more restricted way). We may designate Lounsbury's as a parallel sibling rule, and the new rule as a cross sibling rule.[2]

If such an additional rule is proposed, we will want to see whether its corollary is also applicable: this would be the statement

that a man's sister's or a woman's brother's children, as linking relatives, are equivalent to his or her own children (♂ Ss ... → ♂ s ...,
♂ Sd ... → ♂ d ..., ♀ Bs ... → ♀ s ..., ♀ Bd ... → ♀ d ...). It turns
out that this is indeed valid, and in fact necessary, in explaining the
grandchild terminology. Thus, Tax reports that all of one's sibling's
children's children are called "grandchildren" (no ˙hcihsema); the
basic kin types denoted by the term are ss, sd, ds, dd. Of the derived kin types, those involving a man's brother's or a woman's sister's descendants are handled by Lounsbury's rules: ♂ Bss → ♂ ss by
the merging rule, etc. But a man's sister's or a woman's brother's
descendants (♂ Sss, etc.) are not affected. We may, however, apply
the corollary of our new rule, producing reductions such as the following, all in accord with Tax's data:

1. ♂ Sss → ♂ ss
2. ♂ Sds → ♂ ds
3. ♂ FBdss → ♂ Fdss (by the parallel sibling rule corollary)
   → ♂ Sss (by the half-sibling rule)
   → ♂ ss   (by the cross sibling rule corollary)
4. ♂ FFSss → ♂ FSss (by the skewing rule)
   → ♂ Sss (by the skewing rule again)
   → ♂ ss   (by the cross sibling rule corollary)

There are still other applications of the "grandchild" term,
however, which remain unaccounted for, such as the reference to a
man's father's sister's grandchildren. Thus, we may start a reduction like the following:

♂ FSsss → ♂ Ssss (by the skewing rule)
   → ♂ sss (by the cross sibling rule corollary)

This suggests that ♂ Ssss, ♂ sss, etc., which are not in Tax's gene-
alogical tree, are probably also designated as "grandchildren." But
we cannot complete the reduction to show the equivalence with son's
son. Another rule, then, is needed, stating that one's child's child,
as linking relative, is equivalent to one's child (ss ... → s ..., sd ...
→ s ..., ds ... → d ..., dd ... → d ...). By this rule, we can complete the reduction begun above, with the statement ♂ sss → ♂ ss. In
fact, Tax (1937: 254) confirms that "offspring of grandchildren are
always grandchildren."

The corollary of this rule is, of course, that one's linking relative's parent's parent is equivalent to that linking relative's parent (... FF → ... F, ... FM → ... M, ... MF → ... F, ... MM → ... M). This implies that great-grandparents would be called "grandparents", a practice confirmed by Tax (1937: 253).

This is, then a rule of equivalence between generations. But where Lounsbury's skewing rule equates ego's terminological generation with ascending and descending generations, our new rule only operates between ascending or descending generations. Furthermore, the new rule affects father's kin and mother's kin in the same way. These may both be called <u>lineal merging</u> rules; in what follows, we refer to Lounsbury's skewing rule as the <u>major lineal rule</u> and to our new one as the <u>minor lineal rule</u>.

We now have two types of lineal merging rule, two types of sibling (or collateral merging) rule, and the half-sibling rule, all applicable to the Fox system. It is found, however, that with introduction of additional rules, a new problem arises. Compare, for instance, the following reductions:

1. FMBs → FMB   (by the major lineal rule corollary)
        → FF   (by the cross sibling rule)
2. FMBs → FFs   (by the cross sibling rule)
        → FB   (by the half-sibling rule)
        → F   (by the parallel sibling rule corollary)

Of these two reductions, the first is right and the second wrong; father's mother's brother's son is in fact called "grandfather" in Fox, not "father". We may propose two ways of accounting for this. First, we note that Lounsbury's notation includes a symbol [...] to indicate that linking kin must be involved, but he has no symbol to indicate that they must <u>not</u> be involved; in his material, ♂ B could mean "male ego's brother" or "a male linking kinsman's brother", and the "brother" could be either the designated kinsman or a link to some other kin. We may, then, introduce a boundary marker [#], marking the end of a linkage; [3] thus # ♂ B means "male ego's brother", ♂ B # means "a man's brother as designated kinsman", and # ♂ B # means "male ego's brother as designated kinsman". With this device, we

can rewrite our cross sibling rule to read ... MB # → ... F #,
... FS # → ... M #. The corollaries are # ♂ Ss ... → # ♂ s ..., # ♂
Sd ... → # ♂ d ..., # ♀ Bs ... → # ♀ s ..., # ♀ Bd ... → # ♀ d ... It
can now be seen that reduction 2, as given above, is impossible, since
the cross sibling rule is no longer applicable to FMBs. This leaves
reduction 1, the correct one, as the only one possible.

     Alternatively, we may eliminate reduction 2 not by introduc-
ing a boundary marker, but by prescribing an order of precedence
among rules. In the Fox case, we can give the major lineal rule priority over the cross sibling rule: i.e., where either rule _may_ be applied (as in the first step of reducing FMBs), it is the major lineal
rule which must be chosen, in order to make the correct prediction
of usage.[4]

     Consider further the following pair of reductions:

1. ♂ MBdss → ♂ MSss (by the major lineal rule corollary)
            → ♂ Mss (by the parallel sibling rule corollary)
            → ♂ Bs (by the half-sibling rule)
            → ♂ s (by the parallel sibling rule)

2. ♂ MBdss → ♂ MBds (by the minor lineal rule)
            → ♂ MSs (by the major lineal rule corollary)
            → ♂ Ms (by the parallel sibling rule corollary)
            → ♂ B (by the half-sibling rule)

Again, only the first reduction is correct: the Fox call ♂ MBdss by
the term for "son". And, as before, we can account for this in two
ways. First, we may rewrite the minor lineal rule with a boundary
marker: # ss ... → # s ... (i.e., ego's son's son as link is reduced
to ego's son as link), # sd ... → # s ..., # ds ... → # d ..., # dd ...
→ # d ... The corollaries are ... FF # → ... F #, ... FM # → ...
M #, ... MF # → ... F #, ... MM # → ... M #. The incorrect reduction 2 now becomes impossible, since the minor lineal rule no longer
applies to ♂ MBdss. Or, on the other hand, we need not introduce a
boundary marker if we prescribe that the major lineal rule must have
priority over the minor lineal rule, as it does in reduction 1, to give
a correct result.

Finally, consider the following reductions:

1. ♂ MSdss → ♂ Mdss   (by the parallel sibling rule)
           → ♂ Sss   (by the half-sibling rule)
           → ♂ ss   (by the cross sibling rule corollary)

2. ♂ MSdss → ♂ MSds   (by the minor lineal rule)
           → ♂ Mds   (by the parallel sibling rule)
           → ♂ Ss   (by the half-sibling rule)

Here also, only the first reduction is correct, since the Fox call ♂ MSdss by the "grandchild" term. As above, this can be accounted for by the use of a boundary marker in the minor lineal rule: reduction 2 cannot be carried out if the minor lineal rule is # ds ... → # d .... Again, however, it is possible to eliminate the incorrect reduction by the ordering of rules: we may prescribe that the parallel sibling rule has precedence over the minor lineal rule.

Lounsbury has noted (1964: 388-389, fn. 16) that some kinship systems require that their rules be ranked in an order of precedence. He further notes that the merging rule for Crow and Omaha terminologies

> ... could also have been written in the "Iroquois" fashion which establishes a wider set of equivalences, eliminating links that are same-sex and same-generation kin of any degree of collaterality, and of any kind ("parallel" or "cross"). In this case, however, the rules would have to be listed as an ordered set, the skewing rule always taking precedence over the merging rule.

It appears that, for Fox, such a wider set of equivalences is in fact not merely possible, but necessary; and that either an order of priority, or some other additional descriptive device, is also necessary. Note, however, that the equivalences are restricted in particular ways — e.g., mother's brother is not always equivalent to father, but only as part of a chain of linking kin. If we list the rules as an ordered set, then, we have the following: [5]

    1. Major lineal rule   ⎫
    2. Parallel sibling rule ⎬ in that order
                             ⎭

3a. Minor lineal rule ⎫ after rules 1 and 2, but unordered
3b. Cross sibling rule ⎬ with respect to each other.
 x. Half-sibling rule   unordered with respect to all others.

The importance of ordering for descriptive rules has, of course, been long recognized among linguists, and has recently been re-emphasized by Chomsky and his school. An interesting hypothesis which has been advanced recently by linguists is that the order of rules in a description may correspond in some way to an historical order of development (for a detailed treatment of this idea, see Closs 1965). It would be interesting to see whether the order of rules in a kinship analysis may also reflect historical order. With reference to the Fox system and Central Algonkian systems in general, there is a relevant observation by Hockett (1964: 247) to the effect that "the extension of 'father' and 'mother' to 'parallel-uncle' and 'parallel-aunt' ... seems to be relatively recent." Since this extension of terms is accounted for by the parallel sibling rule, the fact that this rule has a lower priority than the major lineal rule may be a descriptive reflection of its historical recency. If such correlations can be shown in a sufficient number of cases, we will clearly have a powerful tool for reconstructing prehistoric developments in kinship organization.

NOTES

[1] There would be advantages in replacing this notational system with that used by Romney and D'Andrade (1964) and by Hammel (1965); in that case we would write [a + mOf - a] → [aOf - a] or [a + m + x - f - a] → [a + x - f - a]. For ease of comparison with Lounsbury's material, however, we retain his notational conventions.

[2] The terms parallel and cross are here used, for convenience, to mean "of the same sex" and "of the opposite sex" respectively, with reference to siblings.

[3] This is equivalent to the single dot used by Romney (1965: 136) and to the vertical line (meaning "terminal position only") used by Lounsbury (1965: 168-169) in his Trobriand study.

[4] The choice between ordering of rules and narrowing their generality by adding a context restriction (in this case, the boundary marker) is also noted by Lounsbury (1965: 167) for the Trobriand system.

[5]The rules may be restated very economically as an unordered set in a notation based on that of Romney–D'Andrade and Hammel (cf. fn. 1 above). If we let a represent any individual, b an individual of a specific sex, and c an individual of sex opposite to b, then we may write:

Major lineal rule: a + mOf – a → aOf – a
   Corollary: a + fOm – a → a + fOa
Parallel sibling rule: bOb – a → b – a
   Corollary: a + bOb → a + b
Minor lineal rule: #a – a – a – a → #a – a – a
   Corollary: a + a + a + a# → a + a + a#
Cross sibling rule: a + a + bOc# → a + a + c#
   Corollary: #cOb – a – a → #c – a – a
Half-sibling rule: a + a – a → aOa

BIBLIOGRAPHY

Closs, Elizabeth
   1965 Diachronic Syntax and Generative Grammar. Language
      41:402–415.
Hammel, Eugene A.
   1965 "An Algorithm for Crow–Omaha Solutions", in Formal
      Semantic Analysis (ed. by E. A. Hammel), pp. 118–126.
      American Anthropologist, Special Publication, vol. 67,
      no. 5, part 2.
Hockett, Charles F.
   1964 "The Proto Central Algonquian Kinship System", in Ex-
      plorations in Cultural Anthropology: Essays in Honor of
      George Peter Murdock (ed. by Ward H. Goodenough),
      pp. 239–258. New York: McGraw–Hill.
Lounsbury, Floyd G.
   1964 "A Formal Account of the Crow– and Omaha–type Kin-
      ship Terminologies", in Explorations in Cultural Anthro-
      pology: Essays in Honor of George Peter Murdock (ed.
      by Ward H. Goodenough), pp. 351–393. New York:
      McGraw–Hill.
   1965 "Another View of the Trobriand Kinship Categories",
      in Formal Semantic Analysis (ed. by E. A. Hammel),
      pp. 142–185. American Anthropologist, Special Publi-
      cation, vol. 67, no. 5, part 2.

Romney, A. Kimball
    1965 "Kalmuk Mongol and the Classification of Lineal Kinship Terminologies", in Formal Semantic Analysis (ed. by E. A. Hammel), pp. 127-141. American Anthropologist, Special Publication, vol. 67, no. 5, part 2.
Romney, A. Kimball, and Roy G. D'Andrade
    1964 "Cognitive Aspects of English Kin Terms", in Transcultural Studies in Cognition (ed. by A. K. Romney and R. G. D'Andrade), pp. 146-170. American Anthropologist, Special Publication, vol. 66, no. 3, part 2.
Tax, Sol
    1937 "The Social Organization of the Fox Indians", in Social Anthropology of North American Tribes (ed. by Fred Eggan), pp. 243-284. Chicago: University of Chicago Press.

11 | Linguistic Innovations in Karok

Introduction

During the century that the Karok Indians of northwestern California have been exposed to the white man's culture, a considerable number of innovations have been made in their language,[1] under the double stimulus of the Americans' language and culture. Of these innovations a few are matters of phonemic redistribution, but the overwhelming majority are in the lexical field. No morphological or syntactic changes have been found.

The lexical innovations may be divided into three classes: borrowings, new usages, and new formations. Since the new phonemic distributions have arisen principally as a result of borrowing, they will be discussed following the section on loan words.

1. Borrowings

1.1 Following the terminology of Einar Haugen, The Analysis of Linguistic Borrowing, Lg. 26.210-31 (1950), Karok borrowings may be classified into <u>loan words</u> and <u>loan shifts</u> (the type Haugen calls loan blends evidently does not occur). Neither kind is numerous, but loan words constitute the larger group. As would be expected, older Karok speakers with a poor command of English use loan words with complete or partial substitution of native sounds for English ones. Younger persons who speak English well also use these substitutive forms, but in addition use a large number of words with substantially English pronunciation. Since the number of loans in use by the latter group would include practically their entire English vocabulary, this discussion will be limited to the rather small number of words commonly used by the older speakers.

A number of these words designate articles of food, such as 'ápus² apple, apples, pícas peach, peaches, and kó·n corn. In some of these, the English plural form, rather than the singular, is obviously the model. This is probably the result of two facts: 1) English speakers commonly refer to these articles in the mass, rather than as individual items, and so use the plural; 2) the majority of Karok noun forms show no distinction between singular and plural number, so that the Indian might easily err in using the English plural. Yet putíru potato lacks the final sibilant, and ké·ks cake has it where the English plural is probably much less common than the singular. No explanation can be given for these forms.

Another group of words designate some of the most common things in the native Karok culture, but serve as generic terms where Karok originally lacked such. Thus páskit basket may now be used, though before the white man came, a Karok would have had to specify 'ássip bowl-basket, sípnu·k storage basket, 'áttimnam burden-basket or the like. To be sure, there is a reasonable doubt that even the modern Karok speaker feels a need for such a generic term. My informants may have used it with me simply to be accomodating to a white man.

A very few Karok words are known to be loans from languages other than English. The only one that can be traced with much certainty is tákus pelican, from Yurok tₒkus.³ That this word is a borrowing from Yurok to Karok, and not the other way around, is shown by the fact that its phonemic form is not typical for Karok (see 1.3). Furthermore, being a sea-bird, the pelican is common in Yurok territory, but rare in that of the Karok.

Karok loans as a whole show the same kind of distribution by form-class as that given by Haugen (p. 224) for American Norwegian and Swedish. That is, most loans in Karok are nouns; only two loans belong to the class of verbs.⁴ Both of these have English nouns as models: kí·h to lock (< key) and pikča to photograph (< picture). No loans at all are found in the Karok class of particles. But it should be noted that all the classes of lexical innovations in Karok, not only loans but new usages and new formations as well, consist mostly of noun stems. The reason seems to be that the white man brought in more new things than he did new processes, and things are principally designated by noun stems in Karok, as they are in European languages.

1.2. Related to loan words are Haugen's hybrid creations, where English morphemes are put into Karok models. These are not too common. An example of a loan morpheme in a Karok derivational pattern is pússihič cat, where -ič is a suffix of diminutive or affectionate meaning. The same loan stem appears in a native pattern of compounding in pusihtunvê·čas kittens, literally pussy small-plural.

The loaned verbs mentioned in 1.1 enter into derivational formations which should perhaps be included here, though the formation of the derivatives must have occurred after the verbs had already been made part of the Karok language: kî·hår key (literally instrument for locking), pikčáhar camera (instrument for photographing).

1.3. The following phonemic redistributions are found in loan words: /r/ , never word-initial in native words, assumes that position in cases like rápat Robert. Consonant-clusters within a single syllable, never found natively, occur in a word like práms plum(s). In native words, /p t k f θ s š x m n/ occur very rarely in the sequence V̌'CV, but there are loans like 'ápus apple and tákus pelican. This is probably connected (I do not know whether as cause or as effect, or as both) with a tendency among some young Karok to simplify all geminate clusters. [5]

There is another phonological phenomenon in present-day Karok which may be an innovation. It is expressed in the following facts of distribution: /š/ occurs only after /y/ and after a front vowel, long or short, followed or not by any consonant; tí·yšip mountain, čí·š younger sister, pikšip shadow. /s/ occurs frequently in all other positions, as in sáruk downhill, 'á·s water, 'ápsu·n snake. But /s/ also occurs, in a small number of words, after a front vowel; síkspič six bits, kê·ks cake, tasínsir to brush repeatedly, símsi·m metal, knife. Some speakers also fluctuate between /š/ and /s/ in words like naniššára or nanissára my bread. These are the data that make necessary the phonemic separation of /s/ and /š/ . However, there is a historical or morphological reason for each of

the cases cited. Síkspič and ké·ks are obviously borrowings in which
an approximation to English /s/ is made;[6] the situation is like that
reported by Fries and Pike for Mazateco, where siento hundred shows
[t] after nasal, instead of the expected [d].[7] In each of the other examples, a morpheme boundary occurs before the Karok /s/: tasínsir
is a finally-reduplicated derivative from tássir to brush (once). Sím-
si·m is probably a reduplication of a syllable *sim, which has not
been found alone but may be onomatopoetic for the sound of cutting.
Nanissára contains sára bread. The question remains: Why did Karok
speakers ever adopt these pronunciations, which are incompatible
with the one-sibilant phonemic pattern they must have had at one time?
I believe it was a direct result of the bilingual situation. Karok who
learn to speak English at all well learn to differentiate between the
two English sibilants /s/ and /š/ , and are then able to make this distinction not only in loan words like síkspič, but also in those native
words where analogy urges it. The analogical proportions would be
of the type 'ikrak to split (once): 'ikrákrak to split repeatedly: :tássir:
X. Then X = tasínsir, not *tasínšir. This particular innovation, then,
a redistribution of allophones resulting in an additional phonemic contrast, may be due not to loanwords (since they are few) but simply to
the fact of bilingualism in the community.

1.4. Loan shifts in Karok take the form only of loan-trans-
lations or calques, and are infrequent. An example is the use of
fíθθih foot = pedal extremity to mean also foot = 12 inches. A shift
with a more complex history is vírusur, originally bear, now also
pear. Here the Karok speaker's analysis of the English model has
gone astray because of his difficulty in distinguishing between English /p/ and /b/. At least one loan shift contains a hybrid creation
mentioned earlier: pusihíč-ti·v cat's-ears (a kind of flower).

2. New Usages

A second class of lexical innovations is that comprising native words which have acquired new semantic usages. In some the
relation of the new meaning to the old is obvious, as in sá·k, originally arrowhead, now also bullet. In other cases explanation may be re-
quired: 'asáxvuh turtle now also means lock — informants explain that
old-time padlocks looked to the Indians like turtle-shells.[8]

3. New Formations

   3.1. The largest class of innovations is that of new formations. Of several methods of new formation, the least used is onomatopoetic reduplication. This is seen in a number of native words,
such as kačakáˑč blue-jay, púfpuˑf unidentified animal said to whis-
tle, and tíʃptuˑp Eel River Indians (where the name is said to imitate
the sound of their language). None of the elements reduplicated here
occurs alone. In innovations, this process is found only in símsiˑm
knife, metal (see 1.3) and nákišnakiš pig (said to be imitative of the
animal's grunting). Presumably músmus cow was so formed in the
language of its origin, but in Karok it is almost surely a loan word
(see 4.1).

   3.2. A large class of new formations is the derivatives.
Derivation is a common process in Karok, and therefore many new
culture items are labelled with derivatives in various suffixes. Those
derivatives which are believed not to have been used before the white
man came constitute the derivative new formations.

   The commonest derivational suffixes used in innovations form
nouns from verbs, and are as follows:

   -ar is used for names of instruments, as in piθxáhar wash-
board, washing machine, soap, from piθxah to wash. Cf. kíˑhar
and pikčáhar in 1.2. The results are of two semantic types: active,
as in piθxáhar instrument which washes; and passive, as in 'aknupu-
núppar instrument which is thumped, i.e. guitar, from 'aknúppunupˑ
to thump.

   -kir forms names of instruments or occasionally of places,
as in takníhkir wheel from taknih to roll, 'ahóˑkir sidewalk from
'áhoˑ to walk.

   -raˑm ~ -naˑm forms names of places, as in 'irípraˑm
mine from 'írip to dig, 'amnaˑm hotel from 'av ~ 'am to eat. In one
case it is questionable whether an innovation in -raˑm is a new formation or a new usage: 'išraˑm saloon seems to be from 'iš to drink,
but is identical in form with 'išraˑm deerlick.

-aram forms names of places or of receptacles, as in 'imni-šáram <u>kitchen</u> from 'imniš <u>to cook</u>, patváram <u>washbasin</u>, from pá·tva <u>to wash one's self</u>.

-a·n ~ va·n forms names of agents, as in 'ieyúra·n <u>driver</u> from 'ieyur <u>to haul</u>, 'irípva·n <u>miner</u> from 'irip <u>to dig</u>.

A few suffixes are added to noun stems to form other noun stems. Probably the most important is -ič, which sometimes has a diminutive meaning, but at other times is harder to define. In innovations it is generally found added to stems which are already innovations themselves but do not occur alone. An example is pússihič, already seen in 1.2; another is ye·šníhva·nič <u>peddler</u>, where the base is *ye·šríhva·n, the derivative of agent from yé·šrih <u>to sell</u>.

-kuniš <u>like</u> is added to noun stems to form a small number of adjectives (a nominal subclass) in which one can see an accommodation to the way English classifies perceptions, similar to the borrowing of generic terms described in 1.1. The word eúkkinkuniš, literally <u>like bile</u>, means <u>blue</u>, <u>green</u>, or <u>yellow</u>, and originally was probably the only designation for that part of the spectrum. But when asked to translate English <u>blue</u>, an occasional informant will give 'ámku·fkuniš <u>like smoke</u>. In the same way píriškuniš <u>like grass</u> is given for <u>green</u>, and kasčí·pkuniš <u>like porcupine quills</u> (which are dyed yellow for use in basketry) for <u>yellow</u>. But 'ámku·fkuniš, píriš-kuniš and kasčí·pkuniš (like many lexical innovations, see 4) are terms unknown to many speakers. All this leads me to believe that the words are innovations made by bilinguals. Just as when they borrowed the term páskit <u>basket</u> and imitated the ability of English to be more generic than Karok, so here they imitated the ability of English to be more specific. The resultant terms cannot be classed indiscriminately with other new formations, since they describe phenomena which were always known to the Karok, and because it is unlikely that the terms would have come into existence in the absence of bilinguals. On the other hand, since they involve neither morphemic importation nor substitution, they do not come under Haugen's classification of loans. It seems, then, that the type must be recognized as an additional variety of lexical change due to bilingualism — perhaps the term <u>semantic loan</u> could be applied to it.

　　　3.3. The largest class of lexical innovations is that formed by compounding. Karok grammar permits composition of noun stems in two varieties —non-adjective plus adjective, and non-adjective plus non-adjective. The former type has its elements in the order head + attribute, and the adjective may enter the compound in its plural inflected form. The result may be endocentric, as when kuí·sra sun + -'anammahač small gives kusnáh'anammahač clock, or of the exocentric bahuvrihi type, as when tí·v ear + xárahsas long (plural) gives tivxárahsas mule. The type of compound with two non-adjective stems has the order attribute + head and is always endocentric; yúras sea + čiši· dog >yurasčíšši· horse. Note, however, that the precise semantic relation between the parts of such compounds is variable: 'ahup'ássip a vessel made of wood, a box; 'išaha'ássip a vessel to hold water, a bucket.

　　　Many new compounds have as constituents words which are themselves innovations — borrowings, new usages, or new forma- tions, including compounds. Thus the loan word číkin chicken plus the native 'úruh egg gives čikin'úruh (hen's) egg, and this in turn plus the loan word pá·y pie gives čikin'uruhpá·y custard pie.

　　　In some cases the analysis of new compounds into immediate constituents results in forms which do not occur alone, e.g. tikak- vára·r glove, a compound of tí·k hand plus *'akvára·r instrument for putting in (a derivative in -ar). Here, although the synchronic analy- sis is clear, the historical analysis is less so. Did the aboriginally non-existent *'akvára·r have to be conceived of before tikakvára·r could be formed? To me it seems more likely that tikakvára·r was invented as a whole, without reference to its immediate consituents. A similar case (where tí·k has the meaning finger rather than hand) is tikakvánna·č finger-ring. This is to be analyzed as a derivative in -ič from *tikakvára·, a compound of tí·k and 'akvára· putting in.[9] It then differs from the word for glove in being a derivative of a compound, rather than a compound of a derivative.

　　　3.4. An occasional innovation is in the form of a descriptive phrase. Examples are 'ahtáknih muyukúkkuh tire, literally automo- bile (fire-wheel) its shoe, and kusnáh'anammahac 'atrá·x 'unhíkkahi- tih wristwatch, literally clock on the arm it is fastened. Many such expressions are so circumlocutory that their status as lexical units is doubtful, and they are not given in the word-list of this paper: witness the sentence vúra 'u·m tírihšas pe·kxúrik patakunpasnapíšri·hva 'î·riš <u>they're sticking broad pieces of paper down on the floor</u> (i. e. <u>they're laying linoleum</u>).

4. Word List

Following is a list of all the lexical innovations recorded by me.[10] It does not pretend to be exhaustive for the language. Such a goal would be very difficult, for a special reason — that different Karok speakers tend to use different words for new culture objects. That is, there have been repeated borrowings, meaning transfers, and inventions, but many have not diffused widely enough and pushed others out enough to become standard for the language. Thus, when asked the word for <u>wheel</u>, some informants give taknih <u>rolling</u>, while others give taknîhar and still others taknîhkir — these being derivatives meaning <u>rolling-instrument</u>. This is in contrast with a well-established form like čiši· <u>horse</u> (originally <u>dog</u>) which everyone knows and uses.

This list is, then, designed only to furnish further examples of the processes described above, to give an idea of the extent to which each process is used, and to testify to the vigor of derivation and compounding in contemporary Karok grammar. The items are arranged in rough semantic groupings. Each one is marked as l. w. (loan word), h. c. (hybrid creation), l. s. (loan shift), n. u. (new usage), der. (derivative new formation), or cpd. (compound new formation). Forms like tikakvára·r <u>glove</u> and tikakvánna·c <u>ring</u> (see 3.3) are marked as cpd. of der. and der. of cpd. respectively. Following these tags are given the models of borrowings (when not obvious), original meanings of new usages, and literal translations of new formations.

4.1. ANIMALS, <u>Cow</u> (or <u>bull</u>, <u>steer</u>) is músmus, probably a l. w. This form is found in most of Karok's neighbor languages, as well as throughout the Pacific Northwest, so it is difficult to tell exactly where Karok got it. Perhaps the most likely source is Shasta mú·smu·s,[11] since of the tribes with whom the Karok had dealings, the Shasta were closest to the northern area from which the word evidently radiated. Where English speakers would simply say <u>milk</u>,

the cpd. muṣmus'účiš (cow-milk) is used. To moo is 'ikvú·hva (n.u.
to howl).

Horse is čiši· (n.u., dog), yurasčíšši· (cpd., ocean-dog), or
the obsolete 'akǝip'ámva·n (cpd., grass-eater) or tivtunvê·čas (cpd.,
small-ears). This last term contrasts with the words for mule, tivxárahsas (cpd., long-ears) or tivxárahar (der. of cpd., having long
ears). To neigh is 'ikšah (n.u., to laugh).

Cat is pússihič (see 1.2) or tíripus, which is probably a l.w.
from English kitty-puss, used in some dialects for calling cats.[12]
Cf. the Shasta equivalent kiripússi. Kittens are called pusihtunvê·-
čas (1.2). Dog, of the breeds introduced by the white man, is tivár-
arih or tivárarihva (cpd., ear-hanging, as contrasted with the erect-
eared native dog). The diminutives tivánnanihič and tivánnanihvač
are also used.

Chicken is číkin (l.w.). Where English would use simply
egg(s), the cpd. čikin'úruh (chicken-egg) is used; note also čikin'-
uruhpá·y custard pie. To crow (of a rooster) is čú·pha (n.u., to
speak). Other animals are nákišnakiš pig (see 3.1), pišpíšših bee
(n.u., yellowjacket), 'apxantí·čpu·fič sheep or goat (cpd., white-
man deer), and tákus pelican (see 1.1).

4.2. PLANTS AND FRUITS. Peach(es) is píčas (l.w.),
which may be used to illustrate the kinds of compounds common for
fruit names: pičás'as peach-pit (-stone), pičás'a·s peach-juice (-wa-
ter), and pičaspá·y peach pie. Other plant-food l.w.'s are 'ápus ap-
ple(s), 'ápakač apricot(s), kó·n corn, pínšur bean(s) (no reason is
known for the -ur), práms plum(s), tumé·tus tomato(es), and putíru
potato. For the last there is also an obsolete cpd. 'apxanti·čtáyi·ǝ
(white-man Brodiaea). Of other origins are fú·k carrot (n.u., plant
sp. with edible root) and vírusur pear (see 1.4). One new non-edible
plant, probably introduced by accident along with white men's seeds,
is pínhi·č Erodium cicutarium (cpd., make-believe pin, because it
has pin-like seed capsules).

4.3. FOOD (OTHER THAN FRUITS AND VEGETABLES)
AND DRINK. Sugar is 'asúxxi·m (n.u., sugar-pine gum), com-
pounded in 'asuximxanahyá·č candy-cane (very long sugar) and in

'asuximpaxviríxvir <u>rock candy</u> (<u>sugar-sucking</u>), which has the synonym paxviníxvi·nač (der., <u>little repeated-sucking</u>). Wheat flour is
'impur, which is undoubtedly some kind of neologism, since wheat
was introduced by the whites, but is of unknown etymology. The only
form resembling it, 'ikpur <u>acorn flour</u>, cannot be related to it by any
known phonemic alternation.

Other foods are čí·š <u>cheese</u> (l. w.), ké·ks <u>cake</u> (see 1.1 and
1.3), pá·y <u>pie</u> (l. w.), sana'únnuhič <u>biscuit</u> (der. of cpd., <u>little round
bread</u>), saraxútnahič <u>pancake</u> (cpd., <u>thin bread</u>), sarataxunkó·r <u>but-
ter</u> (cpd. of der., <u>bread spreading-on instrument</u>), sú·čakrakas <u>soda
cracker(s)</u> (l. w.). Perhaps classifiable here also are 'ixvínnipač
<u>pill</u> (der., <u>little swallowing</u>) and 'apxanti·č'imšáxvuh <u>chewing gum</u>
(cpd., <u>white-man gum</u>, i. e. <u>plant gum</u>, which the Karok chewed as
we do chicle).

Drinks include 'apxanti·ččampínnišič <u>tea</u> (cpd., <u>white-man
yerba buena</u>).[13] A synonym is tí· (l. w.), forming the cpd. tih'ássip
<u>tea-pot</u> (<u>tea-vessel</u>). Liquor is 'úx'a·s (cpd., <u>bitter water</u>) with the cpd.
'ux'asaye·šríhva·n <u>bartender</u> (<u>liquor-seller</u>). Semantically associated are 'išra·m <u>saloon</u> (see 3.2) and the bivalent stems 'ipxú·spa <u>to
bé sober</u> (der., <u>to have one's mind again</u>) and pahvákkir <u>to be drunk</u>
(n. u., <u>to eat or drink too much</u>), with the der. of agent pahvakíra·n
<u>drunkard</u>.

4.4. TRANSPORTATION. Words connected with travel by
horse are 'iknap <u>horseshoe</u> (n. u., <u>fastening-on</u>) with the synonyms
'ikná·pkar (der., <u>fastening-on-to instrument</u>) and čišihíkna·pkar (cpd.
of der., <u>horse-fastening-on-to instrument</u>); 'išrá·tkir or 'išrá·ttar
<u>reins</u> (der.'s, <u>leading-instrument</u>); 'ativákkir <u>packsaddle</u> (der., <u>car-
rying-on-the-back instrument</u>); 'ikrivtakúkkir <u>saddle</u> (der., <u>sitting-
on instrument</u>); kí·ntako· <u>to ride</u> (der., <u>to sit on</u>, with a different
stem than the preceding item). Note the phrase čiših'ávahkam 'ukú·n-
tako· <u>he's riding horseback</u> (<u>horse-top he's sitting on</u>).

Wagon is vê·kin (l. w.); it has the cpds. ve·kin'ímpa· <u>road</u>
(<u>wagon-trail</u>); also called 'impahtíri (cpd., <u>broad trail</u>), and ve·kin-
'áhyu·m <u>vehicular bridge</u> (<u>wagon-bridge</u>), also called čišiháhyu·m
(cpd., <u>horse-bridge</u>). Wheel is takníhkir or takníhar (der.'s, <u>rolling-
instrument</u>) or taknih (n. u., <u>rolling</u>). The last also means <u>wheeled</u>

vehicle, motor, and forms the cpd. 'ahtáknih automobile (fire-wheel), which has the synonyms 'iɵivɵané·npa·h (cpd., land-boat), ká· (l. w. from English car), and 'iɵyur (n. u., hauling). Other automotive terms are 'iɵyurá'a·h headlight(s) (cpd., auto-lantern), 'e·číprar jack (der., lifting-instrument), 'ikvú·hva horn (n. u., howling), and pišpíšših radiator (n. u., yellowjacket or honeycomb, a radiator being considered to resemble the latter).

Miscellaneous items are 'ahó·kir sidewalk (der., walking-place), 'ahíɵyur locomotive (cpd., fire-car), 'áhpa·h steamship (cpd., fire-boat), and 'ikxipišríhra·m airfield (der., flying-down place).

4.5. TRADES, BUSINESSES, AND PROFESSIONS. 'amna·m hotel (der., eating-place); 'ane·kyáva·n doctor (n. u., sweating sha-man); 'ane·kyavan'ikrívra·m hospital (cpd., doctor-house) with its synonyms 'ane·kyavánni·k (cpd., doctor-place), 'ane·krívra·m (cpd., medicine house), and yikihe·krívra·m (cpd., disease-house); 'araé·-pto·rar census taker (cpd. of der., person-counter); 'ikuke·kyáva·n lumberjack (cpd. of der., log-maker), vuxíčra·m sawmill (der., saw-ing-place); pe·vapíɵva·n storekeeper (der., trader), pe·vapiɵváram or pe·piɵváram store (der., trading-place), with the cpd. pe·piɵv-arámta·y city (many-stores); piykára·n butcher (der., slaughterer), piyka-rára·m slaughterhouse (der., slaughtering-place); supríhva·n surveyor (der., measurer); ye·šníhva·nič peddler (der., little seller).

4.6. MINING TERMINOLOGY. Gold is 'išpuk (n. u., dentalia, money), with cpds. 'išpukasuprávar gold-scales (cpd. of der., gold-measuring-instrument), 'išpuke·mníšra·m gold refinery (cpd. of der., gold-cooking place), and 'išpukappé·n gold-pan (h. c. from išpuk plus English pan).[14] Other terms are 'asó·kir flume (probably a contrac-tion of *'as-ahó·-kir, cpd. of der., water going-place); 'írippar pick-ax (der., digging-instrument), 'irípra·m mine (der., digging-place), 'irípva·n miner (der., digger); 'ixxakaxákkar gold-cradle (der., mak-ing-noise-repeatedly instrument); tanukyánnar shovel (der., scooping-instrument); mítma·ɵva to blast (der., to cause to explode).

4.7. BUILDING TERMINOLOGY: 'asattáran cement (n. u., bedrock), 'ivhanatunvê·čas shingles (cpd., little boards), háma ham-mer (l. w.), ɵivxíššar plane (der., smoothening-instrument), sí· nail (n. u., awl), sihtunvê·čas tacks (cpd., little nails).

4.8. CLOTHING MATERIALS, CLOTHING, AND PERSONAL
EFFECTS. Cloth is makáyva·s (cpd., white-man blanket), with the
cpds. makayvasyukúkkuh tennis shoes (cloth shoes) and makayvase·-
krívra·m tent (cloth house). Cotton is matnus (n.u., bursting out,
because it was seen bursting out of quilts), with cpd. matnusáva·s
quilt (cotton-blanket). Calico is kúkku (n.u., rough) or kukuhmakáy-
va·s (cpd., rough material). Velvet is mur (n.u., mole, because
of the similarity to a mole's fur) or murayáffus (cpd., mole-dress).
Other fabrics are murappó·r corduroy (cpd., mole-pants), sirikayáf-
fus silk (h.c. from English silk plus yáffus dress), and furaxyáffus
satin (cpd., woodpecker-head dress). Lace is xahávik (n.u., spider-
web), with cpd. xahavike·kyá·r crochet needle (lace-tool). Leather
is vastáran (n.u., buckskin), with cpd. vastarankútrah leather jacket (leather-bulging, see the next paragraph). Rubber is 'asáxxu·s
(n.u., steatite, literally smooth rock), with cpd. 'asaxusyukúkkuh
boots (cpd., rubber shoes), also called pú·č (l.w.).

Articles of clothing include kutraháva·s coat (cpd., bulging-
blanket, probably because of the body's bulge underneath it), for
which kutrahar (der., bulging-instrument) is also used. The latter
has cpds. kutnahaná'anammahač jacket (little coat), kutraharaxxára
overcoat (long coat), and several words for raincoat: kutraharáxxu·s
(smooth coat), 'asaxuskútrahar (rubber coat), and paꝋriharakútrahar
(rainy coat). Underwear is surukámsa·nva (cpd., underneath-clothes);
cf. surukampó·r men's underwear (cpd., underneath-pants) and suru-
kamyáffus women's underwear (cpd., underneath-dress). It would be
possible to consider this last group as l.s.'s rather than new formations, the first two based on English underclothes and underpants,
and the third created by analogy to the second. Handkerchief is 'ipčimákkananač, of unknown origin. One informant connected it with a
word 'imákkananač flashy, the existence of which was doubted by other informants. Even assuming the existence of this latter word, no
known derivational or compositional pattern involving it could yield
'ipčimákkananač. Two words for bandanna are cpds. — 'ipčimakanana-
náčka·m (big handkerchief) and 'ipčimakananáč'a·x (red handkerchief).

Miscellaneous items are 'avahkamyukúkkuh rubbers (cpd.,
top shoes, or perhaps a l.s. from English overshoes), 'ifunihe·hyák-
kurih hairpin (cpd., hair sticking-in), 'ikta·tíhar umbrella (der.,

holding-with-a-stick instrument), 'iptasinsĭrar <u>clothes-brush</u> (der.,
brushing-repeatedly instrument), tikakvánna ·č <u>finger-ring</u> (der. of
cpd., <u>little finger-putting-into</u>), tikakvára ·r <u>glove</u> (cpd. of der., <u>hand</u>
<u>putting-into instrument</u>), vo ·nvánna ·č <u>shirt</u> (der., <u>little crawling-into</u>).

4.9. HOUSEHOLD ITEMS. Parts of the house and yard are
pimkúhra ·m <u>sitting-room</u> (der., <u>warming-place</u>), 'imnišáram <u>kitchen</u>
(der., <u>cooking-place</u>), 'avahe ·knívna ·mič <u>pantry</u> (der. of cpd., <u>little</u>
<u>food-house</u>), vurá ·kkir <u>stairway</u> (n. u., <u>ladder</u>), tasačivčaksurúra ·m
<u>gate</u> (cpd., <u>fence-door</u>), 'afiknívna ·mič <u>privy</u> (der. of cpd., <u>little ex-</u>
<u>crement-house</u>).

Various utensils are símsi ·m <u>knife</u> (see 3.1), also meaning
<u>metal</u> of any kind, and some of its cpds. — simsím'a ·n <u>cable</u> (cpd.,
<u>metal rope</u>), simsim'ássip <u>tin box</u> or <u>can</u> or <u>bucket</u> (cpd., <u>metal ves-</u>
<u>sel</u> — see the next paragraph), simsim'ávar <u>table knife</u> (cpd. of der.,
<u>metal eating-instrument</u>), simsim'úhra ·m <u>pipe</u> (for water or the like)
(cpd., <u>metal smoking-pipe</u>, with a l. s. perhaps involved), simsímtas
<u>wire fence</u> (cpd., <u>metal fence</u>), simsimvó ·h <u>sword</u> (cpd., <u>metal ob-</u>
<u>sidian-blade</u>) with its synonym simsimxára (cpd., <u>long knife</u>); sim-
símyu ·p <u>eye-glasses</u> (cpd., <u>metal eyes</u>, probably so named because
of the rims).

<u>Dish</u> is 'ássip, which also means a <u>vessel</u> of any kind (n. u.,
<u>bowl-basket</u>). It also has several cpds. — 'asipsarišríhra ·m <u>dish-</u>
<u>cupboard</u> (cpd. of der., <u>dish-putting-down place</u>) with synonym 'asip-
tayhitíhra ·m (cpd. of der., <u>dish-lying place</u>); 'ikakriha'ássip <u>icebox</u>
(cpd., <u>ice-vessel</u>), 'ahup'ássip <u>wooden box</u> or <u>coffin</u> (cpd., <u>wood-</u>
<u>vessel</u>), 'iөriha'ássip <u>flower-pot</u> (cpd., <u>flower vessel</u>), sak'ássip
<u>bottle</u> or <u>drinking-glass</u> (cpd., <u>obsidian vessel</u>); 'išaha'ássip <u>bucket</u>
(cpd., <u>water-vessel</u>) with synonyms simsim'ássip (cpd., <u>metal ves-</u>
<u>sel</u>) and 'asíkta ·mnam (cpd. of der., <u>water carrying-in-the-hand</u>
<u>receptacle</u>).

Other objects are 'asáxvuh <u>lock</u> (see 2), kĭ ·har <u>key</u> derived
from kí ·h <u>to lock</u> (see 1.1), 'á ·h <u>lantern</u> or <u>electric light</u> (n. u., <u>fire</u>)
with cpd. 'imaxaynumvá'a ·h <u>electricity</u> (<u>lightning-fire</u>); 'axvá ·har
<u>candle</u> (n. u., <u>pitchwood</u>) with cpd. 'axva ·hara ·өkúrit <u>kerosene</u> (<u>can-</u>
<u>dle-grease</u>); kusnáh'anammahač <u>clock</u> (cpd., <u>little sun</u>) with synonym
kusnahkinínna ·sič (cpd., <u>sun-pet</u>); 'ičyununupní ·hvanač <u>needle</u> (der.,

little pulling-through instrument), píˑn pin (l. w.); piθxáhar wash-
board or washing machine or soap (der. , washing-instrument), 'áθθi-
par wringer (der. , wringing-instrument), 'áyan (flat)iron (l. w.), pik-
rupvánnar sewing machine (der. , self-sewing instrument); 'íˑšram
cup (der. , drinking-receptacle), 'amkir table (der. , eating-place),
pimustihvánnar mirror or window (der. , self-looking instrument),
pimkúhar heating stove (der. , warming instrument), patumkiréˑyuˑn-
var pillowcase (cpd. of der. , pillow putting-in instrument), 'ipθeˑm-
šíppar fan (der. , repeated-fanning instrument), patváram bathtub
or washbowl (der. , washing-receptacle), vuhapiθxáhar toothbrush
(cpd. cf der. , tooth-washing instrument). A kind of basketry mat,
not an original type, is called tínnihič (n. u. , flat).

   4.10. FIREARMS. Xuská ˑmhar gun (n. u. , bow), xuskam-
haná'anammahač pistol (cpd. , little gun), sáˑk bullet (n. u. , obsidian,
arrowhead), sakámta ˑp gunpowder (cpd. , bullet-dust), mit to shoot
(n. u. , to pop, explode).

   4.11. MEASURES. In counting money one uses the l. w. 's
túpič two bits, fúpič four bits, síkspič six bits, vánpit (one) penny
(-pit perhaps by analogy with the bit of two bits etc.), and vantára
(one) dollar. For counting more than one dollar, the ordinal numerals are simply used alone, as in 'itrðˑp na'éˑh he gave me five dol-
lars (he gave me five). The same device is used for all measure-
ment of weights: yíθθa 'umáˑθhitih it weighs one pound (it weighs one).

   The term fíθθih foot has been mentioned in 1. 4. Time is
measured with the bivalent stems 'uˑm to be...o'clock (n. u. , to arrive) and 'ipšúppa ˑhpa to be the...-th day of the week (der. , to be
day again). So 'ifyáˑ tu'uˑm what time is it? (how many have arrived?), kuyráˑk tu'uˑm it's three o'clock (three have arrived), 'ik-
rívkih to ˑpsúppa ˑhpa it's Saturday (the sixth day). The l. w. sárari
Saturday has also been recorded.

   4.12. WRITING AND COMMUNICATION. The word meaning
to write, writing, book, letter, or paper is 'ikxúrik, which underlies
most of the other terms in this field: 'ikxuriká'aˑs ink (cpd. , writing-
water), 'ikxúrikkar pencil, pen (der. , writing-instrument); 'ikxurika-
čivčaksurúraˑm postoffice (cpd., letter-door with the synonym 'ikxurika'umúraˑm cpd. of der. , letter-arriving place); 'ikxurikamahyáram

<u>wastebasket</u> (cpd. of der., <u>paper-putting place</u>); 'ikxurike·kšúppa·n
<u>school-teacher</u> (cpd. of der., <u>writing-teacher</u>), 'ikxurike·kšupíhra·m
<u>school</u> (cpd. of der., <u>writing-teaching place</u>); 'ikxuriké·yu·nnamnih
<u>envelope</u> (cpd., <u>letter putting-in</u>); kusre·kxúrik <u>calendar</u> (cpd.,
<u>month-paper</u>). Also to be noted are 'uhyanavára·r <u>telephone</u> (der.,
speaking-into instrument) and its cpd. 'ikxurika'uhyanavára·r <u>tele-</u>
<u>graph</u> (cpd., <u>writing-telephone</u>).

      4.13. RECREATION. 'Akṇupunúppar <u>guitar</u> (der., <u>thumping</u>
<u>instrument</u>) with synonym 'aktumtó·r (der., <u>plucking-instrument</u>);
'ikre·myahvára·r <u>musical instrument</u> of any kind, <u>phonograph</u>, <u>radio</u>
(der., <u>blowing-into instrument</u>, but now applied to the piano, violin,
etc.); ¡ikre·myahvará·va·n <u>musician</u> (der., <u>person who blows into</u>);
'unúhxi·tič <u>baseball</u> (der. of cpd., <u>little unripe round-thing</u> — reason
for this designation not known).

      4.14. NATIONALITIES. <u>White man</u> is called 'apxantínnihič
(cpd., <u>flat-hat</u>, because of the brims on white men's hats), with the
cpd. 'apxanti·čya·s'ára <u>government</u> (cpd., <u>white-man chief</u>) and others listed elsewhere. Obsolete terms for <u>white man</u> are simsimtá·r
(cpd., <u>metal-owner</u>) and mákkay (l.w., from the name of an early
trader, McKay) — the latter surviving mainly in makáyva·s <u>cloth</u>. <u>In-</u>
<u>dian</u> is 'ára·r (n.u., <u>person</u>), with cpd. 'araraya·s'ára <u>Bureau of</u>
<u>Indian Affairs</u> (cpd., <u>Indian chief</u>) and others listed in 4.16. <u>Wiyot</u>
<u>Indian</u> is váyat, a l.w. from Yurok weyet or Wiyot wiyot.[15] A bor-
rowing from English in this case seems unlikely, since the local English pronunciation is wíyàt. <u>Half-breeds</u> were formerly called ke·-
mišá·xxi·č (cpd., <u>devil child</u>). <u>Chinese</u> is 'iptáxxappar (der., <u>having</u>
<u>a braid</u>, i.e. a pigtail).

      4.15. PROPER NOUNS. New place names include ka'timpe·-
piθváram <u>Gent's store in Orleans, Calif.</u> (cpd., <u>upriver edge store</u>,
because it is near the upriver end of town), yu'timpe·piθváram <u>Briz-</u>
<u>ard's store in Orleans</u> (cpd., <u>downriver edge store</u>), 'á·čip vape·-
piθváram <u>Van Pelt and Delaney's store in Orleans</u> (descriptive phrase,
<u>middle store</u>); kapáhra·m, name of a place where a copper mine was
formerly operated (h.c. from English <u>copper</u> plus -ra·m, der. suffix
of place); 'ú·θ <u>Eureka, Calif.</u> (n.u., <u>towards the ocean</u>), 'uθfšši·p
<u>San Francisco</u> (cpd., <u>extreme towards-the-ocean</u>).

Some personal names are má·kič, a woman's name (h. c. from English <u>Margaret</u> plus diminutive -ič); pe·nvári, a man's name (l. w. from English <u>Ben Wilder</u>); pi·txára, a man's name (h. c. from English <u>Pete</u> plus -xára <u>tall</u>); sahvurúmsu·si, a woman's name (h. c. from sahvúrum, a place name, plus English <u>Susie</u>).

One holiday name is known: 'ipmitmíttahiv <u>Fourth of July</u> (der., <u>repeated-popping-time</u>).

4.16. NEW NAMES FOR OLD CONCEPTS. Many of these have been mentioned before, such as the color terms 'ámku·fkuniš <u>blue</u>, píriškuniš <u>green</u>, and kasčí·pkuniš <u>yellow</u> (3.2). To the generic terms like páskit <u>basket</u> (1.1) may be added fiš <u>fish</u>, covering original 'á·mma <u>salmon</u>, 'asku·p <u>trout</u> etc., and tákta <u>doctor</u>, covering original 'é·m <u>sucking shaman</u> and 'ane·kyáva·n <u>sweating shaman</u>. To the l. s.'s like pusihíčti·v <u>cat's-ears</u> (1.4) may be added tahyukúkkuh <u>snowshoes</u>, from tá·h <u>snow</u> and yukúkkuh <u>shoes</u>, existing alongside original yukukuhvíkkapuh, literally <u>woven shoes</u>. The word pikyáviš <u>world-renewal ceremony</u> is a l. w. from local English <u>pikiawish</u>, which in turn was taken from Karok 'iθθívθa·nne·n 'upikyáviš <u>he is going to fix the world</u>, a phrase describing the function of the native priest. It exists alongside the native terms 'ir and 'írahiv. For <u>quartz</u>, 'išpuká'as (cpd., <u>gold-rock</u>) exists alongside native 'asaxyíppit.

Several cpds. of 'ára·r <u>Indian</u> are used to designate native objects whose names now have a wider application. Thus pišpíšših <u>yellowjacket</u> now also means <u>bee</u>, and so to specifically designate the yellowjacket one says 'ararapišpíšših (<u>Indian bee</u>). Similarly 'ararássa·k <u>arrowhead</u> (<u>Indian bullet</u>), 'araraxúska·mhar <u>bow</u> (<u>Indian gun</u>).

4.17. UNCLASSIFIABLE MISCELLANY. 'Axayčakišríhan <u>sheriff</u> (der., <u>seizer</u>), 'axvá·hta·hko <u>blond</u> (cpd., <u>white-head</u>), 'ikxipíxxip <u>flag</u> (n. u., <u>fluttering</u>), 'ikyutríhar <u>plow</u> (der., <u>chopping-up instrument</u>); píkča <u>to photograph</u> or <u>a photograph</u> with its der. pikčáhar <u>camera</u> (see 1.1 and 1.2); tišra·m (<u>cultivated) field</u> (n. u., <u>clearing</u>); tó·nnak <u>in town</u> (h. c. English <u>town</u> plus -ak, suffix of place).

The greeting 'ayukî· <u>hello</u> may or may not be a l. w.; cf. Yurok ʔoyekʷiʔ with the same meaning. I cannot establish the source of this word, but one of my informants claims it was introduced by white men. Furthermore, in J. P. Harrington's publications on Karok, this word is written with a labialized k. This is not normal Karok phonetics, and may indicate that the word was an incompletely assimilated loan in the speech of Harrington's informants.

NOTES

[1] My field work on Karok was done in the spring of 1949 and the summer of 1950 around Orleans, California. My thanks go to the Administration of the University of California for making the work possible, to M. B. Emeneau for his offices in securing the necessary funds, and to Mary R. Haas for advice in the preparation of this paper.

[2] The Karok consonant phonemes are /p t č k ' f θ s š x h v r y m n/; the vowels are /i i· e· a a· o· u u·/. /´/ is stress with high tone except in utterance-final, where it is falling tone and produces glottal interruption of vowels. /ˆ/ is stress with falling tone but no glottalization in any position. A few regular patterns of phonemic substitution, Karok for English, can be noted in the data; for instance, English voiced stops are replaced by Karok voiceless ones. But the rather small number of loans in Karok makes it impossible to work out detailed equivalences.

[3] My thanks go to Robert Robins, of the University of London, for the Yurok data cited here and elsewhere in this paper.

[4] All citations in this paper are stems, but most of them are likewise words, since overt affixation is not necessary for all noun- and verb-forms.

[5] To quote an elderly informant: 'Lots of these half-breeds can talk Indian, but they don't say the words just right; they say 'íša instead of 'íššaha [water].'

[6] English /s/, a blade-alveolar sibilant, is articulated between the positions of Karok /θ/ and Karok /s/, since the former is a blade-dental slit-spirant (or for younger speakers an interdental spirant), while the latter is an apico-alveolar sibilant. Karok whose English is imperfect customarily choose to substitute their /s/ for English /s/, whether speaking English or pronouncing English loan words in Karok such as síkspič. J. P. Harrington's fragmentary Karuk Grammar (Ms 296 in the Franz Boas Collection of Materials for American Linguistics) cites θíkim sic 'em!, but this does not correspond to the usage of my informants.

[7] Coexistent Phonemic Systems, Lg. 25. 29-50 (1949).

[8] Mary Haas furnishes a parallel in Natchez, where ʔolo means both <u>turtle</u> and <u>lock.</u>

[9] Verbal nouns are translated here with English verbs ending in -<u>ing</u>.

[10] Still others may be found in J. P. Harrington, Tobacco among the Karuk Indians of California, Washington, 1932 (BAE-B 94), especially pp. 271-277.

[11] This is one of several Shasta words that can be traced to Chinook Jargon. In respect to its phonemic form, it should be noted that Shasta long vowels are much shorter than Karok long vowels, and so could easily be taken into Karok as short. Cf. Karok 'ápus and Shasta 'á·pu·s <u>apple(s)</u>: these words are probably independent borrowings from English, but show the same equivalence of Shasta long vowel to Karok short.

[12] I am indebted to Jesse Sawyer for evidence of this word's existence in English.

[13] This happens to be the only word found containing /čč/, i. e. [tš̌tš̌], and the only thing that prevents the possible phonemicization of [t·š̌] as /čč/ rather than /tč/. This is then another example of phonemic redistribution (see 1.3).

[14] Because of its identity in pattern with English <u>gold-pan,</u> this is the one Karok word found which would fit into Haugen's class of loan-blends. Rather than establish the class here for it alone, I call it a hybrid creation, the pattern of which it also fits.

[15] The Wiyot word is taken from Kroeber, Handbook of the Indians of California (BAE-B 78) p. 112, where it is said to refer not to the tribe, but to the country around the lower Eel River.

12 | Spanish Words in Patwin

In Collaboration with Elizabeth Bright

Patwin is an American Indian language belonging to the Wintun family and the Penutian stock; it was and is spoken on the western side of the lower Sacramento Valley of California.[1] The Patwin tribe was among the most northerly of those in California to be influenced by Spanish culture. As the Patwin were never missionized, however — the nearest mission being at Sonoma, in Miwok territory—Spanish influence on them was much less than elsewhere. Indeed, almost the only evidence of Spanish contact is provided by linguistic data: although the present-day Patwin do not speak Spanish, some of them have Spanish surnames, and all those speaking Patwin use a language which contains a few loanwords from English, but many more from Spanish.[2]

To indicate the pronunciation of the Patwin words cited below, and to clarify the changes which Spanish words undergo in the process of borrowing, we shall briefly describe the sound system of Patwin. The consonant phonemes are as follows: voiceless unaspirated stops /p t k/, voiceless aspirated stops /ph th kh/, glottalized stops /p' t' k'/, voiced stops /b d/, voiceless fricatives /s λ h/ (respectively retroflex, lateral, and glottal), voiceless alveo-palatal affricate /č/, glottalized affricates /λ' č'/ (respectively lateral and alveo-palatal), nasals /m n/, liquids /l r/, and semivowels /w y/. The vowel phonemes are /i i· e e· a a· o o· u u·/. Of these, the central vowels /e e· o o·/ are peculiar in having a lax quality which makes them seem to fluctuate between the qualities of English [ɪ] and [ʊ] (in bid and book) and those of English [ɛ] and [ɔ] (in bed and balk). The short vowel /a/ resembles the English [ə] in bud, but long /a·/ is comparable with the English [a] in balm. There are no significant phonemes of pitch or stress on the level of the word.

Of the above phonemes, all occur in Spanish loanwords except the aspirated stops, the voiceless lateral fricative /λ/, and the
glottalized stops and affricates. In the transition to Patwin, Spanish
/p t č k/ have not been appreciably changed. Examples are pa·pa 'potato' from papa, čiko·te 'rope' from chicote. The Spanish voiced consonants, however, are less well preserved. Spanish /b/ becomes
Patwin /w/, as in wore·ka 'lamb' from borrega. Spanish /d/ is Patwin /d/ in dewer- 'to owe' from deber,[3] but becomes Patwin /t/ in
sorto 'deaf' from sordo, and is lost in yawlo 'devil' from diablo.
Spanish /y w/ — though they may have had affricate allophones in the
dialect from which Patwin borrowed —[4] always become Patwin semivocalic /y w/, as in ye·wa 'mare' from yegua and wuholo·te 'turkey'
from guajolote. Spanish /g/, lacking any voiced counterpart in Patwin, always becomes /k/, as in ka·tu 'cat' from gato. Of the fricatives, Spanish /f/ is replaced by /p/, as in pa·ha 'leather belt' from
faja 'waistband'; the same example shows the regular Patwin /h/ for
Spanish /x/ — which, however, may have been phonetically [h] in the
dialect involved. Spanish /s/ undergoes retroflexion to become Patwin /s/ in words like kostal 'sack' from costal. Spanish /m n/ are
usually unchanged, as in mansu 'tame' from manso, but Spanish /ñ/
becomes /yn/ in ayno 'year' from año, payno·l 'Mexican' from es-
pañol 'Spanish'. Spanish /l r/ are preserved, but /rr/ coalesces
with /r/: kalera 'ladder' from escalera, but aro·s 'rice' from arroz.
Since initial consonant clusters do not occur in Patwin, those of Spanish are broken up by the insertion of a vowel: tara·po 'cloth' from
trapo 'rag', kalaw 'nail' from clavo.

Accented vowels of Spanish usually become long vowels of
Patwin, as in most of the examples above. Many of the exceptions
are cases where a vowel is followed by /w y/, such as kalaw 'nail',
kawayo 'horse', yawlo 'devil', kanowa 'boat', ayno 'year'; however,
other examples like wute·ya 'glass' from botella 'bottle' prohibit an
all-inclusive statement. In most cases, the approximate qualities of
Spanish nonfinal vowels are preserved in Patwin. The final vowels,
however, present a strange picture. No regular correspondences for
this feature can be found between Spanish originals and Patwin re-
shapings, and different Patwin speakers often use different final vowels. Thus we find both kaye·na[5] and kaye·no 'chicken' from gallina
'hen', awha and awho 'needle' from aguja, pila·te 'dish' from plato,
sapa·te 'shoe' from zapato, winta·no 'window' from ventana, le·če

and le‧čo 'milk' from leche. In the light of these data, nara‧ho 'orange' is probably from the semantically corresponding naranja, rather than from the phonetically more similar naranjo 'orange tree'. A partial explanation of these aberrant vowels may lie in the grammatical interchange between -o and -a; the Patwin, confused by hearing both niño and niña, bueno and buena, may simply have come to feel that final vowels of Spanish words were unpredictably variable. This is surely the process which resulted in the Patwin free variants monču and monča 'much, many', from dial. muncho, -a.

The form of two known borrowings includes the Spanish definite article: lame‧sa 'table' from la mesa,[6] and la‧ča or la‧či 'axe' from el hacha. The word for 'axe' is also found as ha‧če, presumably from dial. jacha.

The main categories of meaning associated with the Spanish loan words in Patwin are those of domestic animals, cultivated plants, and artifacts not known to the Indians before Caucasian contact. Semantic shift can be noted in a few cases: tara‧po 'cloth' from trapo 'rag', ti‧nta 'paint' from tinta 'ink', wute‧ya 'glass' from botella 'bottle', and lewi‧ta 'blouse' from levita 'frock-coat'. A special feature of Patwin is its frequent use of Spanish loan words as synonyms for items of aboriginal vocabulary. Thus ka‧tu 'cat' also means 'wildcat', for which there is an aboriginal term p'amalay. Similarly, the Patwin call 'wild grapes' by the native term khap, and also by owas, from uvas. Such synonymous names exist for a number of artifacts. 'Boat' is either kanowa (from canoa) or wo‧te (from bote); but it is also nu‧, originally a 'tule balsa', but now a synonym of kanowa and wo‧te. In the synonym-set čǔču 'dog' from chucho, alongside aboriginal hayu, the Spanish word may have been used initially only for dogs of European breed.[7] Still other sets of synonyms are harder to account for, such as monču or monča 'much, many', alongside čaket.

Certain Patwin words present etymological problems, either as to whether they are loan words at all, or as to their exact transmission. Meka‧nu 'white man' is undoubtedly a borrowing; but is it from mejicano or americano? The latter answer may be preferred in view of the Patwin variants merka‧nu and mereka‧nu. Serial 'twenty-five cents' contains real 'a bit, 12½ cents; but the word

for 'two' is <u>pampata</u>, not <u>se</u>-, so that the full etymology remains obscure.[8] ('Fifty cents' is <u>watoral</u>, from <u>cuatro reales</u>.) <u>Busway</u> 'onion' may be an unusual metathesized version of <u>cebolla</u>. One Patwin
speaker gave a term <u>sepiraman</u> 'onion', here <u>cebolla</u> may also be involved (though with unusual phonology), but final -<u>man</u> is unanalyzable.

Words of more dubious Spanish órigin include <u>lema·te</u> 'oar'.
If this is from <u>remo</u>, the change of /rr/ to /l/ is unparalleled; the
ending -<u>a·te</u> also poses a problem, though it is reminiscent of <u>pila·te</u>
'dish' and <u>sapa·te</u> 'shoe'. There is also a doubt about <u>sa·r</u> 'salt',
synonymous with aboriginal <u>we·λ</u>. If this is from <u>sal</u>, the change of
/l/ to /r/ is left unexplained — though it does, to be sure, keep the
word distinct from aboriginal <u>sa·l</u> 'clover'. The most dubious etymology to be suggested here is <u>saltu</u> 'spirit, ghost' from <u>santo</u> 'saint';
this word, of great importance in Patwin religion, is found in neighboring languages — Pomo, Lake Miwok, and Maidu —[9] in the meanings 'spirit' and 'spirit impersonator'. Many of these problematic
cases may be due to borrowing through an intermediate Indian language, rather than directly from Spanish. Further studies in the Indian languages of California may be expected to throw light on problems such as the above, as well as upon the Spanish of early California.

NOTES

[1] See A. L. Kroeber, <u>The Patwin and their Neighbors</u>, University of California Publications in American Archaeology and Ethnology, Vol. XXIX: 4 (1932). Field work on the language was done
by Elizabeth Bright in 1952, under the auspices of the University of
California. The informants included Nora Lowell (now deceased),
Ida Mitchum, Sarah Gonzales, Daisy Lorenzo, and Minnie Bill. For
several etymological suggestions incorporated in this paper, we are
indebted to William Shipley, Harvey Pitkin, Sylvia Broadbent, Robert
Oswalt, and Catherine Callaghan.

[2] The borrowings from English include <u>apul</u> 'apple', <u>peces</u>
'peach(es)', and <u>inčinλa</u> 'Indians' (based on the pronunciation /ínjɨn/ ;
the element -λa is unidentifiable). <u>Wanbit</u> 'ten cents' is presumably
from <u>one bit</u>; a citation of this phrase from 1877 in the <u>Dictionary of
American English on Historical Principles</u> (I, 213) includes a remark
that "the dime...passes as a 'bit'...". The Patwin <u>banani</u> 'banana'

is probably not from Spanish, but from English /bənǽniy/. On the
other hand, Patwin ka·tu 'cat' is from gato rather than from English,
on the evidence of the final vowel.

[3] The only case known of a Spanish verb borrowed into Patwin.

[4] The analysis of Spanish phonology used here is that of Bow-
en and Stockwell's "Phonemic Interpretation of Semivowels in Spanish",
Lg., XXXI (1955), 236-240; /y w/ are accordingly recognized as phonemes with more occlusive and less occlusive allophones, like /b d g/.

[5] The actual starting point is Am.-Sp. áuja < aúja (Corominas,
Diccionario Crítico Etimológico de la Lengua Castellana, I, 63a).

[6] This word has been borrowed with the article by many California languages; examples are Gashowu Yokuts lameš and Wikchamni Yokuts dame·sa, supplied by S. Newman, Yokuts Language of California, Viking Fund Publications in Anthropology, II (1944), 16.

[7] Compare other American Indian words for 'dog', from
Karok čiši·h to Aztec chichi; a list of some of the Californian examples is given by Pitkin and Shipley, "A Comparative Study of California Penutian", IJAL, XXIV (1958), 180. Most of these probably have
no connection with Spanish. The Patwin, however, sufficiently resembles chucho to be identified as a borrowing. The etymology of
the Spanish word is obscure; J. Corominas, DCELC, II, 760, con-
nects it with gozque 'perro pequeño y muy ladrador', Ptg. goso 'perrito', Cat. gos 'perro', and with other words in languages from Es-
tonian to Hindustani, all derived from "la sílaba quis, cus, gzzz,
empleada para ahuyentar, azuzar o llamar el perrito". With Patwin
hayu 'dog', compare Pomo and Wappo haiyu, Coast Miwok haiyusa,
given by S. A. Barrett, The Ethno-Geography of the Pomo, Univ.
Calif. Publ. in American Archaeology and Ethnology, VI (1908), 62
and 74.

[8] A morpheme se- 'two' is reported by Harvey Pitkin for the
numeral system of Wintu, a related language.

[9] Kroeber, pp. 365, 377, 379.

13 Animals of Acculturation in the California Indian Languages

1. Introduction

Studies of linguistic acculturation among the American Indians have hitherto been concerned primarily with individual languages (for bibliography, see Haugen 1956:16). Recently, however, data have become available which permit areal surveys of Californian linguistic phenomena. These data derive especially from the field work sponsored by the Survey of California Indian Languages of the Department of Linguistics at the University of California, Berkeley.[1] Within the body of material bearing on linguistic acculturation, items frequently found are those referring to the domestic animals introduced to California by the whites: the terms for 'horse', 'mare', and 'colt', for 'donkey' and 'mule', for 'cow', 'bull', and 'calf', for 'sheep' and 'goat', for 'pig', for 'cat', for 'chicken' and 'rooster', and for 'turkey'. The available terms for each of these animals are presented below, arranged according to their etymologies (as borrowings, as new coinages, or as terms of unknown origin), and according to the languages in approximate north-to-south order. When a language has two terms for the same animal, the second is cross-referenced to the first. The distribution of the better-attested terms is also indicated on outline maps (after Kroeber 1922, map 1).[2] Following the presentation of the data, some general observations will be made.

2. Terms for 'Horse'
(cf. map 1)

2.1 Borrowings from Spanish caballo (cf. Hall 1947).

Yuki kawáyo (Foster 1944:161).[3]
Coast Yuki kaviyu (Barrett 1908:74).

Huchnom   kawaiyū (Barrett 1908:74).
N. Pomo   kawaiyo (Barrett 1908:62).
N. E. Pomo   kawaiyū (Barrett 1908:62).
C. Pomo   kawá·yu (Oswalt).
E. Pomo   kawaiyū (Barrett 1908:62).
S. W. Pomo   kawa·yu (Oswalt).
S. Pomo   kawaiyū (Barrett 1908:62).
S. E. Pomo   kawai (Barrett 1908:62).
Wappo   kawaiyū (Barrett 1908:74).
Nomlaki   kawáyu-t.
Patwin   kawayo.
N. W. Maidu   ka-vá-yo, ka-wá-ya (Curtis 1924b:231).
N. E. Maidu   kawáju.
Nisenan   kawa·yu (Uldall).
Washo   gawá·yɨ?, gawá·yu?.
Lake Miwok   káwaj.
Coast Miwok   kavayu (Baer and Helmersen 1839:250).
Plains Miwok   kawáaju?.
N. Sierra Miwok   kawáyu (Tozzer).
C. Sierra Miwok   kawá·ju-.
S. Sierra Miwok   kawa·ju?.
Soledad Costanoan   cauallo (Henshaw 1955:174).
Antoniano Salinan   kowá·yo.
Migueleño Salinan   kowáy?.
Purisimeño Chumash   cavallo (Henshaw 1955:123).
Barbareño Chumash   kawáyu.
Santa Rosa Island Chumash   caballo (Henshaw 1955:
    123).
Chawchila Yokuts   gawa·yo·/ (Newman 1944:183).
Choynimni Yokuts   gawa·yu'/ (Newman 1944:186).
Chukchansi Yokuts   ka-wá-yu (Curtis 1924b:244).
Gashowu Yokuts   gawa·yu'/ (Newman 1944:185).
Wikchamni Yokuts   gawa·yu/ (Newman 1944:184).
Yawelmani Yokuts   gawa·yo·/ (Newman 1944:168).
N. W. Mono   qawaaju?u.
S. Mono   kabaaju?u.
Panamint   kawaaju?.
Tübatulabal   kawaaju?.
Gabrielino   kavay (Wheeler 1876:447).
Cahuilla   kaváayu?.

Luiseño   kaváyu- (Kroeber and Grace 1960: 239).
Diegueño   ka-vá-yo (Curtis 1926: 174).

2.2 Other possible borrowings.

Yurok   mulah,[4] perhaps from Spanish mula. Although
the Yurok are outside the area of Spanish settlement,
they were visited by Spanish ships during the eighteenth century (Heizer and Mills 1952).
Shasta   sá ·tawac,[5] probably from the Klamath phrase
sátam wats 'dog/horse of the Paiutes' (Barker).
Wintu   sa ·tawas, probably through Shasta from Klamath. The form hos, from English, is given by Curtin in the 1880's (n.d.a: 198) and confirmed by Lee
(1943: 436), but is not reported by Pitkin.

2.3 Adaptations of native terms for 'dog', sometimes also
translated as 'pet' or 'domestic animal'.

Tolowa   ƚ̨ ʔču 'big dog' (Hoijer).
Yurok   tsish ´-uh 'dog', wau-gi chish-eh 'white man's
dog' (Powers 1877: 466-467). The word for 'dog' is
phonemically čišah. Cf. 2.2.
Karok   čiši ·h 'dog', yurasčíšši ·h 'ocean dog'.[6]
Hupa   ƚiŋʔ 'dog'.
Chimariko   sičella 'dog'. Note also sitcilaita (Curtin
1889c: 192), with an unidentified ending.
Bear River Athabaskan   naƚ'i 'dog' (Goddard 1929: 317).
Wailaki   ƚinʔk̯oh 'big dog' (Li).
Kato   hĺĭn=cho (Curtis 1924b:202), apparently 'big dog'.
Wintu   bo-hi ´-neh su-hoh 'big dog' (Powers 1877: 524),
súkuh (Pitkin). Cf. 2.2.
N. Yana   suusu 'dog' (Sapir and Swadesh).
Klamath[7]   wač 'domestic animal'.
Achomawi   jax̯əm 'dog'.
Atsugewi   hoʔmá 'dog'.
N. E. Maidu   sý 'dog' (rare in the meaning 'horse'),
lýkt'akym sý 'riding dog'. Cf. 2.1.
Washo   súkuʔ 'dog' (archaic in the meaning 'horse').
Cf. 2.1.
N. Paviotso   pukkú 'dog'.

S. Paviotso puggú 'dog'.

N. E. Mono puggu. Presumably the original meaning was 'dog, pet', as in other Numic languages.

Panamint puŋgu 'dog'. Cf. 2.1.

Tübatulabal puŋgu ´ñi'i´ŋ 'my horse' (Voegelin 1935:
229). Cf. puñgul 'dog' (Kroeber 1907:81), but puku-
biš-t 'the dog' (Voegelin 1958:225). Cf. also 2.1.

Kawaiisu pugu-zi 'dog', said to be used "sometimes"
for 'horse'. Cf. the entry in 2.6.

Santa Rosa Island Chumash hâ-hâ 'horse and dog...
both being domestic animals' (Henshaw 1955:127,158).

Mohave aha 'ţa (Kroeber 1911:88), elsewhere translated as 'dog' (Kroeber 1943:28). The same stem
probably occurs in the forms ahato-o 'love and hâtoo-
wālǎway (Wheeler 1876:447).

Yuma ʔaxáţ 'dog'.

Diegueño axát 'dog'. Cf. 2.1.

2.4 Adaptations of native words for 'deer' or 'elk'.

Yuki mil-en-ti´-tum. Cf. mi-lōn-te´-tun 'elk' (Powers 1877:486). Cf. 2.1.

Nomlaki kōdit. Cf. kōleţ 'elk' (Barrett 1908:84).
Cf. 2.1.

N. E. Pomo bŏʔŏ-kʰá (McLendon). Cf. bōō-ka 'elk'
(Barrett 1908:62). Cf. 2.1.

C. Pomo kasīzī-tcimaū-kale 'elk for riding', said to
be archaic (Barrett 1908:90). Cf. 2.1.

Luiseño and Cupeño p·á=su-ḳat, said the mean 'water
deer', because they came from the coast (Curtis
1926:174). However, the term is said to mean 'elk'
in some related dialects (Kroeber 1909:242).

Cahuilla pá-sukat, said to be an "old word", probably
from pál 'water' plus súkat 'deer'. Cf. 2.1.

2.5 Descriptive coinages.

Karok ʔakθipʔámva·n 'barley-eater' (archaic), tiv-
tunvê·č 'small-ears' (by contrast with the mule).
Cf. 2.3.

Hupa miḳidahčide·lᶜeʔ 'several sit on top of it'. Cf.
2.3.

Wiyot   talolák^Wiska ʔn 'you mount it' (Teeter).
Chimariko   hiwonanda, perhaps 'for sitting on'. Cf.
    2.3.
Wailaki   ná-nel 'packer' (Curtis 1924b: 202).   Cf. 2.3.
Lake Miwok   ōpōīnī (Barrett 1908: 74) may be identi-
    fied as ʔóppojni 'traveling' (Callaghan).   Cf. 2.1.
Washo   dewdéwluwe ? 'round-hoofed' (archaic).   Cf.
    2.1, 2.3.

2.6   Terms of unknown etymology.

Chimariko   djemtsakta (Curtin 1889c: 192).   Cf. 2.3,
    2.5.
Achomawi   a ʔtsátə.   Cf. 2.3.
S. Pomo ("Gallinomero")   tu-mai ´-i-tun (Powers 1877:
    498).   Cf. 2.1.
Nisenan   ahhanunga (Powers 1877: 593).   Cf. 2.1.
N. E. Mono   pa-tû-za-a (archaic; Curtis 1926: 183).
    Cf. 2.3.
Santa Cruz Costanoan   cu-luk (Henshaw 1955: 171).
Rumsen   čakiyuls.
Obispeño Chumash   her ´-he ´-tcĭ (Henshaw 1955: 118).
Purisimeño Chumash   a-ti ´-ka-mo (Henshaw 1955: 118).
    Cf. 2.1.
Barbareño Chumash   kni-sútap (Wheeler 1876: 447).
    Cf. 2.1.
Chemehuevi   o-a ´rov'-h (Wheeler 1876: 447).
Kawaiisu   wo ʔoda-bi, said to be commoner than pugu-
    zi 'dog' (2.3.).
Serrano ("Takhtam")   pa ´-akhvat, neastamu ´, neatchu-
    u ´ne (Wheeler 1876: 473).
Juaneño   na-a ´-atch (Wheeler 1876: 447).
Diegueño   mo-quuc (Schoolcraft 1853: 103).   Cf. 2.1,
    2.3.

2.7 As can be seen above, more than one term for 'horse'
is available in many languages (cf. map 1). The following patterns
may be noted:

In Karok, Hupa, Chimariko, Wailaki, Achomawi, N. E.
Mono, Kawaiisu, and Diegueño, a descriptive term or a term of

unknown etymology stands alongside one related to the word for 'dog'.
In N. E. Mono and Diegueño, the former types of term are indicated
as the older, appearing only in recordings of some decades past,
whereas modern recordings have the word for 'dog'. In Karok, one
of the descriptive terms is still remembered, but is considered an
archaism.

In Southern Pomo, Lake Miwok, Nisenan, Washo, Barbareño
Chumash, and Diegueño, a descriptive term or one of unknown etymology stands alongside a borrowing from Spanish caballo. The former
types again represent less recent usage than the Spanish loans in all
these languages except Diegueño.

In Yuki, Central Pomo, Nomlaki, and Cahuilla, terms referring to 'deer' or 'elk' appear in older recordings, while adaptations
of caballo appear in modern ones. The reverse situation occurs only
in Northeastern Pomo.

In Yurok, Northeastern Maidu, Washo, Panamint, Tübatulabal, and Diegueño, terms related to the word for 'dog' stand alongside borrowings from Spanish. There is again evidence that the borrowings represent the more modern usage for these languages, with
the exception of Panamint and Diegueño.

In short, there has been a tendency for descriptive terms
and terms of unknown etymology to be replaced over a period of time
by terms meaning 'dog'. In areas outside the Spanish influence, there
has been no further change; that is, borrowing from English has not
generally occurred. [8] In the areas of Spanish settlement, however,
there has been a further tendency to replace all other terms by caballo.

3. Terms for 'Mare'

   3.1 Borrowings from Spanish yegua.

        N. E. Pomo   yé·wă-khằ (McLendon).
        E. Pomo   yé·wà? (McLendon).
        S. W. Pomo   yé·wa (Oswalt).
        Wappo   yɛ ´wa (Radin 1924:38).
        Patwin   ye·wa.

S. Sierra Miwok   je ·wa ?.
Antoniano Salinan   yé ·wa.
Barbareño Chumash   yéwa.

3.2 Other terms.

Hupa   łinče ? 'female dog'.
Shasta   ḱisa ·ḱú ? sá ·tawac 'doe horse' (Silver).
Atsugewi   pestsahara   'female animal' (= 'cow, hen').
Lake Miwok   póccikawaj 'female horse'.
Washo   dalá ʔiŋ dewdéwluwe ? 'female horse'.
Cahuilla   tenil (Seiler), formerly 'antelope' (Kroeber
  1909: 238).

4. Terms for 'Colt'

4.1 Borrowings from Spanish potrillo, potrilla.

S. W. Pomo   potrí ·yu (Oswalt).
Wappo   pɔtrí ·yu ?.
S. Sierra Miwok   potni ·ja ?.

4.2 Other terms.

Klamath   tga ·ẃa-s, tga ʾ w-ḱa. Cf. tge ·w 'older broth-
  er, older child'.
Shasta   čírik 'young elk' (Silver).
Chimariko   sitcǐlai oleta 'little horse' (Curtin 1889c:
  192).
Achomawi   tsauktsa djahóm 'little horse' (Curtin 1889b:
  192).
Atsugewi   tsu ʾktso tsemati ´dse (Gatschet 1877c),
  analysis unknown; hó ʔmá iŋka 'little horse'.
Yana   cu ´cupa (Curtin 1889a: 192), diminutive of the
  word meaning 'dog, horse'.
Wintu   súku poíla 'horse-young' (Curtin n. d. a: 192).
N. W. Maidu   kole ´ 'calf, colt, young' (Gatschet 1877a:
  23).
N. E. Maidu   kawájum tém 'horse child'.
Washo   dewdéwluwe ? ŋá ʔmiŋ 'horse's young'.
Yuki   kawáyo ólsel 'horse-little' (Curtin n. d. c: 192).

E. Pomo pó·šŏřŏkı́č, perhaps from Spanish potro
'colt' (McLendon).
Lake Miwok k̓úččikawaj 'little horse'.
Santa Cruz Costanoan s̈n-mak (Henshaw 1955:186),
etymology unknown.
Panamint cavallo un-dwats-si (Henshaw 1883a:192).
The second element occurs in other names for young
of animals.

5. Terms for 'Donkey'

5.1 Borrowings from Spanish burro.

C. Pomo bú·ru (Halpern).
E. Pomo búřù (McLendon).
S. W. Pomo wú·ru (Oswalt).
S. E. Pomo wúdu (Grekoff).
Wappo wú·ru?.
Lake Miwok wúuru.
Antoniano Salinan špó·lo, țšpó·lo.
Barbareño Chumash wúlu.
Kawaiisu budoo.
Gabrielino buro- (Wheeler 1876:475).
Cahuilla vúwruh.

5.2 Borrowings from other sources.

Klamath limi·l, from Chinook Jargon, which in turn
took the word from French la mule.
N. E. Maidu sekési, from English jackass. The fol-
lowing terms are from the same source.
Washo dzékeš.
S. Sierra Miwok cakac.
N. W. Mono caqahsi.

5.3 New coinages.

Wiyot ławépalukił 'long ears' (Teeter).
Lake Miwok k̓úččimula 'little mule'. Cf. 5.1.
Nisenan bɔnɔ́lʌm 'long ears'.
Washo dawbáksik 'long ears'. Also balá·yut'uwe?,
said to mean 'big ears', but of unknown analysis.

6. Terms for 'Mule'

6.1 Borrowings from Spanish mula.

N. E. Pomo   múlă-kʰà (McLendon).
C. Pomo   mú·la (Halpern).
E. Pomo   múwlà (McLendon).
S. W. Pomo   múlla (Oswalt).
Wappo   mú·lə?.
Lake Miwok   múula, but also wúulu from Spanish bur-
   ro. Cf. wúuru 'donkey' (5.1), a more recent rebor-
   rowing of the Spanish word.
Wintu   mu·la-t.
Nomlaki   mú·la-t.
N. W. Maidu   mula (Gatschet 1877a: 24).
Nisenan   mu·la (Uldall).
Washo   mú·la?, mú·le?.
S. Sierra Miwok   mu·la?.
N. W. Mono   muuhna?a.
Panamint   mu-na (Henshaw 1883a: 192).
Antoniano Salinan   mú·la, mó·la.
Diegueño   moolt (Schoolcraft 1953: 103).

6.2 Other terms.

Yurok   chesh (Heizer and Mills 1952: 113, from a no-
   tation of 1851); this is apparently ƀišah 'dog, horse'.
Karok   tivxárahar, tivxárahsas 'long ears'.
Chimariko   hisā´mitcĭ´ru (Curtin 1889c: 192); cf.
   hisā´m 'ear' (78).
Shasta   ʔú·ƀicu·kini?, said to mean 'long ears', although analysis is unclear.
Achomawi   wawaīsaqdi (Curtin 1889b: 192), apparently
   'large-ear'.
Atsugewi   dju´paua´sma ʾk (Curtin 1884a: 192); cf.
   asma ʾk 'ear' (78).
Yana   tcĭ´lmako (Curtin 1889a: 192), probably phonemic çil-mal?gu 'big-ear'.
Luiseño   chuk-ku-chuk-was (Wheeler 1876: 475), ety-
   mology unknown.
Diegueño   ah-hut (Schoolcraft 1853: 103), undoubtedly
   the same as axát 'dog, horse'. Cf. 6.1.

7. Terms for 'Cow, Cattle'
        (Cf. map 2)

    7.1 Borrowings from Spanish <u>vaca</u>.

        Yuki and Huchnom   paka (Barrett 1908:74).
        Coast Yuki   bāka (Barrett 1908:74).
        N., E., S., and S. E. Pomo   paka (Barrett 1908:62).
        N. E. Pomo   wá·kă-kʰà̀ (McLendon).
        C. Pomo   pa·ka (Oswalt).
        S. W. Pomo   wá·ka (Oswalt).
        Wappo   paka (Barrett 1908:74).
        Lake Miwok   páaka.
        Coast Miwok   paga (Baer and Helmersen 1839:251).
        Nomlaki   pá·kah.
        Patwin   wa·ka.
        N. W. Maidu   pʰák$_\Lambda$. Gatschet also gives le'dshim
          pa'ka (1877a:192), with unidentified first element.
        Nisenan   pa·ká (Uldall).
        Washo   bá·ga?.
        N. Sierra Miwok   pā'ka (Tozzer).
        S. Sierra Miwok   wa·ka?.
        Santa Cruz Costanoan   pak (Henshaw 1955:186).
        Soledad Costanoan   vacca (Henshaw 1955:183).
        Antoniano Salinan   pá·ka.
        Barbareño Chumash   wáka.
        Santa Rosa Island Chumash   wa-ka (Henshaw 1955:129).
        Panamint is said to use the Spanish word (Henshaw
          1883a:192).
        Tübatulabal   paaga?.
        Kawaiisu   bakaa.
        Cahuilla   váaka?.

    7.2 Borrowings from other sources.

    Five languages in northern California have a word for 'cow'
which can be traced to Chinook Jargon <u>moos-moos</u>. These are as
follows:

        Karok   músmus.
        Yurok   musmus.
        Chimariko   musmus.
        Shasta   mú·smu·s.

Klamath   mo·smo·s.
Wintu   mu·smus.

Another set of borrowed terms occurs in the following:

Yuki   wóha (Foster 1944:161).   Cf. 7.1.
Wintu   wuha·-t.   Cf. also mu·smus, above.
Nisenan   wó·hʌ.   Cf. 7.1.
N. E. Maidu   wóha.

Foster suggests that the Yuki is from Spanish oveja 'ewe'. A more
likely source, however, is the regional English term wo-haw 'beef or
cattle for beef, originally so called by the Indians from the "whoa!
haw!" of the drivers of ox teams across the plains' (Mathews 1951:
1883).[9] The reference is to the Plains Indian tribes of the central
United States. However, I have not found the word in the available
vocabularies of Plains Indian languages.

Other probable borrowings are the following:

Wintu   kau (Curtin n. d. a: 192) is the only known borrowing of the English word. Cf. mu·smus and
wuha·-t, above.
S. W. Pomo   kulúweṭʰ 'cattle' is perhaps a borrowing
from Russian koróva (Oswalt). Cf. 7.1.
Washo   gúsu? is thought to be a borrowing from Paviotso kuccú (7.3). Cf. also 7.1.
C. Sierra Miwok   lé·čy- and S. Sierra Miwok   le·cy?
(cf. 7.1) are evidently from Spanish leche 'milk'.
S. Sierra Miwok   kana·to? is from Spanish ganado 'cattle' (cf. 7.1, as well as le·cy?, above). The following
terms may be traced to the same source.
Chukchansi Yokuts   kanna·tu? (Broadbent).
N. W. Mono   qahnaahtu?u.
N. E. Mono   kaanni (etymology more uncertain in this
instance).

7.3 Adaptations of native terms meaning 'deer', 'elk', or
'buffalo'.

Wiyot   hamélakwa?l 'his (i. e., white man's) elk'
(Teeter).

Bear River Athabaskan   djʌsco 'elk' (Goddard 1929:
315).
Yana   tsoréwa 'elk' (Curtin 1889a:109, 192).
C. Pomo   masa´n-pce 'white man's deer' (archaic;
Barrett 1908:90).   Cf. 7.1.
Mutsun   toṭe 'deer, meat' (Mason 1916:429).
Rumsen   toṭ 'deer, meat'.
N. and S. Paviotso   kuccú.   Related words in other
Numic languages have been translated 'buffalo', e.g. ,
Southern Paiute   qu´t·cU (Sapir 1930:645).

7.4 Descriptive coinages.

Hupa   mide ʔ xole·n 'it has horns'.
Shasta   kweká ʔ axti ʔ, said to refer to the sound that
the animal makes (Silver).   Cf. 7.2.
Atsugewi   pestsahara 'female animal'.
Bear River Athabaskan   dɑtcɛ' gɑllin 'her horns she
has' (Goddard 1929:301).
Diegueño   ku·kʷá·yp 'horned animal'.
Yuma   kʷi·kʷáy 'horned one'.

7.5 Terms of unknown etymology.

Achomawi   puwá·wi.
Atsugewi   wipakú·kue·e· (Kroeber 1955:214).   Cf. 7.4.
Wailaki   lá·so·s (Bright).
Purisimeño Chumash   sa-pŭt (Henshaw 1955:118).

8. Terms for 'Bull'

8.1 Borrowings from Spanish toro.

N. E. Pomo   tóȓõ-kʰà (McLendon).
C. Pomo   tó·lo (Halpern).
E. Pomo   tóȓò (McLendon).
S. W. Pomo   tó·ro (Oswalt).
S. E. Pomo   ṭódo (Grekoff).
Wappo   ṭó·roʔ.
Lake Miwok   tóoro.
N. Sierra Miwok   tó´nō (Tozzer).

S. Sierra Miwok   to·ro?.
Antoniano Salinan   tó·lo.
Barbareño Chumash   tólo.
N. W. Mono   too?no?o.
Panamint is said to use the Spanish word (Henshaw
   1883a: 192).
Tübatulabal   to·ro (Voegelin 1935: 216).
Kawaiisu   todoo.
Cahuilla   tóoru?.

8.2 Other terms.

Chimariko   hiteĭ´tŭhŭ´lu (Curtin 1889c: 192), etymol-
   ogy unknown.
Hupa   mič^woĸ xole·n 'it has testicles'.
Klamath   mo·smo·s lag̣i· 'cattle chief'.
Achomawi   wäsŭ´m (Curtin 1889b:192), etymology un-
   known.
Atsugewi   wihá, also meaning 'rooster'. Cf. the Yana
   form following.
Yana   ya´upatcauaia´una (Curtin 1889a: 192), also
   meaning 'rooster', from yau-þa- 'to copulate with'
   (Sapir and Swadesh).
Wintu   bŭl, from English (Curtin n. d. a: 192).
N. E. Maidu   búli, from English.
Washo   ta-bai-âi-kwĭ (Henshaw 1883b: 192), etymolo-
   gy unknown. Modern recordings are demúkweyi?
   bá·ga? 'male cow'; also bá·ga? bú·l. English <u>bull</u>
   has apparently been borrowed to mean 'male animal',
   as in gawá·yɨ? bú·l 'stud horse'.
Yuki   wohamu´yûl (Curtin n. d. b: 192). The first element is wóha 'cattle', but the second is unidentified.
Santa Cruz Costanoan   hŏl´-lĕ (Henshaw 1955: 186),
   etymology unknown.
Rumsen   tūm-nan 'torito' (Pinart 1952: 20), etymology unknown.

9. Terms for 'Calf'

9.1 Borrowings from Spanish <u>becerro</u>, <u>becerra</u>.

N. E. Pomo   wăšéřŏ-k^hà (McLendon).

C. Pomo   wésé·du (Halpern).
E. Pomo   wísěřà? (McLendon).
S. W. Pomo   weseirú (Halpern).
Wappo   wέsselu?.
Lake Miwok   waséelu.
S. Sierra Miwok   pice·no?.
Barbareño Chumash   wesélu.
Kawaiisu   buseduu.
Cahuilla   meséeru?.

9.2   Other terms.

Shasta músmus yěher-qíaq (Curtin 1885:192), some-
thing like 'little cow'. Modern recordings give čírik
'young elk' (Silver), also used for 'colt'.
Klamath   ke·pa·k, from English <u>calf</u> plus diminutive
-'a·k.
Achomawi   buwawi útsilek (Curtin 1889b:192), in
which the first element means 'cow'. A modern re-
cording is kalíj, etymology unknown.
Atsugewi   jóapáp, etymology unknown.
Yuki   woha olsel (Curtin n.d.b:192), in which the first
element means 'cow'.
N. E. Pomo   ši'káʔga· (Halpern), etymology unknown.
Cf. 9.1.
Wintu   käf, from English (Curtin n.d.a:192).
Yana   tsoréwopa (Curtin 1889a:192), diminutive of the
word for 'elk, cow'.
N. W. Maidu   kole´ 'calf, colt, young' (Gatschet 1877a:
23).
N. E. Maidu   wóham tém 'cow child'.
Washo   bá·ga? ŋá·ʔmiŋ 'cow's young'.
Mutsun   l·uopo 'yearling calves' (Mason 1916:428),
etymology unknown.
Panamint   va-ca dwats-itc-Ỷ (Henshaw 1883a:192).
The second element occurs in other names for the
young of animals.

10. Terms for 'Sheep'

10.1 Borrowings from Spanish borrego, borrega.

Yuki wólika (Curtin n. d. b: 192).
N. E. Pomo wǒřékǎ-k^{h}à (McLendon).
C. Pomo welé·ku (Oswalt).
E. Pomo wěřékà (McLendon).
S. E. Pomo wóleeka (Oswalt).
Wappo wâriga' (Radin 1924: 4).
Lake Miwok woléeka.
Patwin wore·ka.
Nisenan wutago (Powers 1877: 598).
Washo wudé·gu?, wedé·gu?, wedé·ge?.
N. Sierra Miwok wotáka (Tozzer).
C. Sierra Miwok muné·kasy-.
S. Sierra Miwok poli·ka?. Also mune·kas.
N. W. Mono pohniihka?a.
Antoniano Salinan polé·ka.
Barbareño Chumash wuléwu.
Santa Rosa Island Chumas wu-le´-hu (Henshaw 1955: 118).
Chawchila Yokuts buliyga·/ (Newman 1944: 199).
Gashowu Yokuts buliyga'/ (Newman 1944: 168).
Yawelmani Yokuts wule·wo·/ (Newman 1944: 105).
Panamint u-de´-wa (Henshaw 1883a: 192).
Kawaiisu badebuu.
Cahuilla vuréewa?.

10.2 Borrowings from English sheep.

Klamath si·p; but Modoc q̓wi·l, etymology unknown.
Shasta sheep (i. e. , the citation uses the English spelling; Curtin 1885: 192).
Achomawi cip, i. e. , [šip] (Curtin 1889b: 192).
Wintu cip, i. e. , [šip] (Curtin n. d. a: 192).
N. W. Maidu shī´pi (Gatschet 1887a: 23).
Washo ší·p. Cf. 10.1.

10.3 Other terms.

Karok   ʔapxantí·čpu·fič 'white man's deer'.
Hupa   mide ʔxole·n nehwa·n 'it looks like cattle'.
Wiyot   tʒonaɣ í ʔdarú·wak 'make blankets' (Teeter).
Atsugewi   wahkú, said to be a rare variant of mahkú 'deer'.
Yana   malilpa 'antelope' (Curtin 1889a: 109, 192).
S. W. Pomo   yama·ni. The origin of this and the following terms is unknown.
Coast Miwok   yamana (Baer and Helmersen 1839: 251).
Washo   magutálsali ʔ típti ʔ (archaic) 'having an old rabbit-skin blanket'. Cf. 10.1, 10.2.
Obispeño Chumash   tcâ-pâ-pâ (Henshaw 1955: 118), etymology unknown.
Juaneño   okhe´-u-ut (Wheeler 1876: 475). See next item.
Luiseño   exí·wut, perhaps from Spanish oveja (Kroeber and Grace 1960: 80).
Mohave   amo-nio-hata, undoubtedly related to amo´ 'mountain sheep' (Wheeler 1876: 475).
Diegueño   ǝmu· (Hayes). Cf. amu´ 'mountain sheep' (Kroeber 1943: 28).

11.   Terms for 'Goat'

11.1 Borrowings from Spanish chivo, chiva.

N. E. Pomo   čí·wǎ-kʰà (McLendon).
S. W. Pomo   čí·wo (Oswalt).
Wappo   čí·wɔʔ.
Lake Miwok   číiwo, číiwa.
N. W. Maidu   tchíwo (Gatschet 1877a: 23).
S. Sierra Miwok   ci·waʔ.
Antoniano Salinan   tšé·po.
Barbareño Chumash   číwu.
N. W. Mono   ciiwuʔu.
Cahuilla   číyvuʔ, číyvaʔ.

11.2 Other terms.

Karok and Hupa use the same term as for 'sheep'.
Shasta ǩahúčučču?, related to a word meaning 'whis-
kers' (Silver).
Klamath go·t, from English.
Nisenan kawrɔ·n (Uldall), from Spanish cabrón 'he-
goat'.
Washo gút, gú·t, gówt (from English).
Kawaiisu cibatuu, from Spanish chivato 'kid'.

12. Terms for 'Pig, Hog'

12.1 Borrowings from Spanish cuchi, cochi, cochino, co-
china.

Yuki kótcit (Curtin n. d. b: 192).
N. E. Pomo kǒ?óčě-kʰà (McLendon).
C. Pomo ko·či (Oswalt).
E. Pomo kó·čǐ (McLendon).
S. W. Pomo koči·na (Oswalt).
Wappo kɔ·tci (Radin 1924: 22).
Lake Miwok kóoči.
Coast Miwok kočina (Baer and Helmersen 1839: 251).
Yana gódji (Curtin 1884b: 192).
Wintu kótcět (Curtin n. d. a: 192).
Patwin ko·ci.
N. W. Maidu kō´tchi (Gatschet 1877a: 23).
N. E. Maidu kóči.
Nisenan kɔ·tʂi (Uldall).
Washo gó·dzi?.
S. Sierra Miwok ko·ci?.
N. W. Mono qohci.
Antoniano Salinan kotšén.
Barbareño Chumash kóči.
Yawelmani Yokuts gɔ·di' (Newman 1944: 14).
Chukchansi Yokuts gɔ·s/ (Newman 1944: 14).
Panamint gâi-tci (Henshaw 1883a: 192).
Kawaiisu kyciina.
Cahuilla kíwči?.

12.2 Other borrowings.

    Klamath   goso, from Chinook Jargon <u>cosho</u>, from
      French <u>cochon</u>. The next five forms have the same
      source, probably with Klamath as intermediary.
    Shasta kúsa.
    Achomawi   gusu (Curtin 1889b: 192).
    Atsugewi   ko'tsa´ (Curtin 1884a: 192).
    Yana   kodja (Curtin 1884b: 192). Cf. 12.1.
    Wintu   ko·ca-t. Cf. 12.1. Yana and Wintu each have
      two forms: one with final i̱, from Spanish; and one
      with final a̱, probably from Chinook Jargon, through
      Klamath and Shasta.
    Lake Miwok   puwérku, also meaning 'dirty', from
      Spanish <u>puerco</u> 'pig'. Cf. 12.1.

12.3 Descriptive terms.

    Karok   nákišnakiš, said to imitate the sound the ani-
      mal makes.
    Hupa   ɫiƙa·w, from –ɫi–...–ƙah, –ƙa·w 'to be fat'.
    Wiyot   puʔžúɫliɫ 'sharp nose' (Teeter).
    Shasta   kwérikaká ʔ (Silver), referring to the animal's
      rooting habits. Cf. 12.2.
    Bear River Athabaskan   yolok', a plural, said to be
      onomatopoetic (Goddard 1929: 317).
    Washo   daʔmósok 'having a split nose' (archaic),
      gikšúyeplu demdéwɨš 'a digger with its nose' (ar-
      chaic), gikšúyep dedíšt'uʔ 'having its nose as a dig-
      ging stick'. Cf. 12.1.

12.4 Terms of unknown etymology.

    Yurok   kʷegeruʔ.
    Bear River Athabaskan   botcwoɫ (Goddard 1929: 317).
      Cf. 12.3.
    Wintu   horó-ichta (Powers 1877: 532). Cf. 12.2.
    Santa Cruz Costanoan   ra´-ra´ (Henshaw 1955: 186).
    Juaneño   tchi-mutch-mutch (Wheeler 1876: 475).
    Cahuilla ("Kauvuya")   tulnik (Wheeler 1876: 475).
      Cf. 12.1.
    Mohave   magua´-kui niu-hata (Wheeler 1876: 475).

13. Terms for 'Cat'
     (Cf. map 3)

13.1 Borrowings from Spanish gato, gata.

N. E. Pomo   ká·tŏ-kʰà (McLendon).
C. Pomo   ga·ṭu (Oswalt).
Lake Miwok   káatu.
Patwin   ka·tu.
Barbareño Chumash   kátu.
Santa Rosa Island Chumash   ka-tu (Henshaw 1955:
     121).
Yawelmani Yokuts   ga·do·/ (Newman 1944:168).
Chukchansi Yokuts   gaadu? (Lamb).
S. Sierra Miwok   ka·to?.
N. W. Mono   qaahtu?u.
Panamint   kaatu?.
Cahuilla   gáatu?.
Diegueño   ká·ta.

13.2 Borrowings from English cat, kitty, and pussy.

Tolowa   bu·sí (Woodward).
Karok   pússihič (with diminutive -ič). Also tíripus,
     from English kittypuss.
Yurok   pusi.
Hupa   bo·se, bo·še.
Wiyot   púsi (Fletcher).
Shasta   pusi (Curtin 1885:192), kíripús (Silver),
     kiripússi.
Klamath   p̓o·si-s, also kidi·.
Atsugewi   kitikitá.
Wintu   kiri.
Nomlaki   kidí·kidi-t.
Yuki   kɨ́'ti (Curtin n.d.b:192).
E. Pomo   pú·č (McLendon).
N. W. Maidu   kídi (Gatschet 1877a:24).
N. E. Maidu   kíki. Also két'i [kǽ·t'i], from cat.
Washo   kí·di, bú·ši.
S. Sierra Miwok   pu·ci?, pu·si?. Cf. 13.1.
S. Paviotso   kidí?i.

N. W. Mono   kitiiʔi. Cf. 13.1.
N. E. Mono   kidi.
S. Mono   kidiʔi.

13.3   Other borrowings.

S. W. Pomo   kúška, from Russian <u>kóška</u> (Oswalt).
Washo   tum-ce´-gɨl (Henshaw 1883b:192). Cf. 13.2.
    This and the following four terms can be traced to
    dialectal Spanish <u>tonche</u>.[10]
S. E. Pomo   tónče (Grekoff).
Wappo   tɔ´ntci (Radin 1929:189).
Plains Miwok   tónčiʔ.
Tcholovone Yokuts   tonjē, recorded by Pinart in 1880
    (Merriam 1955:137).
Esselen   mǐ´s-ka-tas (Kroeber 1904:55). This and
    the following terms seem to reflect Spanish <u>mis</u>, a
    syllable used for calling cats. The remainder of
    the Esselen form may represent <u>gata</u>.
Antoniano Salinan   smíš.
Migueleño Salinan   iṣmiṣ.
Obispeño Chumash   mi-si´-nă (Henshaw 1958:118).

13.4   Terms derived from words for 'wildcat' or 'mountain
lion'.

Hupa   mindiȝ nehwa·n 'it looks like wildcat'. Cf.
    13.2.
Shasta   tchuaí (Gatschet 1877b), to be identified with
    ʔícwey 'wildcat'. Cf. 13.2.
Achomawi   tadžālə 'mountain lion'.
N. Paviotso   tuhúʔu 'wildcat', táibuʔu tuhúʔu 'white
    man's wildcat'.
Patwin   pu-mal-ai-eh (Powers 1877:530), phonemi-
    cally pamalay 'wildcat'. Cf. 13.1.
Barbareño Chumash   anakpuk (Wheeler 1876:485), to
    be identified with a-năk-pu´ 'wildcat' (Henshaw
    1958:106). Cf. 13.1.
Ventureño Chumash   as-hai´, al-hai´-ya, to be iden-
    tified with as-hai´-yi 'wildcat' (Henshaw 1955:106,
    118).

Cahuilla ("Kauvuya") tukut (Wheeler 1876:473), the
same as dukut 'wildcat' (Kroeber 1909:238).
Mohave nu´me (Wheeler 1876:475), otherwise 'wildcat' (Kroeber 1943:28).

13.5 Terms of unknown origin.

Achomawi ki´nīwaka (Curtin 1889b:192). Cf. 13.4.
Bear River Athabaskan bᴏttcinɛs (Goddard 1929:
314), conceivably from English pussy.

The Costanoan family of languages share a term:

Santa Cruz Costanoan pe-něk (Henshaw 1958:186).
Mutsen penie, penik (Mason 1916:428).
Rumsen penek.

Three Uto-Aztecan languages also share a term:

Panamint na´-tu (Henshaw 1883a:192). Cf. 13.1.
Tübatulabal na·di+? 'the cat' (Voegelin 1958:224).
Kawaiisu naata.

14. Terms for 'Chicken, Hen'

14.1 Borrowings from Spanish gallina 'hen'.

N. E. Pomo kʰàyí·na-kʰà (McLendon).
C. Pomo gáyi·na (Halpern).
E. Pomo kě?énà (McLendon).
S. W. Pomo kayi·na (Oswalt).
S. E. Pomo káynu (Grekoff).
Wappo kayi´na (Radin 1924:10).
Lake Miwok kajína.
Coast Miwok kayina (Baer and Helmersen 1839:251).
Patwin kaye·na, kaye·no.
Plains Miwok kajína.
S. Sierra Miwok kaji·na?.
N. W. Mono qajiïhna?a.
Esselen kai-yi´-nap-ca (Kroeber 1904:55).
Antoniano Salinan kayé·na.
Barbareño Chumash kayína.

Cahuilla   gayíyna?.
Luiseño   gayí·nami 'hens' (Kroeber and Grace 1960:
    239).
Diegueño   gaịen.

14.2 Borrowings from English.

Karok   číkin.
Yurok   ciki.
Klamath   ǰigin.
Shasta   tci 'kĕn (Curtin 1885:192).
Yana   tcǐ 'kĕn (Curtin 1884b:192).
Wintu   ciken.
N. E. Maidu   cikíni.
Washo   dzí·gin.
Yuki   chicken (cited in English spelling; Curtin n.d.b:
    192).

14.3 Adaptations of native vocabulary.

Hupa   ǩiya·W; cf. diminutive ǩiyasᶽ 'bird'.
Atsugewi   pestsahara 'hen', also 'cow, mare, fe-
    male animal'.
Patwin   mansu cip 'tame bird' (with Spanish manso
    'tame'). Cf. 14.1.
Yawelmani Yokuts   'ɔ·we·'ič, originally 'one who is
    crowing' (Newman 1944:31).
Luiseño   cajàl 'quail' (Tagliavini 1928:909). Cf.14.1.

14.4 Terms of unknown etymology.

Achomawi   wastsí 'hen' (Curtin 1889b:192).
Nisenan   tɔtɔyka (Uldall).
Washo   pat-se-en-neh (Simpson 1876:470), ta-la-iñ
    (Henshaw 1883b:192). More modern recordings
    are ?awá?wulu?, ?awá?wɨle?, said by informants
    to be a Miwok word and to be archaic. Cf. 14.2.
Santa Cruz Costanoan   lĕl-lo 'hen' (Henshaw 1955:
    186).
Ventureño Chumash   ö-kö´-ya 'hen' (Henshaw 1955:
    118).

Panamint   ka´-ka-wŭt-a (Henshaw 1883a:192).
Kawaiisu   kakawyty. Cf. the preceding item.
Juaneño   ga-khaut (Wheeler 1876:476). Cf. the two
   preceding items.
Cahuilla ("Kauvuya")   khanamu´ (Wheeler 1876:476).
   Cf. 14.1.
Mohave   kvalo-yau´va (Wheeler 1876:476).
Yuma   x^Walayáw. Cf. the Mohave form.

15. Terms for 'Cock, Rooster'

15.1 Borrowings from Spanish gallo.

Ν. Ε. and S. W. Pomo   gá´yu (Halpern).
Wappo   ga´yo (Radin 1924:28).
Lake Miwok   gáaju.
Cahuilla   gáayu?.
Luiseño   ga´yi (Kroeber and Grace 1960:239).

15.2 Terms meaning 'male chicken'.

Shasta   tci´kĕn ăwa´ti´k^Wai´-o (Curtin 1885:192).
Wintu   wíte tcíkin (Curtin n.d.a:192).
Yuki   chicken iwup (Curtin n.d.b:192).
Ν. Ε. Pomo   k^hayínabìkĭ (McLendon). Cf. 15.1.
C. Pomo   gayí´na báya (Halpern).
E. Pomo   kĕ?énăkák (McLendon).
S. Sierra Miwok   naŋ´a?kaji´na?.

15.3 Other terms.

Wiyot   wuto?lĭl 'talks'.
Achomawi   kusáwi (Curtin 1889b:192), etymology
   unknown.
Atsugewi   wihá, also meaning 'bull'.
Yana   yaupatcauaiauna 'bull' (Curtin 1889a:192). For
   this and the preceding term, cf. 8.2.
Washo   tĕm-nu-kwĭ´ (Henshaw 1883b:192).
Ventureño Chumash   a-ta-hatc´ (Henshaw 1958:
   118).

16. Terms for 'Turkey'

16.1 Borrowings from Mexican Spanish <u>guajolote</u> (from Aztec we ʔšolotl).

> N. E. Pomo   wŏló·tĕ-kʰà (McLendon).
> C. Pomo ("Yo-kai ʹ-a")   wa-ha-lo ʹ-teh (Powers 1877: 498).
> E. Pomo   bŏhólŏtó (McLendon).
> S. W. Pomo   waholó·ţe (Oswalt).
> S. Pomo ("Gallinomero")   o-ho-lo ʹ-teh (Powers 1877: 499).
> Wappo   waholó·ţɛ ʔ.
> Lake Miwok   wolohóote (note metathesis).
> Patwin   wuholo·te.
> N. W. Maidu   waholo ʹte (Gatschet 1877: 25).
> Nisenan   wa ʰal-loh (Powers 1877: 592).
> Antoniano Salinan   xoló·te, woxoló·te.
> Barbareño Chumash   woxolóti.
> Yokuts   wo-ho-lo ʹ-tih (Powers 1877: 576).
> S. Sierra Miwok   wohlo·te ʔ.
> Mohave   oŏrōwtă (Wheeler 1876: 449), or-rót (Curtis 1908: 124). The second form may be reduced from the first.
> Yuma   or-rŭ̃t (Curtis 1908: 124). Cf. the Mohave forms.

16.2 Other borrowings and coinages.

> Wiyot   ͜wutoronóʔtatṛaʔla 'long nose' (Teeter).
> Hupa   kiya·W, the same as 'chicken' (14.3).
> Klamath   sqoľo·-s. Cf. sqoľe 'meadowlark', said to be named from its call.
> N. W. Maidu   hük ʹ-wa (Powers 1877: 592). Cf. N. E. Maidu hýkwo 'grouse'.
> N. E. Maidu   ku-lok ʹ-ku-lok (Powers 1877: 592), apparently onomatopoetic, although perhaps with influence of Spanish <u>guajolote</u>.
> Washo   tɨ·gi, tɨ·ki, from English.
> N. W. Mono   ʔotoʔotohnaʔa, from ʔotoʔoto 'cry of the turkey'.

16.3 Terms of unknown etymology.

Achomawi   kol-kol´-lis-seh (Powers 1877:604).
Yuki   chi-met hoⁿt (Powers 1877:486).
Pomo (variety not identified)   ma-ba´-deh (Powers 1877:498).
Washo   ou-wha-wee-ap (Simpson 1876:471). Cf. 16.2.

17. New Terms for 'Dog'
    (cf. map 4)

Linguistic data regarding the dog remain to be considered. This animal was not, to be sure, introduced to California by Europeans. Nevertheless, the words denoting it in the Californian languages show signs of extensive borrowing and lexical innovation. The spread of forms such as Karok čiši·h, Yurok čišah, Chimariko sičela, N. W. Maidu sý, Nisenan suku, Yana suusu, Nomlaki sukut, Chukchansi Yokuts če·xa, and C. Sierra Miwok čukí꞉ 'dog' has been remarked on by previous writers (Dixon and Kroeber 1903:16, Pitkin and Shipley 1955:180). Another instance of lexical spread among genetically unrelated languages is found in the term hayu 'dog', occurring in all varieties of Pomo except Northeastern, in Wappo, in Patwin, in Lake Miwok, in Southern Sierra Miwok, and — in the form haiyūsa — in Coast Miwok (Barrett 1908:62, 74, 84; Broadbent; Callaghan). All these languages, except for the surprisingly distant Southern Sierra Miwok, are spoken in the area to the north of San Francisco Bay — the part of California in which dogs were reportedly rare in aboriginal times (Kroeber 1941).

Californian names for the dog were apparently influenced in still further ways by European contact. For one thing, as seen above, old words for 'dog, pet' were often transferred to the horse; in some languages a new term for 'dog' then made its appearance. Another factor was the introduction of European breeds of dogs; several tribes came to distinguish the erect-eared Indian dog from the lop-eared hound of the white man. In many Spanish-settled parts of the area, the Spanish word chucho was borrowed, although it is not clear whether or not it was used to distinguish European dogs from native ones. The following are the recorded neologisms for 'dog'.

17.1 Borrowings from Spanish <u>chucho</u>.

> C. Pomo ("Yu-kai") chu´-chu (Powers 1877: 499),
> alongside hayu.
> Patwin cucu, alongside hayu.
> Coast Miwok tshutshu (Powers 1877: 552), alongside
> haiyɑsa.
> Plains Miwok čúuču?.
> Santa Clara Costanoan choó-cho (Powers 1877: 545).
> Esselen šoošo (Pinart 1952: 79), alongside utc-mas,
> hu´-tcu-mas, can-â´-co (Kroeber 1904: 55).
> Luiseño tcutcec, alongside aboriginal awal (Kroeber
> 1907: 81).

17.2 Other types of innovation.

> Karok tivárarih 'ear-hanging', alongside aboriginal
> čiši·h 'dog, horse'.
> Shasta ʔí·pitaktak 'ear-floppy' (Silver), alongside
> aboriginal ʔá·psu.
> Chimariko sitčí´la wa´we, wówairup (Curtin 1889c:
> 109, 192). Cf. wowoin 'to bark' (Dixon 1910: 378).
> Klamath wača·k 'little pet'. Cf. wač, now meaning
> 'horse'.
> Achomawi áts-li-mu-kí, said to mean 'lop-ear' (Cur-
> tis 1924a: 254), alongside aboriginal jaxə̄m 'dog,
> horse'.
> Wintu ma·t-ɬaqas 'floppy ears', alongside aboriginal
> sukuh 'dog, horse'.
> Central Yana ȝaxdu-malʔgu 'hanging ears' (Sapir
> and Swadesh), alongside aboriginal (N. Yana) suusu
> 'dog, horse'.
> N. W. Maidu hɛ́nom sy· 'coyote pet', alongside ab-
> original sy·.
> N. E. Maidu wépam sý 'coyote pet', alongside sý
> 'dog, horse'.
> Washo dewdɛ́tsuwe?, dulé·tsuwe?, describing the
> animal's foot (cf. dewdéwluwe? 'round-foot, horse'),
> alongside súku? 'dog, horse'.
> N. Paviotso sogóbukkù; cf. pukkú 'dog, horse'. The
> first element may be compared with Nisenan suku
> 'dog'.

S. Paviotso   tooga, from English <u>dog</u>. Cf. puggú
'dog, horse'.

N. E. Mono   toogy, from English; also k^Widappuggu,
perhaps 'excrement-pet'. Cf. puggu 'horse'.

S. Mono   ʔissabukku 'coyote-pet'.

Mohave   aha ́t·tcoqa (Kroeber 1911: 88), containing
aha ́t·a 'dog, horse', but with the second part unidentified.

18. Conclusions

18.1 The Spanish loanwords in the above data permit certain conclusions about the Spanish spoken in early California. The
terms <u>caballo</u>, <u>yegua</u>, <u>vaca</u>, <u>toro</u>, <u>gato</u>, <u>gallina</u>, and <u>gallo</u> are found
to occur here, as throughout the Spanish-speaking world. The term
for 'turkey', <u>guajolote</u>, agrees with Mexican usage, as might be expected. In the remaining instances, however, Californian Spanish evidently used only one of several terms known in Spain and Latin Amer-
ica. Thus 'colt' is <u>potrillo</u> rather than <u>potro</u>, 'donkey' is <u>burro</u> rather
than <u>asno</u>, 'calf' is <u>becerro</u> rather than <u>ternero</u>, 'pig' is usually <u>cochi</u>
or <u>cochino</u> rather than <u>puerco</u>, and 'dog' is <u>chucho</u> rather than <u>perro</u>.
In several instances, the Californian languages reflect one Spanish
term, while other American Indian languages reflect another (the contrasting data is from Kiddle): 'mule' is <u>mula</u> rather than <u>macho</u> (which
appears in Keres, Tewa, Cora, and Kekchi); 'sheep' is <u>borrego</u> rather than <u>carnero</u> (in Southern Paiute, Hopi, Keres, Tewa, Zuni, Nahuatl, Kekchi, and in South America) or <u>oveja</u> (in Navaho, Keres, Yaqui, Mixtec, and in South America); 'goat' is <u>chivo</u> rather than <u>cabra</u>
(in Keres, Cotoname, Black Carib, and in South America). Finally,
it is interesting to note that Spanish <u>mis</u>, used to call a cat, has provided a name for the animal in a long list of Middle and South American languages, but in California is found only in Esselen, Salinan, and
Obispeño Chumash, adjacent languages of the central Californian
coast.

18.2 In the terms for 'horse', it has already been noted that
there was a tendency, in Spanish-settled areas, for the loanword <u>ca-
ballo</u> to replace all other terms. Scattered instances of the same tendency may be found in the other animal names: in C. Pomo, pa·ka
'cow' replaces masa ́n-pce 'white man's deer'; in Washo, gawá·yɨʔ

'horse' replaces súku? 'dog' and dewdéwluwe? 'round–hoofed', while
gó·dzi? 'pig' replaces da?mósok 'split–nose' (and similar terms); in
Cahuilla, kúwči? 'pig' replaces tulnik (etymology unknown); in Patwin,
Barbareño Chumash and Cahuilla, <u>gato</u> 'cat' replaces native words
meaning 'wildcat'; and in Cahuilla, gayíyna? 'hen' replaces khanamu´
(etymology unknown). In addition, there are the instances where
Spanish <u>chucho</u> has replaced, at least in part, the aboriginal words
for 'dog'. This tendency may be explained in the terms proposed by
Casagrande (1954: 217–218): among the various types of lexical innovation, the extension of old meanings (as 'dog' to 'horse') and the coin-
age of new descriptive terms are classified as "primary accomodation"; they "make use of only native linguistic resources and may potentially be used in the earliest stages of linguistic adjustment to culture contact." As time passes, however, the language of the imping-
ing culture becomes more familiar; bilingualism arises, and "secondary accomodation" may take place, by which loanwords are acquired.

     18.3 In contrast to the large number of Spanish loanwords
in the languages of southern California, the number of borrowings
from English in the northern quarter of the state is quite small. There
are no borrowings at all of English <u>mare, colt, mule,</u> or <u>pig</u>. <u>Horse</u>
and <u>cow</u> appear only in Wintu; <u>bull</u> only in N. E. Maidu and Washo;
<u>cat</u> only in N. E. Maidu; <u>turkey</u> only in Washo; <u>goat</u> only in Klamath
and Washo; and <u>calf</u> only in Klamath and Wintu. Terms of wider extension are <u>jackass</u> in N. E. Maidu, Washo, S. Sierra Miwok, and
N. W. Mono; <u>sheep</u> in Klamath, Shasta, Achomawi, Wintu, N. W.
Maidu, and Washo; and <u>chicken</u> in Karok, Yurok, Klamath, Shasta,
Yana, Yuki, N. E. Maidu, and Washo. The only animal regularly
designated by an English loanword in northern California is the cat,
represented by <u>kitty</u> in Klamath, Atsugewi, Yuki, Wintu, Nomlaki,
N. W. Maidu, N. E. Maidu, Washo, S. Paviotso, and Mono; by <u>pus-
sy</u> in Tolowa, Karok, Yurok, Hupa, Wiyot, Klamath, Shasta, Washo,
S. Sierra Miwok, and E. Pomo; and by <u>kittypuss</u> in Karok and Shasta.
It is interesting that these are all words used more to call a cat than
to refer to the animal. Thus they could probably be heard and learned,
even by a monolingual Indian, much more readily than the reference
term <u>cat</u>.

     The evident resistance which the northern languages display
to borrowing from English may be associated with a lower incidence

of bilingualism in the north, and this in turn may be caused by the
fact that the period of contact of the northern languages with English
has not been as long as that of Spanish influence in the south. Yet a
century seems long enough for borrowing to occur, if there were any
tendency for it to do so.[11] Other reasons must be sought for its fail-
ure to occur, and some linguists have connected resistance to borrowing with grammatical patterns of the receiving language. Thus Haugen
(1956: 66) paraphrases Sapir as suggesting that "loanwords are easily
accepted by languages with unified, unanalyzed words, but not by languages with active methods of word compounding." This hypothesis
seems to fail when applied to Karok and Yurok: the former has elaborate machinery for derivation and compounding, while the latter
has practically none; yet both languages are slow to borrow from
English. [12]

A different type of hypothesis is offered by Dozier (1956),
who contrasts the heavy borrowing of Spanish words by Yaqui with
the resistance to Spanish loans in Tewa. The explanation is sought
in the differences of early Spanish policy toward the two tribes. The
policy applied to the Yaqui was permissive and relaxed; the result
was "that a fusion of Spanish and Yaqui cultural elements took place
in a comparatively short time," both language and nonlinguistic culture entering into the fusion. Spanish policy toward the Tewa, however, was harsh and oppressive, so that "up to the present time
Spanish and Rio Grande Pueblo cultural patterns have remained distinct" (157), and linguistic borrowing from Spanish is minimal. This
suggests that the Californian situation might also be explained in sociocultural terms, rather than in terms of linguistic structure alone.

The copious materials of Cook (1943), concerning the relations between Indians and whites in California, present a far from
happy picture of Indian life under the Spanish mission system, showing "how the racial fiber of the native decayed morally and culturally,
how confinement, labor, punishment, inadequate diet, homesickness,
sex anomalies, and other social or cultural forces sapped his collective strength and his will to resistance and survival" (22.37). In
spite of this, however, "the missionaries, whatever the shortcomings
of their temporal system, were imbued with a powerful desire for the
spiritual and material betterment of the native race" (22.1). Furthermore, "among the Ibero-Americans, the Indian was regarded, if not

with definite attachment, at least with tolerance and sympathy, as perhaps not yet an equal but as a human being entitled to the rights and privileges of his class. His life was almost as sacred as that of a white man; his soul was entitled to salvation" (23.4). To the Anglo-American, however, "all Indians were vermin, to be treated as such ... The native's life was worthless, for no American could even be brought to trial for killing an Indian... Finally, since the quickest and easiest way to get rid of his troublesome presence was to kill him off, this procedure was adopted as standard for some years" (23.5). Thus, although the California Indians did not fare as well at Spanish hands as did the Yaqui, they were at least treated by the Spanish in a manner aimed at their acculturation. Their treatment by the Anglo-Americans, on the other hand, had no goal other than to get them out of the way, by genocide if necessary. The relative hospitality of the southern and central Californian languages to Spanish loanwords, and the relative resistance of the northern languages, may be due to just this difference in sociocultural relations.

NOTES

Acknowledgments: A large part of the previously unpublished material presented here was made available by colleagues, whose coöperation I wish to acknowledge with thanks. The following list of languages, in approximate north-to-south order, gives the names of the linguists who provided data on each.

Tolowa: Harry Hoijer and Mary Woodward.
Hupa: Mary Woodward.
Wiyot: Stuart Fletcher and Karl Teeter.
Chimariko (reconstituted): George Grekoff.
Klamath-Modoc: Phillip Barker.
Shasta: Shirley Silver.
Achomawi and Atsugewi: D. L. Olmsted.
Mattole and Wailaki: Fang-Kuei Li.
Pomo: A. M. Halpern, Robert Oswalt, Sally McLendon, and George Grekoff.
Wappo: Jesse O. Sawyer, Jr.
Wintu and Nomlaki: Harvey Pitkin.
Patwin: Elizabeth Bright.

Maiduan: William Shipley.
Washo and Antoniano Salinan: William H. Jacobsen, Jr.
Lake Miwok and Plains Miwok: Catherine Callaghan.
Central Sierra Miwok: L. S. Freeland.
Southern Sierra Miwok and reconstituted Rumsen: Sylvia
    Broadbent.
Paviotso, Mono, Panamint, and Tübatulabal: Sydney Lamb.
Chukchansi Yokuts: Sylvia Broadbent and Sydney Lamb.
Kawaiisu: Sheldon Klein.
Cahuilla: Hansjakob Seiler.
Barbareño Chumash: Madison Beeler.
Dieguefio: Alfred S. Hayes.
Yuma: A. M. Halpern.

In the body of this paper, the above sources are cited only for the languages on which more than one linguist has provided data.

Collection of this material was initiated in a class taught by
Mary R. Haas in 1955. More recently, unpublished vocabularies
from the Bureau of American Ethnology Archives were consulted in
the form of microfilms, obtained by Professor Haas especially for
the Survey of California Indian Languages. I am especially grateful
to Professors Mary Haas and William Shipley for valuable assistance
and advice.

[1] See note above.

[2] The boundary between Paviotso and Mono which is shown by
Kroeber has been changed in accordance with the findings of Sydney
Lamb (1958).

[3] All data are cited as they appear in their sources. It has
not been possible to standardize the notations, which range from the
phonetic (both amateur and skilled) through the phonemic to the morphophonemic. In the recordings of Miwok by Broadbent and Callaghan,
of Kawaiisu by Klein, of Uto-Aztecan languages by Lamb, and of
Maiduan by Shipley, the symbol ʝ represents a palatal semi-vowel,
while y̱ is a high nonfront unrounded vowel. Where similar terms
are given by more than one source, I cite phonemic transcriptions in
preference to phonetic ones. Between more than one phonetic record-
ing, I cite a published one in preference to an unpublished one.

[4] All Yurok forms are from the lexicon in Robins (1958) unless otherwise stated.

[5] Shasta forms are from the word list of Bright and Olmsted,
unless otherwise stated.

[6] All Karok forms are from the lexicon in Bright (1957).

[7] Of Oregon; used in place of the closely related Modoc, for which very few data were available.

[8] The only exception is Wintu, which (as recorded by Curtin) shows more animal names borrowed from English than any other Californian language.

[9] The exclamation <u>whoa haw</u> 'a cry of command to a draft animal' is attested from 1848 (Craigie and Hulbert 1944: 2482).

[10] <u>tonche</u> is reported from Jalisco (Ramos i Duarte 1898: 487), and is said to stem from the extinct Coca Indian language (Dávila Garibi 1935: 290). The word was brought to my attention by Mr. Robert A. Thiel.

[11] It is noteworthy that S. W. Pomo acquired at least twelve loan words from Russian during only twenty-nine years of contact (Oswalt 1958).

[12] The role of structural resistance to borrowing is also de-emphasized by Weinreich (1953: 62).

BIBLIOGRAPHY

Abbreviations used:

AA	American Anthropologist
BAE-A	Bureau of American Ethnology Archives
CNAE	Contributions to North American Ethnology
IJAL	International Journal of American Linguistics
UC-AR	University of California Anthropological Records
UC-PAAE	University of California Publications in American Archaeology and Ethnology
UC-PL	University of California Publications in Linguistics

Baer, K. E. von, and Gregor von Helmersen
    1839. Beiträge zur Kentniss des russischen Reiches, vol. 1. St. Petersburg.
Barrett, S. A.
    1908. The ethno-geography of the Pomo and neighboring Indians. UC-PAAE, 6: 1-332.
Bright, William
    1957. The Karok language. UC-PL, 13: 1-458.

Bright, William, and D. L. Olmsted
    1959. A Shasta vocabulary. Kroeber Anthrop. Soc. Papers,
        20:1-55.
Casagrande, Joseph B.
    1954. Comanche linguistic acculturation II. IJAL, 20:217-
        237.
Cook, S. F.
    1943. The conflict between the California Indian and white
        civilization. Ibero-Americana, 21:1-194, 22:1-55,
        23:1-115, 24:1-29.
Craigie, Sir William A., and James R. Hulbert
    1944. A dictionary of American English on historical prin-
        ciples. Chicago.
Curtis, E. S.
    1908. The North American Indian, vol. 2. Cambridge, Mass.
    1924a. The North American Indian, vol. 13. Norwood, Mass.
    1924b. The North American Indian, vol. 14. Norwood, Mass.
    1926. The North American Indian, vol. 15. Norwood, Mass.
Dávila Garibi, J. Ignacio
    1935. Recopilación de datos acerca del idioma coca y de su
        posible influencia en el lenguaje folklórico de Jalisco.
        Investigaciones Lingüísticas, 3:248-302.
Dixon, R. B.
    1910. The Chimariko Indians and language. UC-PAAE, 5:
        293-380.
Dixon, R. B., and A. L. Kroeber
    1903. The native languages of California. AA, 5:1-26.
Dozier, Edward P.
    1956. Two examples of linguistic acculturation. Language,
        32:146-157.
Foster, George M.
    1944. A summary of Yuki culture. UC-AR, 5:155-244.
Goddard, Pliny E.
    1929. The Bear River dialect of Athapascan. UC-PAAE, 24:
        291-324.
Hall, Robert A., Jr.
    1947. A note on Taos k´owena horse. IJAL, 13:117-118.
Haugen, Einar
    1956. Bilingualism in the Americas: a bibliography and re-
        search guide. Publ. of the Amer. Dialect Soc., no. 26.

Heizer, Robert F. , and John E. Mills
        1952. The four ages of Tsurai. Berkeley and Los Angeles.
Henshaw, H. W.
        1955. California Indian linguistic records: The Mission In-
               dian vocabularies of H. W. Henshaw, ed. by R. F.
               Heizer. UC-AR, 15: 85–202. (Recordings of the 1880's.)
Kroeber, A. L.
        1904. Languages of the coast of California south of San Fran-
               cisco. UC-PAAE, 2: 29–80.
        1907. Shoshonean dialects of California. UC-PAAE, 4: 65–
               165.
        1909. Notes on Shoshonean dialects of Southern California.
               UC-PAAE, 8: 235–269.
        1911. Phonetic elements of the Mohave language. UC-PAAE,
               10: 45–96.
        1922. Elements of culture in native California. UC-PAAE,
               13: 260–328.
        1941. Salt, dogs, tobacco. UC-AR, 6: 1–20.
        1943. Classification of the Yuman languages. UC-PL, 1: 21–
               40.
        1955. An Atsugewi word list. IJAL, 24: 213–214.
Kroeber, A. L. , and George William Grace
        1960. The Sparkman grammar of Luiseño. UC-PL, 16: 1–258.
Lamb, Sydney
        1958. Linguistic prehistory in the Great Basin. IJAL 24: 95–
               100.
Lee, D. D.
        1943. The linguistic aspect of Wintu⸴ acculturation. AA, 45:
               435–440.
Mason, J. Alden
        1916. The Mutsun dialect of Costanoan. UC-PAAE, 11: 399–
               472.
Mathews, Mitford M.
        1951. A dictionary of Americanisms. Chicago.
Merriam, C. Hart
        1955. Studies of California Indians. Berkeley and Los Ange-
               les.
Newman, Stanley
        1944. Yokuts language of California. Viking Fund Publ. in
               Anthrop. , no. 2.

Oswalt, Robert
  1958. Russian loan words in Southwestern Pomo. IJAL, 24: 245-247.
Pinart, Alphonse
  1952. California Indian linguistic records: The Mission Indian vocabularies of Alphonse Pinart, ed. by R. F. Heizer. UC-AR, 15:1-84. (Recordings of 1878).
Pitkin, Harvey, and William Shipley
  1958. Comparative survey of California Penutian. IJAL, 24: 174-188.
Powers, Stephen
  1877. Tribes of California. CNAE, vol. 3.
Radin, Paul
  1924. Wappo texts. UC-PAAE, 19:1-147.
  1929. A grammar of the Wappo language. UC-PAAE, 27:1-194.
Ramos i Duarte, Feliz
  1898. Diccionario de mejicanismos, segunda edición. Méjico.
Robins, Robert
  1958. The Yurok language. UC-PL, 15:1-300.
Sapir, Edward
  1930. The Southern Paiute language. Proc. of the Amer. Acad. of Arts and Sciences, vol. 65.
Sapir, Edward, and Morris Swadesh
  1960. Yana dictionary. UC-PL, 23:1-267.
Schoolcraft, Henry Rowe
  1853. Information respecting the history, condition and prospects of the Indian tribes of the United States, vol. 2. Philadelphia.
Simpson, J. H.
  1876. Report on explorations across the Great Basin of Utah. Washington, D. C.
Tagliavini, C.
  1928. Frammento d'un dizionarietto luiseno-spagnuolo. Proc. of the 23rd Intern. Congr. of Americanists, pp. 905-917.
Voegelin, C. F.
  1935. Tübatulabal texts. UC-PAAE, 34:191-246.
  1958. Working dictionary of Tübatulabal. IJAL, 24:221-228.

Weinreich, Uriel
          1953. Languages in contact. Publ. of the Ling. Circle of
                N. Y., no. 1.
Wheeler, George
          1876. Annual report upon the geographical surveys west of
                the one hundredth meridian, vol. 7. Washington, D. C.

                        UNPUBLISHED DATA

                           Microfilms

Curtin, Jeremiah
          1884a. Atsugewi vocabulary. BAE-A, MS no. 2059.
          1884b. Yana vocabulary. BAE-A, MS no. 2060.
          1885. Shasta vocabulary. BAE-A, MS no. 709.
          1889a. Yana vocabulary. BAE-A, MS no. 953.
          1889b. Achomawi vocabulary. BAE-A, MS no. 1454.
          1889c. Chimariko vocabulary. BAE-A, MS no. 1451.
          n.d.a. Wintun vocabulary. BAE-A, MS no. 841.
          n.d.b. Yuki, Achomawi, and Maidu vocabularies. BAE-A,
                MS no. 1452.
Gatschet, Albert
          1877a. Maidu vocabulary (Chico). BAE-A, MS no. 646-A.
          1877b. Sasti-English and English-Sasti dictionary. BAE-A,
                MS no. 706.
          1877c. Achomawi vocabulary. BAE-A, MS no. 620.
Henshaw, H. W.
          1883a. Panamint vocabulary. BAE-A, MS no. 786.
          1883b. Washo vocabulary. BAE-A, MS no. 963-6.

                          Manuscripts

Barker, Phillip   Klamath-Modoc.
Beeler, Madison S.   Barbareño Chumash.
Bright, Elizabeth   Patwin.
Bright, William   Wailaki and Migueleño Salinan.
Broadbent, Sylvia   Reconstituted Rumsen.
                           Southern Sierra Miwok and Chukchansi
                                Yokuts.
Callaghan, Catherine A.   Lake Miwok and Plains Miwok.

Fletcher, Stuart   Wiyot.
Freeland, L. S.   Vocabulary file of Central Sierra Miwok,
                                    ed. by Sylvia Broadbent. (In files of
                                    the Survey of California Indian Lan-
                                    guages, Berkeley.)
Grekoff, George   Reconstituted Chimariko, based on data
                                    of Edward Sapir and others. (In files
                                    of the Survey of California Indian Lan-
                                    guages, Berkeley.)
                                    Southeastern Pomo.
Halpern, Abraham   Pomo. (In files of the Survey of Califor-
                                    nia Indian Languages, Berkeley.)
                                    Yuma.
Hayes, Alfred S.   Diegueño.
Hoijer, Harry   Tolowa.
Jacobsen, William H., Jr.   Salinan and Washo.
Kiddle, Lawrence B.   Spanish loan words in American Indian
                                    languages. (Read at the summer meet-
                                    ing of the Linguistic Society of Ameri-
                                    ca, 1958.)
Klein, Sheldon   Kawaiisu.
Lamb, Sydney   Uto-Aztecan and Chukchansi Yokuts.
Li, Fang-Kuei   Mattole and Wailaki.
McLendon, Sally   Eastern and Northwestern Pomo.
Olmsted, D. L.   Achomawi and Atsugewi.
Oswalt, Robert   Southwestern and Central Pomo.
Pitkin, Harvey   Wintu and Nomlaki.
Sawyer, Jesse O., Jr.   Wappo.
Seiler, Hansjakob   Cahuilla.
Shipley, William   Maiduan.
Silver, Shirley   Shasta.
Teeter, Karl   Wiyot.
Tozzer, A. M.   Northern Sierra Miwok. (Data recorded
                                    in 1908, now in the files of the Survey
                                    of California Indian Languages, Ber-
                                    keley.)
Uldall, H. J.   Nisenan. (In files of the Survey of Cali-
                                    fornia Indian Languages, Berkeley.)
Woodward, Mary   Hupa and Tolowa.

KEY TO MAPS

ATHABASCAN FAMILY
Oregon group
 1a. Rogue River (uninhabited)
Tolowa group
 1b. Tolowa
Hupa group
 1c. Hupa
 1d. Chilula
 1e. Whilkut
Mattole group
 1f. Mattole
Wailaki group
 1g. Nongatl
 1h. Lassik
 1i. Sinkyone
 1j. Wailaki
 1k. Kato
ALGONKIN FAMILY
Yurok
 2a. Yurok
 2b. Coast Yurok
 3. Wiyot
YUKIAN FAMILY
 4a. Yuki
 4b. Huchnom
 4c. Coast Yuki
 4d. Wappo
LUTUAMIAN FAMILY
 5. Modoc
HOKAN FAMILY
Shasta
 6a. Shasta
 6b. New River Shasta
 6c. Konomihu
 6d. Okwanuchu
 6e. Achomawi (Pit River)
 6f. Atsugewi (Hat Creek)
Yana
 7a. Northern Yana (Noze)
 7b. Central Yana (Noze)
 7c. Southern Yana
 7d. Yahi
 8. Karok
 9. Chimariko
Pomo
 10a. Northern
 10b. Central
 10c. Eastern
 10d. Southeastern
 10e. Northeastern
 10f. Southern
 10g. Southwestern
 11. Washo
 12. Esselen
Salinan
 13a. Antoniano
 13b. Migueleño
 13c. Playano (doubtful)
Chumash
 14a. Obispeño
 14b. Purisimeño
 14c. Ynezeño
 14d. Barbareño
 14e. Ventureño
 14f. Emigdiano
 14g. Interior (doubtful)
 14h. Island
Yuman
 15a. Northern (Western) Diegueño
 15b. Southern (Eastern) Diegueño

15c. Kamia
15d. Yuma
15e. Halchidhoma (now Chemehuevi)
15f. Mohave
PENUTIAN FAMILY
Wintun
 Dialect groups:
 16a. Northern
 16b. Central (Nomlaki)
 16c. Southeastern (Patwin)
 16d. Southwestern (Patwin)
Maidu
 Dialect groups:
 17a. Northeastern
 17b. Northwestern
 17c. Southern (Nisenan)
Miwok
 18a. Coast
 18b. Lake
 18c. Plains
 18d. Northern
 18e. Central
 18f. Southern
Costanoan
 19a. Saklan (doubtful)
 19b. San Francisco
 19c. Santa Clara
 19d. Santa Cruz
 19e. San Juan Bautista (Mutsun)
 19f. Monterey (Rumsen)
 19g. Soledad
Yokuts
 Dialect groups:
 20a. Northern Valley (Chulamni, Chauchila, etc.)
 20b. Southern Valley (Tachi, Yauelmani, etc.)
 20c. Northern Hill (Chukchansi, etc.)
 20d. Kings River (Choinimni, etc.)
 20e. Tule-Kaweah (Yaudanchi, etc.)
 20f. Poso Creek (Paleuyami)
 20g. Buena Vista (Tulamni, etc.)
UTO-AZTEKAN (SHOSHONEAN) FAMILY
Plateau branch
 Mono-Bannock group:
 21a. Northern Paiute (Paviotso)
 21b. Eastern Mono (Paiute)
 21c. Western Mono
 Shoshoni-Comanche group:
 21d. Koso (Panamint, Shoshone)
 Ute-Chemehuevi group:
 21e. Chemehuevi (Southern Paiute)
 21f. Kawaiisu (Tehachapi)
Kern River branch
 21g. Tübatulabal (and Bankalachi)
Southern California branch
 Serrano group:
 21h. Kitanemuk (Tejon)
 21i. Alliklik
 21j. Vanyume (Möhineyam)
 21k. Serrano
 Gabrielino group:
 21l. Fernandeño
 21m. Gabrielino
 21n. Nicoleño
 Luiseño-Cahuilla group:
 21o. Juaneño
 21p. Luiseño
 21q. Cupeño
 21r. Pass Cahuilla
 21s. Mountain Cahuilla
 21t. Desert Cahuilla

158

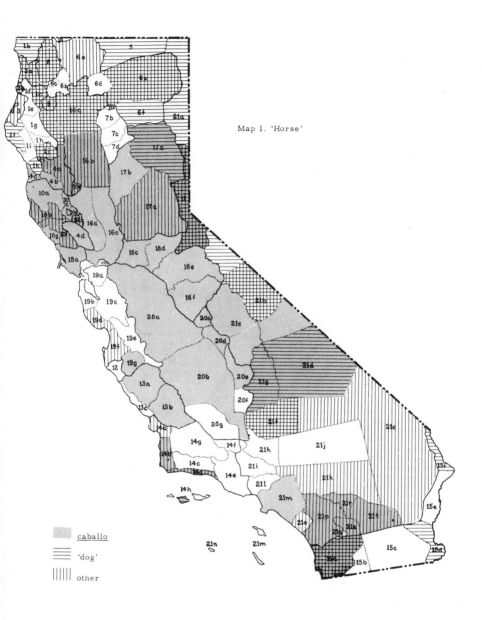

Map 1. 'Horse'

caballo

'dog'

other

159

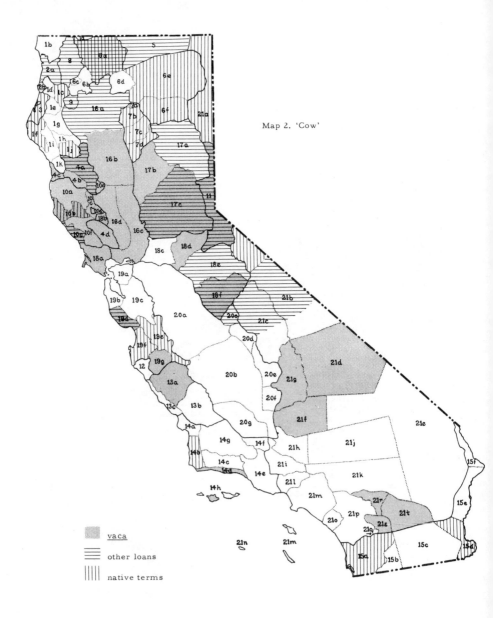

Map 2. 'Cow'

vaca

other loans

native terms

160

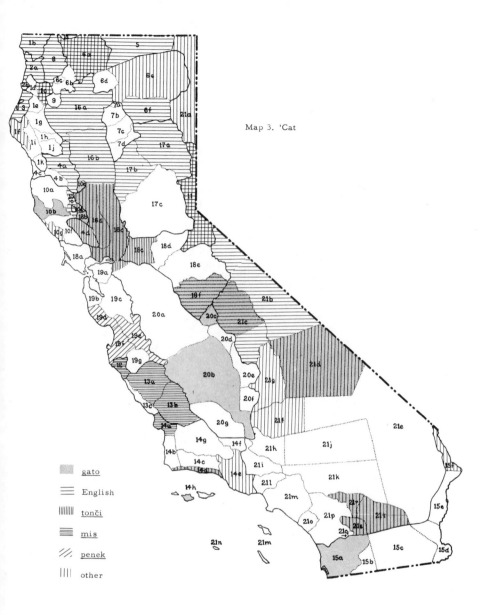

Map 3. 'Cat

gato

≡ English

||||||| tončï

≡ mis

/// penek

|||| other

161

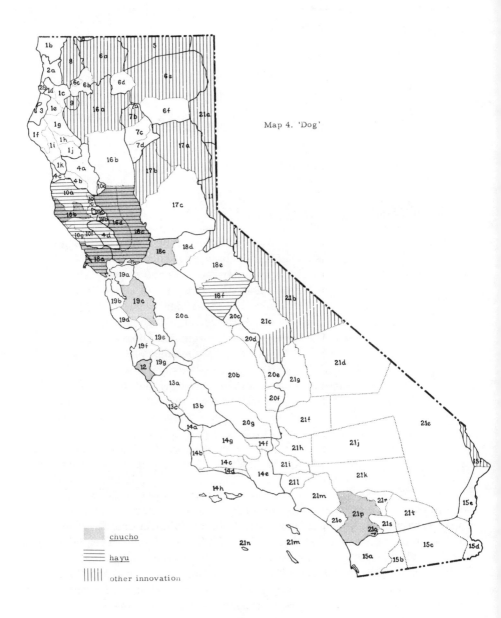

Map 4. 'Dog'

chucho

hayu

other innovation

162

14 The Linguistic History of the Cupeño

In Collaboration with Jane Hill

The Cupeño People

Several Uto-Aztecan groups are found in Southern California. Three of these, the Cahuilla, Luiseño, and Cupeño, are closely related, but the exact nature of the relationship is problematic. The Cupeño were one of the smallest tribes in California in aboriginal times; Kroeber (1925, p. 689) estimates their maximum strength at 500. They were encountered by the Spanish in the 18th century, living in two villages near Warner's Hot Springs in San Diego County. These villages, Cupa and Wilakalpa, were permanent sites; Gifford (1926, p. 395) states that Cupa, the larger village, was a "self-sufficient political unit" inhabited by members of seven patrilineages, "which, although living in a single village and therefore bound by certain territorial ties, nevertheless maintained their distinctness, each lineage having its own land upon which wild products were gathered, each having its patriarchal chief, and each keeping fresh the story of its origin". The seven lineages in Cupa were divided into two exogamous moieties, Coyote and Wildcat. Three of the Coyote lineages, the Kaval, Blacktooth, and Norte, were said to be the "original" Cupeño lineages, descended from the three sons of the hero-founder of Cupa. Two Coyote lineages were said to be of Cahuilla origin. The Wildcat lineages were all said to be "foreign", of Luiseño, Diegueño, and Cahuilla derivation. The smaller Cupeño village, Wilakalpa, had two lineages, both of Wildcat affiliation. Gifford points out that Wilakalpa men were forced to seek wives outside their village, and that Wilakalpa thus was not "independent" in the sense that Cupa was.

The Cupeño lived in their two villages until 1902, when the Warner's Hot Springs site was sold to a white man to be developed

as a resort. The Cupeño were then evicted from their land and re-
moved to the Luiseño town of Pala. The remnants of the tribe are
now scattered through several towns in Southern California.

The ethnographic data collected by Gifford and Kroeber provide a clue to the affiliations of the Cupeño with their neighbors. The
Kaval, Blacktooth, and Norte lineages of the Cupeño, descended from
three sons of a single father, and further fitting the criteria of terri-
toriality, group consciousness, and linguistic unity, may be considered a patri-sib like those described for the Cahuilla by Bean (1960).
It is possible that the Cupeño are originally a patri-sib which became
detached from the larger body of the Cahuilla.

Kroeber considers evidence from mythology, ceremony, and
linguistics in his discussion of Cupeño origins. He finds their mythology close to that of the Cahuilla, but their ceremonialism closely
resembling the Luiseño forms. The Cupeño language, he finds, is
clearly an independent one, although closer to Cahuilla than to Luiseño. He suggests that the Cupeño, in order to have developed an independent language, must have experienced a period of isolation from
the Luiseño and Cahuilla, and must have split off early from an undifferentiated Luiseño-Cahuilla group.

Two explanations have thus been offered concerning the Cupeño relationship with the Cahuilla and Luiseño. The ethnographic
evidence suggests that they are a southern offshoot of the Cahuilla.
But Kroeber proposed, on the basis of linguistic data, that the Cupeño "detached from the still somewhat undifferentiated Luiseño-
Cahuilla group at some former time" (1925, p. 690). The evidence
from a systematic comparison of the three languages should suggest
a decision between the two possibilities, or offer a third solution:
that the Cupeño split off from the Luiseño after the Luiseño-Cahuilla
split.

The Use of Linguistic Evidence

The use of rigorous comparative linguistic techniques can
often clarify historical relationships between peoples when other
methods prove inadequate. When a proto-language has been recon-

structed, the comparativist examines the innovations that appear in
the daughter languages. Where he finds that certain daughter languages share an innovation from the proto-language, he must assume
that they share a period of common history.

Two factors complicate this procedure, however. First is
the problem of borrowing: two languages may diverge, but the speakers may maintain contact, and borrowings from one language into the
other may occur after the initial split. Such loan words will resemble cognate pairs between donor and receiver language. The second
problem is that of "drift", the phenomenon described by Sapir, who
noted that some language groups exhibit an apparently "built-in" tendency to change in certain directions — tendencies perhaps determined by stresses in the pattern of the proto-language. Drift phenomena may be confused with shared innovations. However, both borrowings and resemblances due to drift may usually be distinguished from
true cognates because they stand out from the pattern of regular correspondences determined by comparative techniques.

Ideally, a strict application of comparative techniques should
include treatment of grammar and lexicon as well as phonology. In
the present case, however, it is necessary to restrict the discussion
mainly to phonology, since complete morphological and syntactic descriptions of the languages concerned are not available. Our procedure, then, is as follows: By comparison of cognate sets in Cahuilla,
Cupeño, and Luiseño, we reconstruct the phonemic system of their
ancestor language. We then consider features that represent innovations from the reconstructed proto-language. If two of the languages
share an innovation not found in the third, we assume that they shared
a period of common history after separating from the third language.
Finally, we make a preliminary survey of lexical data to support the
findings based on phonology. [1]

The Cupeño Phonemes

The Cupeño data presented here are from the speech of Miss
Rosinda Nolasquez, a native of Cupa, now living in Pala, California.
The following are Miss Nolasquez's Cupeño phonemes:

Consonants:							Short vowels:		

Consonants:

p	t	c	k	kw	q	ʔ
(f)	s	ṣ	x	xw		h
v	(d)	y	(g)	w		
	l	ly				
	r					
m	n	ny	ŋ̣			

Short vowels:

	i		u
	(e)	ə	(o)
		a	

Long vowels:

i:		u:
(e:)	ə:	(o:)
	a:	

Primary stress:

Phonemes in parentheses occur only in Spanish loan words.

Cupeño has four syllable types: CV and CVC (stressed or unstressed), CV: and CV:C (stressed only). Consonants in the first position in syllables are said to occur initially; those in the second position are said to occur finally. The following consonants occur in both positions, except as otherwise stated.

/p/ is a voiceless bilabial stop: p<u>ív</u>ət "tobacco", n<u>ə́</u>ʔəp "I (realized aspect)".

/t/ is a voiceless dental stop: t<u>úkut</u> "wildcat".

/c/ is voiceless and alveopalatal. In syllable-final position it has the sibilant allophone [š], elsewhere it is the affricate [č]: ʔácly<u>ə</u>m "cattle", c<u>íciq</u>ə "he is gathering".

/k/ is a voiceless velar stop: k<u>íʔut</u> "elderberry", t<u>úk</u> "will sleep".

/q/ is a voiceless back-velar stop: q<u>əsíly</u> "sagebrush", p<u>ə́nəq</u> "he came".

/kw/ is a voiceless stop with simultaneous lip-rounding, extremely rare in final position. Before unaccented /a/ it is back-velar, like /q/; elsewhere it is velar, like /k/: kw<u>ə</u>ʔïc "food", kw<u>áq</u>ə "he is eating", n<u>əsəlákwn</u>ən "I scratched".

/ʔ/ is a glottal stop: nə́ʔət "basket", n̥íʔyə "go away".

/f/ is a voiceless labiodental spirant, occurring only in loanwords: fó:sforo "match".

/s/ is a voiceless alveolar sibilant: nəʔásismə "my brother's daugher".

/ṣ/ is a voiceless retroflex sibilant: ṣanəṣáneyəqə "it is fuzzy", nə́nəṣ "my mother's elder sister".

/x/ is a voiceless velar spirant: wáxəcily "frog", máx "will give".

/xw/ is a voiceless velar spirant with simultaneous lip-rounding, very rare in final position: páxwit "blister", ʔísəxw "will sing a man's song".

/h/ is a voiceless glottal spirant, and relatively rare: həwváqə "he is smelling", wíh "two".

/v/ is a voiced labiodental spirant, never occurring in word-initial position except in loanwords: návət "cactus sp.", táv "will put it down", vá:ka "cow".

/d/ is voiced and dental; after nasals it is a stop, elsewhere it is a spirant [ð]. It occurs only in loanwords, and never in word-final position: dyé:go "Diego", səndí:yə "watermelon".

/y/ is a voiced palatal glide, sometimes devoiced in word-final position: yun̥ávic "buzzard", pəyúy "it snowed".

/g/ is a voiced velar fricative [ɣ]. It occurs in only one native Cupeño morpheme, and never occurs finally: gəyí:nə "chicken", tə́gələm "take it away (pl.)".

/w/ is a voiced labiovelar glide, sometimes devoiced in word-final position: wáwəm "far", nəwíw "my acorn gruel".

/l/ is a voiced alveolar lateral, devoiced in word-final position. It is rare in word-initial position: láwiq "he's flicking it", ʔálwit "crow".

/ly/ is a voiced alveopalatal lateral, devoiced in word-final position. It is rare in word-initial position: lyáwyəxwənət "hole", tə́vily "spark".

/r/ is a voiced alveolar flap. It occurs in Spanish loans and in a very few native words: ʔətírə "very", kwəxá:r "to sour".

/m/ is a voiced bilabial nasal: mánit "toloache drink", ʔíslyəm "coyotes".

/n/ is a voiced alveolar nasal: nə́ʔən "I".

/ny/ is a voiced alveopalatal nasal, not occurring finally: nyímiqə "he's folding it", wányic "flood".

/ŋ/ is a voiced velar nasal: ŋán "will cry".

/i/ is a high front vowel. It is slightly lowered before /t c s/ , and when unstressed after consonants other then /q h ʔ/: míʔi "which", híc "what".

/e/ is a mid-front vowel. It occurs in unstressed syllables of Spanish loanwords: ló:te "ear of corn".

/u/ is a high-back rounded vowel. It tends to be lowered and centralized in unstressed syllables: túkut "wildcat".

/o/ is a mid-back rounded vowel. It occurs in unstressed syllables of Spanish loanwords: ló:ko "crazy, drunk".

/ə/ is a mid-central vowel, slightly raised and rounded after /ṣ/: mə́mət "ocean", pəṣə́ʔə "flower".

/a/ is a low-central vowel: támit "sun", ʔəxwáʔaw "over there". It occurs in unstressed syllables only before /y w/ and in reduplicated syllables; otherwise it is morphophonemically replaced by /ə/: compare kwáqə "he is eating", but kwəʔíc "food".

Long vowels occur only in stressed syllables. The mid vowels /e: o:/ (only in loans) are slightly higher than the corresponding short vowels; other long vowels have the same qualities as the corresponding short vowels do when stressed. Examples of long vowels are: ní:ntəm "pregnant women", ʔiglé:sə "church", mə́:t "gopher", pá:nət "tarantula", mú:t "owl", ló:ko "crazy".

In addition to the primary stress /ˊ/, there is a phonetic secondary stress. Although it tends to occur on alternate syllables counting from the primary stress, fully adequate rules for its prediction have not yet been formulated.

The Cahuilla Phonemes

Cahuilla data have been obtained principally from Mrs. Katherine Saubel, a speaker of the Mountain dialect. Her speech corresponds closely to the Desert Cahuilla described by Seiler (1957). The phonemes of Mrs. Saubel's Cahuilla are as follows:

Consonants:							Short vowels:		
p	t	č	k	q	qw	ʔ	i		u
(f)	s	š	x		xw	h	e		
v	(d)	y	(g)		w			a	
	l	ly					Long vowels:		
	r						i:		u:
m	n	ny	ŋ				e:		o:
Stress: ˊ								a:	

The values of the symbols listed above are similar to those described for Cupeño. Fuller information on Cahuilla phonetics and on Cahuilla historical phonology can be found in Bright (1965a). It is relevant here, however, to point out certain distributional and historical peculiarities of the Cahuilla phonemes.

1) The alveopalatal affricate and fricative, which are in complementary distribution in Cupeño, are not quite so in Cahuilla. To be sure, /č/ occurs only before vowels, and /š/ occurs mostly before consonants or word-finally; but there are a few occurrences of /š/ before vowels, for example, ʔínyišily "little". There is frequent morphophonemic alternation between /č/ and /š/, for example,

in púčily "eye", hépuš "his eye". All these facts suggest that we might set up a pre-Cahuilla phoneme *c, with allophones like those of Cupeño /c/.

2) The only labiovelar stop phoneme in Cahuilla has back-velar occlusion; hence the writing /qw/, contrasting with a rare intervocalic cluster of /k/ plus /w/, as in túkwet "mountain lion".

3) Of the consonants /v d g f/, /d g f/ and word-initial /v/ occur only in Spanish loans. Word-medial /v/ occurs in native words, however, just as in Cupeño.

4) The alveolar flap /r/, as in Cupeño, occurs in Spanish loans and in a small number of other items, for example, wíːru- "to blow a flute".

5) The phoneme /l/ is common in medial position, but (again as in Cupeño) is rare initially; examples are laméːsaʔ "table" and lúmuʔily "measles".

6) Cahuilla /e/ is clearly a front vowel when stressed, but is centralized when unstressed, approaching the sound of Cupeño /ə/. Cahuilla /a/ also has a schwa-like allophone when unstressed, but contrast with /e/ is preserved. Cahuilla is thus more conservative in this matter than Cupeño, which merges unstressed /a/ and /ə/.

7) Long vowels are rare in Cahuilla. They occur as the result of contractions, for example, in píːly "fur" from *píhily; as the replicas of accented vowels in Spanish loan words, for example, inʼ vúːru "donkey"; and in a few other words, for example, sáːmsa- "buy", which may be loans from other Indian languages.

8) Cahuilla /oː/, with no short counterpart, occurs only in Spanish loans like tóːruʔ "bull", and in móːmat "ocean", presumably a borrowing from Luiseño móːmat.

9) The position of Cahuilla stress is, for the most part, morphologically predictable: it falls on stem-initial syllables, but moves to prefixes before monosyllabic stems, for example, in ʔáčily "pet", but néʔaš "my pet". Departures from this rule are suspect of

being loans, for example, paxá: ? "red racer snake, assistant chief" (cf. Luiseño paxá?).

The Luiseño Phonemes

The Luiseño data used here were originally taken from the works of Harrington (1933), Kroeber and Grace (1960), and Malécot (1963, 1964). Most of them, however, have been checked with Malé-cot's informant, Mrs. Gertrude Chorre. The phonemic inventory is as follows (cf. Bright, 1965b):

Consonants:								Short vowels:	
p	t		č	k	kw	q	qw	?	i	u
(f)	s	ş	š	x	xw			h	e	o
v	d		y	(g)	w				a	
l									Long vowels:	
r									i:	u:
m	n			ŋ					e:	o:
Stress:									a:	

The following comments are relevant to our comparative treatment:

1) Luiseño /č/ and /š/ are in near-complementary distribution, as in Cahuilla, with /č/ before vowels and /š/ elsewhere; however, the pattern is broken by a few examples such as páčxam- "to wash (clothes)". There is frequent morphophonemic alternation, for example, in wá: ?iš "meat", plural wá?čum "cattle".

2) The fricatives /v d/ are never initial in native words, though they may be in Spanish loans; /f g/ occur only in loans.

3) Basic /ş r/ are replaced by /s d/ respectively in diminutive forms: şú: kat "deer", súkmal "fawn"; ŋarúŋruš "jar-shaped", diminutive ŋadúŋdumal.

4) There is no contrast in unstressed syllables between /i/ and /e/, or between /u/ and /o/; we write only /i/ and /u/.

5) Vowel length in Luiseño is predictable to a considerable extent: vowels in stressed open syllables are usually long, those in

stressed closed syllables or in unstressed syllables are usually short,
as in mó:mat "ocean" vs. its derivative mómyum "white men". But
there are exceptions to this pattern, for example, nukín "my sack"
vs. nusú:n "my heart", yá?qa "it's running" vs. pá:?kal "sunflower",
sú:kat "deer" vs. táka:t "straight". The historical background of
these cases has not been completely worked out, though many of the
Luiseño long vowels are clarly due to contraction, as in kwí:la "oak
sp." as compared to Cupeño kwínily, Cahuilla qwíñily, or as in móm-
ŋa:š "white man" as compared with its alternative form mómŋaxwiš.

Comparative Phonology

    The comparison of apparent cognates in Cupeño, Cahuilla
and Luiseño reveals a set of systematic phonological correspondences,
which in turn indicate the major outlines of the phonemic system of
the prehistoric parent language. The languages are here indicated
by abbreviations: Cu[peño], Ca[huilla], and Lu[iseño]. The reconstructed proto-language is called Cupan, after Cupeño and the aboriginal town of Cupa; this nomenclature is based on the geographical
central position of Cupeño, on its conservatism in certain phonological respects (such as the preservation of *ə), and on the desire to
pay some belated tribute to the much-abused people of Cupa. (We
reject, on esthetic grounds, the term "Luisish" suggested by Lamb
(1962).)

    Only a few cognate sets are given in this section to exempli-
fy each correspondence; a fuller presentation of cognates is given in
the Appendix to this paper. Hyphens are used to set off verb stems
and bound noun stems; as elicited from informants, the latter normally have possessive prefixes attached.

    Cu /p/, Ca /p/, Lu /p/ = Cupan *p: Cu -pi, Ca -pi?, Lu
-pi? "breast"; Cu kúp-, Ca kúp-, Lu kúp- "sleep". The P[roto] U[to-]
A[ztecan] correspondence, as reconstructed by Voegelin and Hale
(1962), is *p; for example, *pi "breast", *kuup(i) "close eyes, sleep".

    Cu /t/, Ca /t/, Lu /t/ = *t: Cu -tə, Ca tá-t, Lu ?a-tá? "sin-
ew"; Cu -təm?ə, Ca táma-l, Lu -tamá "tooth, mouth". PUA has *t,
as in *ta- "sinew", *taşma "tooth".

Cu /c/, Ca /č ~ š/, Lu /č ~ š/ = *c̣: Cu c̣ə́m, Ca čə́m, Lu
čá: ʔam "we"; Cu -puc̣, Ca púči-ly, -puš, Lu pú: či-l, púš-la, -púš
"eye". PUA has *s̱ in *puₙsi "eye", but most other Cupan terms containing this correspondence have not yet been traced to PUA. One set,
in which Cahuilla is not represented, has PUA *c̣: Cu c̣ív, Lu čí: v-
"bitter", PUA *c̣is̱pu.

Cu /k/, Ca /k/, Lu /k/ = *k: Cu kít, Ca kít, Lu kít "fire";
Cu túkmet, Ca túkmaš, Lu tú: kumit "night". PUA has *k, as in *ku
"fire", *tus̱ki "night". In a few words, Cu has /q/ corresponding to
Ca and Lu /k/; see "bite" (PUA *kɨ), "fish" and "nettle" in the Appendix.

Cu /kw/, Ca /qw/, Lu /kw/ = *kw: Cu -kwál̕ə, Ca qwál-
ma-l, Lu -kwalma "armpit"; Cu kwínily, Ca qwínyily, Lu kwí: la "oak
sp. " Reliable PUA cognates are not available.

Cu /kw/, Ca /qw/, Lu /qw/ = *qw: Cu kwás̱ic, Ca qwásiš,
Lu ʔá-qws̱a "cooked, ripe"; Cu kwa-, Ca qwa-, Lu qwaʔ- "eat".
PUA has *k̲ᵂ, as in *kᵂaᵤs̱ɨ "cooked", *kᵂa(ʔa) "eat".

Cu /q/, Ca /q/, Lu /q/ = *q: Cu -qa, Ca -qaʔ, Lu -qaʔ "paternal grandfather"; Cu náqəl, Ca náqal, Lu náqla "ear". PUA has
*k before low vowels, as in *kas̱ku "father's mother"; or *k after
*Vₙ, as in *naₙka "ear". In a few cases, Cu has /k/ corresponding
to Ca and Lu /q/; see "buckwheat", "fox", "quail", "rat", and "rock"
in the Appendix.

Cu /ʔ/, Ca /ʔ/, Lu /ʔ/ = *ʔ: Cu ʔás̱-, Ca ʔáʔas- (reduplicated), Lu ʔás̱- "bathe"; Cu wáʔ- "to roast", wáʔic "meat", Ca
wáʔiš "meat", Lu wá: wa- "to roast", wá: ʔiš "meat". PUA has *ʔ,
as in *ʔasi "bathe", *was̱ʔi "to roast".

Cu /v/, Ca /v/, Lu /v/ = *v, reconstructed only in word-
medial position: Cu pívət, Ca pívat, Lu pí: vat "tobacco"; Cu návət,
Ca návet, Lu ná: vut "prickly pear". PUA has *p after *Vs̱, as in
*pis̱pa "tobacco", *nas̱pɨ "prickly pear".

Cu /s/, Ca /s/, Lu /s̱/ = *s̱- (i. e. , word-initial *s): Cu
súʔul, Ca súʔ-wet, Lu súʔla "star"; Cu sílyi-, Ca sílyi-, Lu s̱í: li-

"pour". PUA has *s̱, as in *su̱ "star". But Lu has unexplained initial /s/ in two cases: see "buy" and "one" in the Appendix.

Cu /s/, Ca /s/, Lu /s/ = *-s- (i.e., word-medial *s̱). It is hypothesized that this correspondence represents noninitial occurrences of the same proto-Cupan *s̱ which was set up in the preceding paragraph. Examples are Cu qusá-, Ca híkus-, Lu hakwí:s- "breathe" Cu ʔíswit, Ca ʔíswet, Lu ʔíswut "wolf". PUA again has *s̱, as in *hikʷɨsɨ "breathe".

Cu /ṣ/, Ca /s/, Lu /ṣ/ = *ṣ: Cu -ṣú:n, Ca -sun, Lu -ṣú:n "heart"; Cu kuṣ-, Ca kús-, Lu kuṣáni- "take". The PUA of Voegelin and Hale has *s̱, as in *sula "heart", *kʷɨs̱si "take". A problem that remains unsolved is whether rules can be formulated to show when PUA *s̱ becomes Cupan *s̱, and when it becomes *ṣ. Or must the PUA system be revised to recognize separate *s̱ and *ṣ?

Cu /x/, Ca /x/, Lu /x/ = *x, reconstructable only in noninitial position: Cu ʔətáxʔə, Ca táxlis-wet, Lu ʔatá:x "man, person"; Cu háx, Ca háxʔi, Lu háx "who". PUA has medial *k after *a (other than *aₙ), as in *taka "man", *haki "who".

Cu /h/, Ca /h/, Lu /h/ = *h: Cu húyəl, Ca húyal, Lu hú:la "arrow"; Cu páh, Ca páh, Lu pá:hi "three". PUA has *h, as in *hu "arrow", *pahi "three".

Cu /w/, Ca /w/, Lu /w/ = *w: Cu wáxni-, Ca wáx-, Lu wáxni- "to dry"; Cu təw-, Ca téw-, Lu tów- "see". PUA has *w, as in *waki "dry", *tɨwa "find".

Cu /l/, Ca /l/, Lu /l/ = *l, reconstructable only in word-medial or word-final position: Cu -sulʔə, Ca sálul, Lu sulát "fingernail, claw"; Cu məlál, Ca málal, Lu malá:l "metate". PUA has medial *t, as in *suₙtu "fingernail". Although Cupan *l and *t both derive from PUA *t, they appear to contrast, at least in final syllables; cf. Cu pú:l, Ca pú:l, Lu pú:la "doctor" with Cu mú:t, Ca mú:t, Lu mú:ta "owl".

Cu /ly/, Ca /ly/, Lu /l/ = *l after *i: Cu kwínily, Ca qwínyily, Lu kwí:la "oak sp."; Cu -qílyʔə, Ca -qílyʔi, Lu -qli "nape".

Cu /l/, Ca /l/, Lu /r/ is attested only in Cu mə́ləkwi-, Ca méli-, Lu mó:ri- "twist"; and in Cu čǝ́li- "cut", Lu čóri- "chop wood". A reconstruction *r may be indicated, but there is no evidence to relate this to PUA *r.

Cu /y/, Ca /y/, Lu /y/ = *y: Cu -yə, Ca -ye?, Lu -yo? "mother"; Cu yúy-, Ca yúy-, Lu yúy- "to snow". PUA has *y, as in *yɨʔɨ "mother".

Cu /m/, Ca /m/, Lu /m/ = *m: Cu muha-, Ca múh-, Lu mu?án- "shoot"; Cu támit, Ca támit, Lu timét "sun". PUA has *m, as in *muhu "shoot".

Cu /n/, Ca /n/, Lu /n/ = *n: Cu kínə-, Ca ná- or kína-, Lu ná?- "burn" (intr.); Cu sá:nǝt, Ca sá:nat, Lu sá:nat "gum". PUA has *n and *l, as in *naṇʔa "to burn", *sala "sticky, gum". Some Cu and Ca examples have /ny/ next to *i: see "bend" and "river".

Cu /ŋ/, Ca /ŋ/, Lu /ŋ/ = *ṇ : Cu ṇan-, Ca ṇá:ṇ-, Lu ṇá:- "weep"; Cu ṇíy-, Ca ṇíy-, Lu ṇé- "go away". PUA has *ṇ, as in *ṇola "return".

Note that no correspondences have been found for the following consonant phonemes: Cu /xw g r ny/ and initial /x l/; Ca /xw r ñ/ and initial /x l/; Lu /xw d/ and initial /x l/.

Cu /i/, Ca /i/, Lu /i/ = *i: Cu wíly, Ca wíly, Lu ?a-wí? "fat"; Cu ?í?i ~ ? iví, Ca ?í? ~ ?ív?i, Lu ?iví? "this". PUA has *i, as in *wi- "fat", *?i "this". Most of the Cupan examples are in stressed syllables; elsewhere, less regular correspondences are found. Thus Cu has /ə/ instead of /i/ in Cu ?əyál, Ca ?íyal, Lu ?iyá:la "poison oak".

Cu /i/, Ca /i/, Lu /e/ = *e: Cu wíh, Ca wíh, Lu wéh "two"; Cu pít, Ca pít, Lu pét "road". PUA has *o, as in *wo- "two", *po "road". Before *x, Ca has /e/ instead of /i/: Cu wəxítit, Ca wéxet, Lu wixé?tut "pine" (PUA *woṣko).

Cu /ə/, Ca /e/, Lu /o/ = *ǝ: Cu qǝ́-, Ca ké-, Lu kó?i- "bite"; Cu mǝ́nily, Ca ménily, Lu móyla "moon". PUA has *ɨ, as

in *kɨ "bite", *mɨya "moon". When unstressed, Lu forms have /u/
instead of /o/: Cu tə́vət, Ca tévat, Lu tuvát "conifer sp. ".

Cu /a/, Ca /a/, Lu /a/ = *a: Cu pál, Ca pál, Lu pá:la "water"; Cu -ma, Ca -ma, Lu -ma? "hand". PUA has *a, as in *pa "water", *ma "hand". In unstressed position, Cu has /ə/ instead of /a/:
Cu náqmə-, Ca náqma-, Lu náqma- "hear".

Cu /u/, Ca /u/, Lu /u/ = *u: Cu túl, Ca túl, Lu tú:la "charcoal"; Cu -mu, Ca -mu, Lu -mú:vi "nose". PUA has *u, as in *tu
"black", *muṣpi "nose". In unstressed position, Cu sometimes has
/ə/ instead of /u/: Cu hənúvət, Ca húnuvat, Lu hunú:vat "Yucca mohavensis".

Cu /V/, Ca /V/, Lu ∅ in unstressed medial syllables = *V
of the quality indicated by Ca: Cu ʔə́wəl, Ca ʔéwil, Lu ʔówla "blood"
point to reconstructed *ʔə́wila.

Cu ∅, Ca ∅, Lu /V/ in unstressed final syllables = *V of the
quality indicated by Lu. This is illustrated by the final vowel of the
preceding example. The historical loss of unstressed vowels, reflected in this and the previous correspondence, also plays an important role in the morphophonemic alternations of the present-day Cupan
languages, as in Cu ʔísily "coyote", plural ʔísly-əm; Lu kamíisa
"shirt", nu-kmíisaki "my shirt".

Words in which all three languages have initial stress are
reconstructed as having initial *⌣́, as in Cu ʔáʔalxi-, Ca ʔáʔalxi-,
Lu ʔá:alvi- "tell a story", and other examples above. No supraseg-
mental phonemes have been reconstructed for PUA, and the earlier
history of Cupan *⌣́ is not known at present.

Words in which Cu and Lu have stress on the second syllable, and Ca has stress on the first syllable, are reconstructed with
*⌣́ on the second syllable: Cu ʔəwál, Ca ʔáwal, Lu ʔawá:l "dog"; Cu
kəváʔmal, Ca kávaʔmal, Lu kaváʔmal "pot".

In a few sets of cognates, Cu and Lu show different stress
patterns; such sets will not fit either of the above correspondences.
Examples are Cu támit, Ca támit, but Lu timét "sun"; Cu qəṣíly, Ca
qásily, but Lu qá:ṣil "sagebrush".

Conclusion

This study has applied the methods of linguistic comparison
and reconstruction to three Uto-Aztecan languages of Southern California, which apparently form a genetic grouping. By reconstructing
features of their common ancestor — the language we have named
Proto-Cupan — we have hoped to shed light on the specific relationships of the languages to each other, and specifically to choose between the following possible patterns of descent:

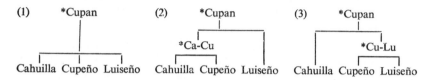

The criterion for choice is that of shared innovations: if two of the
languages share a feature that is not in the third and not in the proto-
language, then they are assumed to have had a period of shared history and to constitute a separate subbranch. By this criterion we can
find two reasons for gouping Cahuilla and Cupeño as a separate subbranch of Cupan. One is the development of *l̲ to Ca and Cu /ly/ after *i̲, where Lu retains /l/; the other is the merger of *e̲ and *i̲ to
Ca and Cu /i/, where Lu retains contrasting /e/ and /i/. On these
bases, family tree 2 seems the most likely.

Grammatical and lexical comparisons are desirable, of
course, to support the hypothesis of a historical Cahuilla-Cupeño unity. In the area of lexicon, we find the following classes of terms:

1) Those in which the three languages show no relationship,
for example, Cu mí?aw-, Ca píš-, Lu wukó:?a- "arrive".

2) Those in which Cu and Ca have related terms, whereas
Lu has an unrelated form, for example, Cu ?ísily, Ca ?ísily, Lu
?anó? "coyote".

3) Those in which Cu and Lu agree, whereas Ca has an unrelated form, for example, Cu -múc?ə, Lu -mú:ṣi, but Ca yultámal
"beard".

4) Those in which Ca and Lu agree, whereas Cu has an unrelated form, for example, Ca ʔíŋily, Lu ʔéŋla, but Cu yə̣wál "salt".

Of the stem-lists available to us from the three languages, we find
two-language agreement for Cupeño and Cahuilla in 64 cases, for Cupeño and Luiseño in 42 cases, and for Cahuilla and Luiseño in 10
cases. Although this lends some support to our belief that Cupeño
and Cahuilla form a genetic unit, further study of individual vocabulary items should be made. At present only one lexical set will be
mentioned: in the meaning "west", Cu has kə̣wí-kə̣ and Ca qáwi-ka,
while Lu has payó:-m. The Cu and Ca forms can be etymologized as
"toward the mountains" (Cu kə̣wí-c, Ca qáwi-š "rock", Lu qawí:-ča
"mountain".) The Lu form perhaps contains pá:-la"water" and yó-t
"big", referring to the ocean. These forms suggest that Cahuilla and
Cupeño once shared a common home in the deserts to the east of the
Coast Range. Cahuilla social organization has recently been described (Bean, 1960) in terms of patri-sibs, that is, groups of lineages
with a shared territory, a distinctive dialect, and a consciousness of
group identity. The Cupeño may well have originated as one such sib
of a larger Cahuilla-Cupeño entity.

APPENDIX: LIST OF COGNATES

The following is a list of forms believed to be cognate in the
three languages, Cupeño, Cahuilla, and Luiseño, together with their
proto-Cupan reconstructions, so far as these can be made. Where a
corresponding proto-Uto-Aztecan form has been reconstructed by
Voegelin and Hale, it is given along with its reference number from
the appendix of their work.

Absolute suffix (1): Cu -t (as in mú:t "owl"), Ca -t (as in mú:t
    "owl"), Lu -ta (as in mú:ta "owl") or -t (as in kút "fire"):
    *-ta.
Absolute suffix (2): Cu -c (as in kíc "house"), Ca -š (as in kíš
    "house"), Lu -ča (as in kí:ča "house") or -š (as in suʔíš
    "jack-rabbit"): *-ca.
Absolute suffix (3): Cu -l (as in pú:l "doctor"), or -ly (as in múkʔily
    "a sore"), Ca -l (as in pú:l "doctor") or -ly (as in múkily "a
    sore"), Lu -la (as in pú:la "doctor") or -l (as in mú:kil "a
    sore"); *-la.

Acorn mush: Cu wíwic, Ca wíwiš, Lu wí: wiš (wíw- "cook acorn
    mush"): *wíw-.
Agave: Cu ʔəmúl, Ca ʔámul, Lu ʔamú: l: * ʔamúl.
And: Cu mə, Ca mán "well, ... ", Lu man "and, also": *ma-.
Ant: Cu ʔánət, Ca ʔánet, Lu ʔá: nat: * ʔánVt.
Armpit: Cu -kwálʔə, Ca qwálmal, Lu -kwálma: *kwál-.
Arrow: Cu húyəl, Ca húyal, Lu hú: la; *hú-. PUA *hu (78).
Artemisia dracunculus (a plant): Cu wácic, Ca wáčiš, Lu wá: čiš:
    *wácic.
Ashamed, be: Cu həmán-, Ca sunháman- (with sun- "heart"), Lu
    ha-mó:ya-; *hamV-.
Augmentative suffix: Cu -wit, Ca -wet, Lu wut: *-wət? PUA *wɨ-
    "big" (100). (For an example of the suffix, see "wolf".)
Aunt, maternal: Cu -nəš, Ca -nes, Lu nóš: *-nəš.
Aunt, paternal: Cu -pah, Ca -pa, Lu -pá:-may: *-pa.
Awl: Cu ʔívic, Ca ʔíviš, Lu ʔé: viš: * ʔévic.
Bathe: Cu ʔáš-, Ca ʔáʔas- (with reduplication), Lu ʔáš-: * ʔáš-.
    PUA * ʔasi (139).
Be (1): Cu qáʔ, Ca qál, Lu qál-: *qá-. PUA *kaṣtɨ "sit" (42).
Be (2): Cu míyəxwə "there is ..., hello", Ca míyaxwe "there is ...,
    hello", Lu mí: x- "be", míyu "hello": *mí-.
Bear: Cu húnwit, Ca húnwet, Lu húnwut: *húnwət. (This is apparent-
    ly the augmentative (q. v.) of "badger", Ca húnal, Lu hú: nal.)
Bear fruit: Cu tú-, Ca tú-, Lu tú:-ʔaviš "barren": *tú-.
Bend: Cu nyími-, Ca nyími- (cf. lámi- "to fold"), Lu né: mi-: *némi-?
Bewitch: Cu píʔ-, Ca pí-, Lu piʔáni-: *pi-.
Bite, to: Cu qə́-, Ca ké-, Lu kóʔi-: *kə́-ʔ. PUA *kɨṇ(ʔi) (43).
Blood: Cu ʔə́wəl, Ca ʔéwil, Lu ʔówla: * ʔə́wila.
Bloom, to: Cu ṣə́- (cf. pəṣə́ʔə "flower"), Ca sé- (séʔiš "flower"),
    Lu ṣo: ʔ-: *ṣə́-.
Blue bird sp.: Cu cáʔic, Ca čáʔiš, Lu čá: ʔiš: *cáʔic.
Body: Cu -táxwi, Ca táxawily, Lu -tá: xaw: *táxawi-. (Cf. "person".)
Borrow: Cu tə́ʔə-, Ca téʔe-, Lu tó: ʔ-: *tə́ʔ-.
Bread, to make: Cu ṣáw- (cf. ṣáwic "bread"), Ca sásaw- (with re-
    duplication, cf. sáwiš "bread"), Lu ṣá: wka-: *ṣáw-.
Breast: Cu -pi, Ca -piʔ, Lu -piʔ: *pi. PUA *pi (6).
Breathe: Cu qusá- (cf. hiqsáʔ- "to sigh"), Ca híkus- (cf. -híkusʔa
    "breath"), Lu hakwí: s- (híkwsa-š "breath"): *hikwVsa-?
    PUA *hikᵂɨsɨ (55).
Bring: Cu yáw-, Ca yáw- "catch", Lu yá: w- "have, hold, take":
    *yáw-.

Brother, elder: Cu -páṣmə, Ca -pas, Lu -pá: ʔaṣ: *-paṣ?

Buckwheat: Cu wilákəl, Ca húlaqal, Lu wuláqla: *huláqala?

Burn (intr.): Cu kínə-, Ca ná-, kína-, Lu ná ʔ-: *na-. PUA *naᵤʔa
    (95b).

Burrow, a: Cu təkic, Ca tékiš "cave", Lu tóvkiš "storage cave":
    *təkic?

Buy: Cu sámsə-, Ca sá: msa-, Lu sá: msa-: *sámsa-? (The unex-
    pected long vowel of Ca and the initial /s/ of Lu suggest bor-
    rowing from some non-Cupan language.)

Buzzard: Cu yuṇávic, Ca yúṇaviš, Lu yuṇá: viš: *yuṇávic.

Carry a load: Cu túku-, Ca túk-, Lu tukwáni-: *tuk-.

Ceremonial enclosure: Cu wámkic, Ca wámkiš "brush lean-to", Lu
    wámkiš: *wámkic.

Charcoal: Cu túl (cf. túlnək-ic "black"), Ca túl (túlek-iš "black"),
    Lu tú: la: *túla. PUA *tu "black" (23).

Chia: Cu páṣəl, Ca pásal, Lu pá: ṣal: *páṣal.

Chief: Cu nə́: t (long vowel unexplained), Ca nét, Lu nó: ta: *néta.

Child: Cu kí: -mal "boy", Ca kíat "child", Lu kihá: t "small": *kiha-.

Chipmunk: Cu səkáwit, Ca síkawet, Lu ṣuká: wut "tree squirrel":
    *sVká-wət.

Cholla cactus: Cu mútəl, Ca mútal, Lu mú: tal: *mútal.

Claw/nail: Cu -sul ʔə, Ca sálu-l, Lu -ṣla, ṣulá-t: *ṣula (with appar-
    ent metathesis of vowels in Ca). PUA *suᵤtu (26).

Come: Cu mənmáx-, Ca ménvax-, Lu mon-: *mən-.

Conifer sp.: Cu tə́vət, Ca tévat, Lu tuvát: *tevat.

Cooked/ripe: Cu kwáṣic, Ca qwásiš, Lu ʔá-qwṣa: *qwaṣ-. PUA
    *kʷaᵤsɨ (50).

Crow: Cu ʔálwit, Ca ʔálwat, Lu ʔálwut: *ʔálwVt.

Daughter of man: Cu -ṣuṇámə, Ca -súṇama, Lu -ṣawá: may (cf.
    ṣuṇá: l "woman"): *ṣuṇáma? (apparently the diminutive
    (q. v.) of "woman").

Deer: Cu súqət, Ca súqat, Lu ṣú: kat: *súqat?

Dig: Cu wáli-, lyáw-, Ca wáli-, Lu láwi-: *wáli-, with metathesis
    in Cu and Lu.

Diminutive suffix: Cu -mə, -mə-l, Ca -ma, -ma-l, -ma-ly (cf. -mál-
    yu ʔa "woman's son"), Lu -mal, -may: *-ma-l? PUA *mala
    "child (with female reference)" (84).

Doctor: Cu pú: l, Ca pú: l, Lu pú: la: *púla (with Cu and Ca long vow-
    els unexplained).

Doctor, to: Cu tíŋələ?əc "medicine", Ca tíŋ?aypiš "medicine", Lu
  téŋal- "to doctor", téŋal-kat "doctor": *téŋ-.

Dog: Cu ?əwál, Ca ?áwal, Lu ?awá:l: *?awál.

Dove: Cu məxíly, Ca máxily, Lu mixé:l: *mVxél.

Down/below: Cu tə́- (cf. təmál "earth"), Ca témal "earth", Lu tó:-ŋax
  "down" (cf. tó:-ta "stone", tó:-mal "small stone"?): *tə-
  "down", *tə-mal "earth".

Drink: Cu pá-, Ca pá-, Lu pá:?-: *pa-. (Cf. "water".)

Dry, to: Cu wáxni-, Ca wáx-, Lu wáxni-: *wáx-. PUA *waki (99).

Eagle: Cu ?áṣwit, Ca ?áswet, Lu ?áṣwut: *?áṣwət.

Ear: Cu náqəl, Ca náqal, Lu náqla: *náqala. PUA *naⁿka (47).

Eat: Cu kwa-, Ca qwa-, Lu qwa?-: *qwa-. PUA *kʷa(?a) (48).

Egg: Cu -pánic "testicle", Ca pánet, Lu pá:nil: *pán-.

Eye/seed: Cu -puc, Ca púčily, -puš, Lu púšla, -púš: *púcila. PUA
  *puⁿsi (5).

Fat: Cu wíly, Ca wíly, Lu ?a-wí?: *wí-. PUA *wi- (102).

Father: Cu -na, Ca -na?, Lu -na?: *-na.

Fire: Cu kút, Ca kút, Lu kút: *kút. PUA *ku (137).

First/before: Cu múluk, Ca múlu?uk, Lu ?amú:la: *múl-.

Fish: Cu qəyúl, Ca kíyul, Lu kiyú:l: *keyúl?

Flat: Cu takətákə?əc "bald", Ca táka- "be flat", Lu táka:t "straight":
  *táka-.

Flea: Cu məkwác, Ca múkaš, Lu mukwá?čiš: *mukwác?

Fox: Cu kəwís?ic, Ca qáwi?siš, Lu qiwé:wiš: *qawé...ic?

Foxtail grass: Cu wávic, Ca wá:viš, Lu wá:viš: *wávic.

Frog: Cu wáxəcily, Ca wáxačily, Lu waxáw?la (cf. waxá:-wut "frog
  sp."): *waxa-.

Girl: Cu nəwíc-məl (cf. nəwíkət "wife"), Ca náwiš-maly (cf. náwi-
  taly "teen-age girl"), Lu nawí:l "young woman", nawít-mal
  "girl": *nawí-.

Give: Cu max- (cf. nə́məx- "sell"), Ca máx-, Lu námxan- "give
  away": *max-. PUA *maṣka (83).

Go away: Cu ŋíy-, Ca ŋíy-, Lu ŋe-: *ŋe-. Cf. PUA *ŋola, *ŋowa
  "return" (152).

Goose: Cu lə́?əl, Ca lá?la?, Lu lá?la: *lá?ala?

Gopher: Cu mə́:t, Ca mé:t, pl. méht-am, Lu mó:ta: *mə́həta.

Gourd: Cu níxic, Ca néxiš, Lu né:xiš: *néxic.

Grandfather, maternal: Cu -kwa, Ca -qwa?, Lu -kwá?: *-kwa. PUA
  *kʷa?a (127).

Grandfather, paternal: Cu -qa, Ca -qa?, Lu -qá?: *-qa. Cf. PUA
    *ka_ᵍku "father's mother" (170).

Grass: Cu səmát, Ca sámat, Lu ṣá:mut: *samVt.

Gum: Cu sánət, Ca sá:nat, Lu ṣá:nat: *sanat. PUA *sala (147).

Guts: Cu -ṣá?i, Ca sá?ily, Lu ṣá?iš "excrement": *sá?i-.

Hair of body: Cu -pí?i, Ca -píh?i, pí:ly, Lu ?a-pé? "feathers": *pé?
    (but Ca -h- is unexplained).

Hand: Cu -ma, Ca -ma, Lu -ma?: *-ma. PUA *ma (128).

Hat: Cu yúmə?ət, Ca yúmu?- "put on hat", Lu yumú?i- "put on hat":
    *yumu- "put on hat".

Hear: Cu náqmə-, Ca náqma-, Lu náqma-: *naqma-, from *naqa-
    "ear".

Heart: Cu -ṣú:n (long vowel unexplained), Ca -sun, Lu -ṣú:n: *-ṣún.
    PUA *sula (98).

Heat, to: Cu sə́xi- "burn" (tr.), sə́xnə- "cook"; Ca séx- "cook",
    séxi? "hot springs", Lu ṣéxli- "to warm water": *sə́x-.

Hell: Cu tə́lmikiš, Ca télmikily, Lu tólmik: *tə́lmik.

Horned toad: Cu cəláke, Ca čálaka?, Lu čaláka: *caláka.

House: Cu kíc, Ca kíš, Lu kí:ča: *kíca.

Hull, to: Cu si?áy- "to hull acorns", si?áyic "hulled acorns", Ca
    sí?ay- "to peel", Lu sí:?awiš "hulled acorns": *si?a-.

Hunt: Cu ?ámu-, Ca ?ámu-, Lu ?á:mu-: *?ámu-.

I: Cu ná̧, Ca né?, Lu nó:: *nə̧.

Jackrabbit: Cu sú?ic, Ca sú?iš, Lu ṣu?íš: *su?ic.

Jackrabbit, young: Cu páwxət, Ca páxwut, Lu pá:xut: *páxwut?

Jealous, to be: Cu náwi-, Ca náwa:n-, Lu ná:win-: *náw-. (Cf. also
    Cu ná?aw- "blame", náwvi- "fight".)

Kill: Cu mə́qə-, Ca méqa-, Lu mókna-: *mə́q-?

Leach: Cu pácik-, Ca páčik-, Lu páška-: *pácik-.

Leaf: Cu -pəl?ə, Ca pálat, Lu pávlaš (from reduplicated *pa-pala-):
    *pala-.

Left (hand): Cu ?icvá-wit, Ca ?íšva:x, Lu -?éčva: *?ecva-.

Lizard sp.: Cu yú?əl, Ca páyul (with pá- "water"?), Lu yulú?:
    *yu...l.

Look for: Cu hál-, Ca há:l-, Lu há:l-: *hál-.

Manzanita: Cu kə́ləl, Ca kélil, Lu kó:lul: *kə́lVl.

Metate: Cu məlál, Ca málal, Lu malá:l: *malál.

Mistletoe: Cu cáymə, Ca cáyal, Lu ?ačá:yaka: *cáy-.

Mockingbird: Cu təmáwit, Ca támawet, Lu tamá:wut: *tamá-wət
    "mouth-big".

Moon: Cu mǽnily, Ca ménily, Lu móyla: *mǽnila? PUA *mɨya (158).

Mortar, bedrock: Cu ʔílyǝpǝl, Ca ʔílypalʔa, Lu ʔé: lapal: *ʔélapal?

Mother: Cu -yǝ, Ca -yeʔ, Lu -yoʔ: *-yǝ. PUA *yɨ-ʔɨ (106).

Mouth/tooth: Cu -tǝmʔǝ, Ca -támʔa, Lu -tamá: *-tama. PUA
      *taѕma "tooth" (29).

Nape: Cu -qílyʔǝ, Ca -qílyʔi, Lu -qli, qilá-t: *qel-. Cf. PUA
      *kuѕta "neck" (154)?

Net, carrying: Cu ʔíkǝt, Ca ʔíkat, Lu ʔí: kat: *ʔíkat.

Nettle: Cu síciqily, Ca číkišily, Lu ѕakíšla. (Metathesis and irreg-
      ular correspondences make it impossible to reconstruct a
      proto-form.)

Night, to pass: Cu túk- (cf. túkmǝt "night"), Ca túk- (túkmaš "night"),
      Lu tú: k- "to camp out" (tú: kumit "night"): *túk-. PUA
      *tuѕki "night" (144).

Nit: Cu sáʔwǝt, Ca sáʔwa-, Lu ѕáʔwut: *sáʔwV-.

North: Cu tǝmám-, Ca témam-, Lu tumá: m: *tǝmám.

Nose: Cu -mu (cf. -muv "snot"), Ca -mu (-muv "snot"), Lu -mú: vi:
      *-mu(v). PUA *muѕpi (15).

Oak sp. (1): Cu kwínily, Ca qwínyily, Lu kwí: la: *kwínila?

Oak sp. (2): Cu wíʔǝt, wiʔáwlǝt "oak spp.", Ca wíʔat, wíʔasily "oak
      spp.", Lu wiʔá: ѕal: *wiʔa-.

Old man: Cu nǝxáncuʔvǝl (cf. nǝxánic "man"), Ca náxaluʔvel (náxa-
      niš "man"), Lu naxán-mal (cf. naxá: ča- "become old"):
      *naxá-.

Old woman: Cu níclyǝvǝl, Ca níšlyuʔvel, Lu néšmal: *néc-.

One: Cu súplǝwit, súlit, Ca súplyiʔ (cf. súpul "other"), Lu supúl:
      *su-. Cf. PUA *sɨ- (65).

Owl: Cu mú: t, Ca mú: t (plural múht-am), Lu mú: ta: *múhuta.

Palm tree: Cu má: wǝl, Ca mául, Lu má: xwal, má: xul: *máxwal?

Person: Cu ʔatáxʔa, Ca táxlis-wet (cf. táx "self"), Lu ʔa-tá: x "per-
      son, self": *tax. PUA *taka "man" (145).

Pet: Cu -ʔác (cf. ʔácily "cow"), Ca -ʔaš, ʔácily, Lu -ʔá: š, ʔášla:
      *ʔáci(la).

Pine: Cu wǝxítit, Ca wéxet, Lu wixéʔtut: *wexét-. PUA *woѕko (142).

Poison oak: Cu ʔǝyál, Ca ʔíyal, Lu ʔiyá: la: *ʔiyála.

Possession: Cu -míxǝn, Ca -méxan, Lu -mí: x: *míx. Cf. "be" (2).

Pot: Cu kǝváʔmǝl, Ca kávaʔmal, Lu kaváʔmal: *kaváʔmal.

Pour: Cu sílyi-, Ca sílyi-, Lu ѕí: li-: *síli-.

Pregnant woman: Cu nít, Ca nít, Lu nét: *nét.

Prickly pear: Cu návǝt, Ca návet, Lu ná: vut: *návǝt. PUA *naѕpɨ
      (16).

Pull out: Cu xúwi-, Ca hú:-, Lu hú:yaki-: *hú-?

Push: Cu núli-, Ca nú?aqan-, Lu nú:li: *nú-.

Put: Cu táv_ən-, Ca táve-, Lu taváni-: *tav-.

Put on: Cu yúl- "string beads", yúti- "build", Ca yúl- "string beads,
  build", Lu yú:li- "put on": *yú(l)-.

Quail: Cu k_əxál, Ca qáxal, Lu qaxá:l: *qaxál?

Raccoon: Cu ?ayám_əl, Ca ?áyamal, Lu pá?yamal (with pa- "water"?):
  *?ayámal.

Race, to: Cu námi- (cf. n_ənmi- "chase"), Ca némí- "chase", Lu
  ná:mi- "race" (nánmi- "chase"): *námi-, reduplicated
  *ná-nami-?

Racer snake: Cu p_əxá?_ə, Ca paxá:?, Lu paxá?: *paxá?.

Rat: Cu káw_əl, Ca qáwai, Lu qáwla: *qáwala?

Rattlesnake: Cu s_əwit, Ca séwet, Lu s_əó:wut: *s_əw_ət.

Raw: Cu sáwit, Ca sáwit, Lu sawút: *sawit?

Reed: Cu s_əyily, Ca séyily, Lu s_əóyla: *s_əyila.

River: Cu wányic "flood", Ca wániš, Lu waníš: *wanic.

Road: Cu pít, Ca pít, Lu pét: *pet. PUA *po (4).

Roadrunner: Cu púwic, Ca púwiš, Lu púypuy: *púwi-?

Roast, to: Cu wá?- (cf. wá?ic "meat"), Ca wá?iš ("meat", Lu wá:wa-
  "to roast" (wá:?iš "meat"): *wá- "to roast", *wá?ic "meat".
  PUA *wa_s?i "to roast" (162).

Rock: Cu k_əwíc, Ca qáwiš, Lu qawí:ča "mountain": *qawíca?

Rot, to: Cu písá?ic "rotten", Ca pís?iš "rotten", Lu pisá?- "to rot":
  *pisá?-.

Run: Cu yá?-, Ca yá?i- "run fast", Lu yá?-: *ya?-.

Sagebrush: Cu q_əsíly, Ca qásily, Lu qá:sil: *qasil.

Say: Cu ya-, Ca yá-, Lu ya-: *ya-.

See/find: Cu t_əw-, Ca téw-, Lu tów-: *t_əw-. PUA *ti-wa "find" (21).

Sew: Cu ?ú?l_ə-, Ca ?ú?la-, Lu ?ulá?na-: *?ula-. The Cu and Ca
  forms may be from reduplicated *?ú-?ula-.

Shoe: Cu wáq_ət, Ca wáqat, Lu wáčxat: *wá...at.

Shoot: Cu muha-, Ca múh-, Lu mu?án-: *muh-? PUA *muhu
  (81).

Shoulder: Cu -s_ək?_ə, Ca -sék?a, Lu -s_əó:ka: *s_əka.

Sinew: Cu -t_ə, Ca tá-t, Lu -tá?: *ta. PUA *ta (125).

Sister, elder: Cu -qísm_ə, Ca -qis, Lu -qé:?is: *qé...s.

Sky: Cu túkv_ə?_əc, Ca túkvaš, Lu tú:paš: *tú...ac.

Sleep: Cu kúp-, Ca kúp-, Lu kúp-: *kúp-. PUA *ku_ŋp(i) "close eyes"
  (153).

Smoke: Cu mí?ət, Ca mí?at, Lu kú:mit (cf. kú-t "fire"): *mi-.
Smoke, to: Cu pívat "tobacco", Ca pív- "to smoke", pívat "tobacco",
    Lu pí:vat "tobacco": *pív- "to smoke", *pívat "tobacco".
    PUA *piṣpa "tobacco" (12).
Snow, to: Cu yúy-, Ca yúy-, Lu yúy-: *yúy.
Sore, a: Cu múk?ily, Ca múkily, Lu mú:kil: *múkil?
South: Cu kicám-, Ca kíčam-, Lu kí:čam: *ḳicam.
Springtime: Cu táṣpə, Ca táspa, Lu táṣpa: *táṣpa.
Spruce: Cu yúyily, Ca yúyily, Lu yúyla: *yúyila.
Squirrel: Cu qíŋic, Ca qíŋic, Lu qé:ŋic: *qéŋic.
Star: Cu sú?ul, Ca sú?-wet, Lu ṣú?la: *sú?-. PUA *ṣu (71).
Sting: Cu súyi-, Ca súyily "scorpion", Lu ṣúyla "scorpion": *ṣúyi-
    "sting", *ṣúyila "scorpion".
Stir: Cu wəláwəli- "irrigate", Ca wáluš- "to hoe", Lu wá:li- "stir",
    waláwali- "irrigate": *wal-.
Suck: Cu mís-, Ca mímiš- "chew" (with reduplication), Lu mé:či-
    "chew": *mé-.
Sumac: Cu nákwit, Ca nákwet, Lu nákwut: *nákwət.
Summer: Cu táwpə, Ca táwpa?, Lu táwpa: *táwpa.
Sun/day: Cu támit, Ca támit, Lu timét: *tVmet.
Sunflower: Cu pá?əqily, Ca pá?akal, Lu pá:?qal: *pá?aq-?
Sweat oneself: Cu háclə- (cf. háclə?əc "sweathouse"), Ca háslava?al
    "sweathouse", Lu hášla- (hášlaš "sweathouse"): *hácla-.
Sweep: Cu wáqi-, Ca wáka?a-, Lu wá:qi-: *wáq-?
Sycamore: Cu səvíly, Ca sívily, Lu sivé:la: *sevéla.
Tail: Cu -kwəṣ, Ca -qwas, Lu pí-qwsiv: *-qwas? PUA *kʷaŋsi (51).
Take: Cu kuṣ-, Ca kús-, Lu kuṣáni-: *kuṣ-. PUA *kʷɨ-ṣi (52).
Teardrop: Cu -?is, Ca -?is, Lu -?és: *-?es.
Tell a story: Cu ?á?alxi-, Ca ?á?alxi-, Lu ?á:?alvi-: *?á?al-.
That: Cu pə́ "he", Ca pé? "that", Lu pó:? "he": *pə.
This: Cu ?í?i, ?iví-, Ca ?í?, ?ív?i, Lu ?iví?: *?i(ví).
Three: Cu páh, Ca páh, Lu pá:hi: *pah-. PUA *pahi (1).
Throw away: Cu wícəxi-, Ca wíčahan-, Lu wí:či-: *wíc-.
Thunder: Cu táwṣənvə (="autumn"), Ca táwvat, Lu táwṣuŋva "autumn":
    *táw-.
Tick (the animal): Cu mácily, Ca máčil, Lu ?amáča: *mác-?
Tie, to: Cu túcin-, Ca túčin-, Lu tú:či-: *túci-.
Track, to: Cu tə́pi-, Ca tétpi- (reduplicated), Lu tópi-: *tə́pi-.
Turtle: Cu ?áyily, Ca ?áyily, Lu pá:?ila (perhaps from *pá-?ayila,
    with pa- "water"): *?áyila.

Twist: Cu mə́ləkwi-, Ca méli-, Lu mó:ri-: *mə́ri-?
Two: Cu wíh, Ca wíh, Lu wéh: *wéh.
Urine: Cu síc ə- "defecate", Ca síʔily "urine", Lu síʔiš: *sí-. PUA
　　　*si (67).
Wake: Cu kwáti-, Ca qwápi-, Lu kwáta-: *kwa-.
Wash: Cu qáyə, Ca qáyi-, Lu qá:yi-: *qáyi-.
Water: Cu pál, Ca pál, Lu pá:la: *pála (cf. "drink"). PUA *pa (123).
We: Cu cə́m, Ca čém, Lu čá:ʔm: *c...m.
Weep: Cu ŋə́ŋ, Ca ŋá:ŋ-, Lu ŋá:-: *ŋa-.
What: Cu híc, Ca híčʔa, Lu hí:ča: *híc-.
When: Cu mípə, Ca mípaʔ, Lu mí:ki-ŋa: *mí-.
Who: Cu háx, Ca háxʔi, Lu háx: *háx-. PUA *haki (138).
Wildcat: Cu túkut, Ca túkut, Lu tú:kut: *túkut.
Wing: Cu -wíkʔi, Ca -wákʔa, Lu -wki, -kawí, kawí-t: *kawí-?
Wolf: Cu ʔíswit, Ca ʔíswet, Lu ʔíswut: *ʔíswət. This is apparently
　　　the augmentative of "coyote" (Cu ʔísaly, Ca ʔísily).
Wood, to gather: Cu kə láw- (kə láwət "wood"), Ca kélaw- (kélawat
　　　"wood"), Lu kulá:w- (kulá:wut "wood"): *kə láw- "gather
　　　wood", *kə láwat "wood".
Yes: Cu hə́:hə:, Ca hé:heʔ, Lu ʔuhó:: *hə.
You: Cu ʔə́, Ca ʔéʔ, Lu ʔóm: *ʔə.
Yucca mohavensis: Cu hənúvət, Ca húnuvat, Lu hunú:vat: *hunúvat.
Yucca whipplei: Cu pənál, Ca pánal, Lu paná:l: *panál.

NOTE

[1] Data on Cupeño used in this paper were collected by Jane
Hill in 1962 and 1963, with support from the Survey of California
Indian Languages, Department of Linguistics, University of Califor-
nia, Berkeley, and from the Center for Research in Languages and
Linguistics, University of California, Los Angeles. The data on
Cahuilla were collected between 1961 and 1963 by William Bright,
with support from the Department of Anthropology and from the
Committee on Research of the University of California, Los Angeles.
Data on Luiseño were collected by William Bright in 1965, with the
aid of a grant from the Penrose Fund of the American Philosophical
Society.

BIBLIOGRAPHY

Bean, Lowell,
> 1960, "The Wanakik Cahuilla", Masterkey, 34: 111-210 (Los
> Angeles).

Bright, William,
> 1965a, "The history of the Cahuilla sound system", Inter-
> national Journal of American Linguistics, 31: 241-244.
> 1965b, "Luiseño phonemics", International Journal of Amer-
> ican Linguistics, 31: 342-345.

Gifford, E. W.,
> 1926, "Miwok lineages and the political unit in aboriginal
> California", American Anthropologist, 28: 389-401.

Harrington, John P.,
> 1933, "Annotations", in Chinigchinich, by Gerónimo Boscana
> (Santa Ana, California, Fine Arts Press), pp. 91-228.

Kroeber, A. L.,
> 1925, Handbook of the Indians of California (= Bureau of Amer-
> ican Ethnology, Bulletin 78) (Washington, D. C., Gov-
> ernment Printing Office).

Kroeber, A. L., and George W. Grace,
> 1960, The Sparkman grammar of Luiseño (= University of
> California Publications in Linguistics, vol. 16) (Ber-
> keley and Los Angeles, University of California Press).

Lamb, Sydney M.,
> 1962, "Language classification and Uto-Aztecan", in Studies
> in Californian linguistics, ed. by William Bright (=
> University of California Publications in Linguistics,
> vol. 34) (Berkeley and Los Angeles, University of
> California Press), pp. 106-125.

Malécot, André,
> 1963, "Luiseño, a structural analysis, I, Phonology", Inter-
> national Journal of American Linguistics, 29: 89-95.
> 1964, "Luiseño, a structural analysis, III: Texts and lexi-
> con", International Journal of American Linguistios,
> 30: 14-31.

Seiler, Hansjakob,
> 1957, "Die phonetischen Grundlagen der Vokalphoneme des
> Cahuilla", Zeitschrift für Phonetik, 10: 204-223.

Voegelin, C. F. and F. M. , and K. L. Hale,
        1962, "Typological and comparative grammar of Uto-Aztecan:
        I (Phonology)", <u>Indiana University Publications in An-
        thropology and Linguistics; Memoir 17 of International
        Journal of American Linguistics</u> (Bloomington).

15 | Archaeology and Linguistics in Prehistoric Southern California

In Collaboration with Marcia Bright

At the time of historic contact, the coastal area of Southern California was occupied by three language families: Chumash, represented by Ventureño, Barbareño, Island Chumash, etc.; Uto-Aztecan, represented by Fernandeño, Gabrielino, Luiseño, and Juaneño; and Yuman, represented by Diegueño (see map on page 205). Chumash and Yuman are further related in that they both belong to the Hokan stock. The present paper deals with the prehistoric movements of these peoples, as inferred from both archaeological and linguistic evidence, which led to the distribution seen at contact. The discussion is divided into the following parts: (1) Kroeber's outline of the prehistoric movements, (2) Presentation of the archaeological evidence, (3) Presentation of the linguistic evidence, and (4) Interpretation.

1. According to Kroeber, California culture history can be divided into four periods. Regarding the topic of this paper, he says that, in the First Period,

> The people of this area almost certainly comprised
> the ancestors of the modern Hokans, perhaps of the
> Penutians. Algonkians and Athabascans are more
> doubtful; Shoshoneans had not yet entered (Heizer
> and Whipple 1951: 109).

In the Second Period,

> The Shoshoneans were probably spreading out of the
> Great Basin across the deserts toward the coast.
> They may have reached the ocean toward the close
> of this period. Here and there bodies of them that
> had come into intimate advance guard contacts with

aliens were specializing their speech to become the
ancestors to groups like the Tübatulabal or Cupeño.
Culturally the Shoshoneans carried little into Cali-
fornia: they could of had but little in the Basin.
They did separate the Southern from the Central
Hokans...during this period (Op. cit., 111).

In the Third Period, "the Shoshoneans no doubt continued to press
southward" (Op. cit., 112). Finally, the Fourth Period saw the flour-
ishing of coastal cultures, those encountered by the Spanish at historic
contact.

Kroeber is reluctant to put dates on these periods, but at
one point he states: "the first of the four culture phases might be set
roughly in the time between 2,000 - 1,500 B.C. and 500 B.C.; the second as continuing from about 500 B.C. to 500 A.D.; the third until
approximately 1,200 A.D.; and the fourth from then on" (Op. cit. 119).
According to these dates the Shoshonean speakers reached the coast
about 500 A.D., where they found Hokan speakers already occupying
the area.

Elsewhere, Kroeber (1923: 578-9) states:

The languages of the southern California branch (of
Shoshonean languages) are sufficiently specialized
to make it necessary to assume a considerable period for their development. This specialization could
hardly have taken place without either isolation or
alien contacts in a marginal location, such as the
branch is subject to now. Then, the ramifications
of this branch imply a residence of some duration;
there are three fully differentiated languages and
a dozen dialects in southern California. How long
it would take these to spring up it is impossible to
say; but 1,000 years of location on the spot does
not seem an excessive figure, and perhaps it would
be conservative to allow 1,500 years since the Shoshoneans first began to reach the coast. The languages of the Yuman and Chumash peoples, whom
the Shoshoneans have apparently split apart in their
shoreward drift, are so extremely different from

each other now that this period is certainly the
minimum that can be assumed for their separation.

We will here examine the archaeological and linguistic evidence to
see what there is to support or refute the assumption that the south
coast of California was populated, in an unbroken line, by Hokan
speakers, and that Shoshonean speakers reached the coast about 500
A.D., driving a wedge through the existing Hokan population.

2. The area of concern is the coastal strip from Point Conception to the Mexican border, including the Channel Islands. All of
the archaeological sites used in the sequence are less than 20 miles
from the coast, and most are coastal lagoon sites. Since we know of
no throrough survey of this archaeological area, the information presented here is based on our own interpretation of published sources.

The first task is the archaeological establishment of a common cultural substratum that underlies all of the historical coastal
cultures. This may have been a cultural uniformity represented linguistically by Hokan speakers. More will be said of this below.

The oldest radiocarbon dates on the coast come from a cultural stratum known as the San Dieguito culture, found only in San
Diego County. It dates at more than 6,000 B.C. This was a desert-
type hunting culture characterized by stone equipment for hunting and
a complete lack of the seed grinding equipment which characterized
the later cultures on the coast. At present no transitional material
has been found between the San Dieguito and the later culture. It is
possible that the San Dieguito hunting people were the first Hokan
speakers on the coast, and that they developed the later seed gathering culture, or that the seed gatherers (Millingstone Culture) were
another group who came to the coast with their culture already developed along these lines. At this point, due to the lack of evidence, it
is impossible to say.

The earliest horizon represented over the entire area has
been called the Millingstone Horizon (Wallace 1954). Although there
are some variations due to differences in the physical environment,
the cultures all display likenesses in a dominance of millingstones
and mullers, crude stone work, and a scarcity of bone and shell; the

focus of the economy is on seed gathering. Radiocarbon dates show
this culture to be fully developed by 5,000 B.C. in the form of the La
Jollan Culture in the south, with comparable dates or comparative
evidence in the north.

From this more or less uniform millingstone horizon, there
developed three regional variations. Moving from south to north,
these cultures show an increasing degree of marine orientation. The
northern area reaches from north of Point Conception to Malibu Creek,
and included the northern Channel Islands. The diaries of the early
Spanish explorers tell of great villages and large ocean-going canoes
on the Santa Barbara coast and northern Islands. The Chumash developed the most elaborate culture on the California coast south of the
Northwest Coast Culture area, made possible by their highly developed
technology for exploiting the sea. The Island cultures were completely dependent on the sea, while the mainland cultures still continued to exploit plant resources and take game.

The southern area, from the San Luis Rey River south to the
Mexican border and beyond, [1] was occupied at contact by the Diegueño,
who speak a Yuman language of the Hokan stock. Their culture appears to have been developing toward a marine-oriented economy,
but never reached great elaboration. At contact there were no coastal
villages such as were seen by the early Spanish in the northern area.
It has been postulated (Warren et al. 1961) that the reason for the
lack of development of a marine economy lay in an ecological change:
that about the time the millingstone culture was beginning to exploit
the lagoons, a climatic change took place which resulted in the silting
up of the lagoons, ruining them as a source of shellfish, which had
been simply gathered by hand. Instead of developing a technology that
would allow them to use the open sea, i.e. canoes and fishhooks, the
Indians moved back from the coast and returned to a millingstone culture, only occasionally visiting the lagoons thereafter.

The central area from Malibu Creek to the San Luis Rey River and Santa Catalina and San Nicolas Islands were occupied at contact by Uto-Aztecan speakers: the Gabrielino, Luiseño and Juaneño.
The Indians of this area had a varied economy. From the archaeological evidence this central area appears to be a cultural hybrid, re-

lying heavily on seed gathering, but also exploiting the ocean. It is believed that Santa Catalina and San Nicolas Islands were inhabited by Gabrielino speakers. The archaeology shows that a high level of culture was reached on the islands (Rozaire 1959, Reinman & Townsend 1960, Reinman 1964). These island cultures, like those to the north, must have been marine-oriented, as the islands are too poor to support a population from their own fauna and flora. Now assuming that the Uto-Aztecan speakers came out of the Great Basin, one of the following could be true: (1) They arrived on the coast during the millingstone period, when their culture would have been so much like that of the coastal culture that a difference between the two cultures would not have been discernible archaeologically. They then developed a marine culture, as the Chumash did to the north, but did not reach as great a reliance on the sea due to the continual revitalization of the seed-gathering complex by people continuing to come out of the Great Basin through the linguistic corridor. Alternatively, (2) they migrated to the coast much later, but the migration was so slow that it was more of an infiltration than a migration. Both Hokan and Shoshonean speakers could have lived side by side, each borrowing from the other and developing together, again with the continuing seaward drift of Shoshoneans acting as a brake on marine orientation. Unfortunately the type of archaeological site found in California does not leave tell-tale strata like those found in the Southwest. From the archaeological evidence alone, we may never know what the condition of the culture was on the coast at the time the Shoshoneans arrived.

3. The linguistic evidence is presented in the following table, set up in such a manner that the languages can be compared to each other and to Proto-Uto-Aztecan. The table should be read in the following manner: Moving from left to right, the first column contains the English glosses; column two contains Proto-Uto-Aztecan as reconstructed by Voegelin and Hale 1962; column three, Gabrielino from unpublished data collected by J. P. Harrington; column four, Luiseño words from W. Bright 1968; column 5, Chumash forms provided by Richard Applegate (personal communication); [2] and finally, column 6 contains Diegueño from Couro & Hutcheson 1973. Phonetic symbols of our sources (the Diegueño in particular) have been modified for easier comparability.

		Proto-Uto-Aztecan	Gabrielino	Luiseño	Chumash	Diegueño
1.	anus	*ʔato	-kóoteʔ	-kúpča	-tiwis	kapsul
2.	arrow	*hu	húu-r	húu-la	ya	ʔəpal
3.	arroyo	*aki	paxáay-t	waní-š	maha	kuṭap
4.	ask	*tani	máa-	todyúŋe-	aqut-asɨw	akəkwii
5.	bathe	*ʔasi	—	ʔás̩-	kep'	ɬyup
6.	be	*kaₛtɨ	xáa	qáal	ʔil	-yuu, yi
7.	big	*wɨ-	-w-t	-wo-t	xax'	ʔiikuu
8.	bite	*kɨ_uʔi	—	kóʔe	axsii	čuukuw
9.	bitter	*cɨₛpu	tepóoʔ	číiv-ot	kut'ó, šon'	ʔəxkwaq
10.	black	*tu_u	yopíixa	yovátaat	šošoy	nyiɬy
11.	bone	*oho	-ʔée-n	-koláaw	-se	aq
12.	breast	*pi	-píipe-n	-piʔ	-kutet	nyəmay
13.	breathe	*hikʷɨsi	—	hakíis-	enhes	yaas
14.	burn	*na_uʔa	—	náʔ-	ixut	aaraw
15.	cactus	*naₛpɨ	náavo-t	náavo-t	ʔitat'	ʔəxpaa
16.	cave	*tɨso	—	tóvke-š	mup	ɬəxup
17.	claw	*su_utu	-čúur	s̩olá-t	-ixway'	salyəxwuuw
18.	cold	*sɨ_upi	ʔočóo	s̩ovóoya	ʔipeyu	xəčuur
19.	come	*ki_uma	kimá	haqwáačem	yɨti	-yiw
20.	cooked	*kʷa_usɨ	—	ʔá-kws̩a	ipšeɬ	pəɨyəmaa
21.	cut	*tɨₛki	—	wóke-	-n'oqš	aakaṭ
22.	die	*mu_uki	—	píʔ-muk-	aqšan	məlay
23.	dog	*puₙku	wosiʔ	ʔawáa-l	čtɨn'	ʔəxaṭ
24.	drink	*hiₛ-	páa-	páaʔe-	aqmil	-sii
25.	dry	*waki	hokée-	wáx-	axsɨw	saay

194

		Proto-Uto-Aztecan	Gabrielino	Luiseño	Chumash	Diegueño
26.	eagle	*kʷa-	ʔašáw-t	ʔáṣwo-t	slow'	ʔixpaa
27.	ear	*naₙka	-náanax	náq-la	-tu	xₑmał
28.	eat	*kʷaʔa	kwaʔáa	kwaʔ-	ʔuw	-saaw
29.	egg	*no-	-xáaxe-n	páane-l	štum	ʔur
30.	enter	*paₛki	pakóo	čolúpe-	tap	wₑxap
31.	excrement	*kʷiᵤta	wyóoʔer	-sáaʔ	waxan-ɨš	—
32.	eye	*puₙsi	čóočo-	púš-la	tɨq	-yiiw
33.	eyebrow	*sɨₛ-po	—	kíimesa-š	-išmek'ew	—
34.	fall	*wɨₛci	poríi-	holúka-	xmen	-nał
35.	fat	*wi-	witáa	ʔa-wíʔ	—	-šay
36.	fire	*ku	-čáav	-kúíʔ	nɨ	ʔaaw
37.	flea	*tɨᵤpu	motíuče-y	mokwáʔče-š	step	ʔₑwił
38.	(to) fly	*nɨʔi	—.	wíla-	xoxoyon	-man
39.	food	*kʷi	-kwáʔe-n	náačaxone-š	ʔuw-mu	ʔₑsuw
40.	foot	*tala	-néev	ʔé-t	-tem'	-mily
41.	fur	*po	-héha-n	-peʔ	-šuš	lₑmis
42.	go	*simi	myáa	hatíʔa-	nal'	waa
43.	grandfather (maternal)	*kwaʔa	-kwáaʔ	-kwáʔ	Y -nono	-nₑkwaaw
44.	grandfather (paternal)	*kaₛku	-káaka	-káʔ	Y -popoč'	-nₑpaaw
45.	grandmother (maternal)	*suʔu	-šúuk	-túíʔ	B -nen'e Y -nebeʔ	-nₑmaaw
46.	grind	*tuᵤsu	peráa-	póyʔe-	iwex, mexwe	taawaa, -tuṭ
47.	guts	*si	-šíi-n	-sɨ́i	-ʔaxšɨw	pₑxaa
48.	hand	*ma	-máa-n	-máa	-pu	-sały

195

		Proto-Uto-Aztecan	Gabrielino	Luiseño	Chumash	Diegueño
49.	hair	*co(ni)	—	-yúʔ	-ʔoqwon	xǝɬytaa
50.	head	*moʔo	-pwáa-n	-yúʔ	-yɨwɨš	xǝɬytaa
51.	hear	*kahi	naxáakwa-	náqma	itaq	yip
52.	heart	*sula	šúun-ar	-súun	-poš	iičix, -yay
53.	heavy	*pɨutɨ	—	wíma-xat	Y xulxul	wǝnah
54.	hill	*touno	hemúuve-t	qawíi-ča	Y wošlo-lomol	matǝkun
55.	horn	*ʔawa	-ʔáʔa-n	-ʔáw	-hap	-kwaa
56.	house	*ki	kíi-y	kíi-ča	ʔap	ʔǝwaa
57.	husband	*kuŋa	—	-kúuŋ	-hin-pakɨwaš	-čuuy
58.	kill	*mɨʔa	—	mókna-	B/Y siniweʔ, alawan	-muuč
59.	knee	*toŋo	—	-qáxme	-istukun	mǝxǝtun
60.	know	*mati	—	ʔayále-	poš-oč	-yaaw
61.	laugh at	*aci	yée-	—	šu-qon'-ɨšpi	uusay
62.	leaf	*sawa	—	pávla-š	s-qap	—
63.	leg	*kasi	—	-qáaṣe	-ʔɨl'	-mily
64.	light a fire	*naya	—	tíke-	aqtɨp, api-wil	-tuɬ
65.	liver	*nɨsma	—	-nóoma	-ʔal	čǝpǝsii
66.	louse	*ʔatɨ	-ʔáar	ʔoláa-t	šik	ǝmiɬy
67.	lung	*soŋno	-šáar	—	—	čǝxwaaɬ
68.	man	*taka	-táaxa-t	ʔa-táax	ʔat'axač	ʔiikwič
69.	meat	*tuuku	hoɲíi-y	wáaʔ-eš	-ʔam'amɨ	kukwaayp
70.	moon	*mɨya	mwáa-r	móy-la	ʔawhay'	xǝɨyaa
71.	mortar	*tɨupa	tokwíi-š	tóopa-l	ʔalqap	ʔǝxmuu
72.	mother	*yɨʔɨ	-óok	-yóʔ	-teteʔ	-taly

196

		Proto-Uto-Aztecan	Gabrielino	Luiseño	Chumash	Diegueño
73.	mouth	*tɨ_uni	-tóoye-n	-tamá	-ʔɨk	aa
74.	name	*tɨ_nwa	-twáanya-n	túŋ-la	-tɨ	čəxič
75.	navel	*si_sku	-úuʔa-n	-tíide	-topo	milyəpuu
76.	neck	*ku_sta	-ŋóoŋ	-xáara	-ni	-yəpuk
77.	night	*tu_ski	yáawke	túukome-t	ulkuw	xuṇ
78.	no	*ka	xáy	qáy	mɨ, mu-	umaaw
79.	nose	*mu_spi	-móope-n	múuve-l	-nuxš	-xuu
80.	one	*sɨ	pokíuʔ	sopúl	paketʼ	ʔəxink
81.	owl	*tukur(i)	múuho-t	múu-ta	muhu	ʔuʔuu
82.	pine	*wo_sko	wěsyáaxa-r	wexéʔto-t	cʼɨkʰɨnɨn	ʔərpuu
83.	put	*tɨ_ska	tavóo	taváne-	sinay	tap
84.	rabbit	*tokʷi	tóove-t	tóove-t	kunʼ, ma	xəɨyaaw
85.	rain	*yuku	wakóo-	xíla-	tuhuy	ʔəkwiy
86.	red	*sɨta	kwahóoxaʔ	ʔávʔaat	uqštahay	ʔəxwaṭ
87.	reed	*pa_ska	šwáa-r	ṣóy-la	kawɨyɨš, swa	ʔəxtaa
88.	road	*po	pée-t	pé-t	ʔaliyaš	ʔuunyaa
89.	roast	*wa_sʔi	hoŋáa-	wáawa-	oxtokok	-hiɨ
90.	root	*ŋa	-wíiwe-n	kwíinamo-š	-ʔaxpilil	pəhəmaa
91.	salt	*ʔo_sŋa	ʔoŋóo-r	ʔeŋ-la	tip	ʔəsily
92.	shine, sun	*toŋa-la	—	qwáata-	—	-ṭuw
93.	shoot	*muhu	—	moʔán-	wɨl	-ṭim
94.	sinew	*ta-	-táa-n	ʔa-táʔ	-ʔaxpilil	pəxəmaa
95.	sleep	*ku_upi	—	kúp-	we	xəmaa
96.	small	*tɨma	čenúuhoʔ	keháa-t	mitʼi	ʔəstik
97.	smoke	*kʷi_sci	ʔačyáan	kúume-t	tow	uuxuy

197

		Proto-Uto-Aztecan	Gabrielino	Luiseño	Chumash	Diegueño
98.	snow	*hɨ̲ₛpa	ywáa-t	yúuye-t	iwaw	aalap
99.	star	*su	šúu-r	súʔ-la	ʔaqiwo	kwənməsaap
100.	stomach	*poka	—	téeʔ-la	-qɨp	-tuu
101.	summer	*taᵤca	ʔoróore-vet	táwpa	čišaw-l	ʔiipaɬ
102.	tail	*kʷaᵤsi	-póoke-n	pí-qwsev	-teleq	xəyuɬ
103.	take, have	*kʷɨ̲ₛ(sɨ)	—	yáw-	hin	-yuuw
104.	this	* ʔi	menée	ʔevíʔ	kaki	pəyaa
105.	three	*pahi	páaheʔ	páahe	masɨx	xəmuk
106.·	tobacco	*pispa	šúuke-y	píiva-t	šow	ʔup
107.	tongue	*lɨ̲ŋi	-nóoŋe-n	-wéeye	-ʔelew	ənəpaɬ
108.	tooth	*taₛma	-táama-n	tamá-	-sa	-yaaw
109.	two	* wo-	wehéeʔ	wéh	ʔiškom'	xəwak
110.	urinate	*siᵤʔi	síiʔ-iy	síiʔ-eš	oxšol	pəsiw
111.	water	*pa	páa-r	páa-la	ʔo	ʔəxaa
112.	white	*toᵤsa	ráawroʔ	xwáyaat	ʔowow	nəməšap
113.	who	*ha(ki)	hakɨi	háx	ʔasku	maap
114.	wing	* ʔaᵤŋa	-máaša-n	kawí-t	-qawawhan	wirewír
115.	winter	*toᵤmo	očóočeve	sovóo-wot	cway'i	xiičur
116.	yellow	* ʔoha	—	ʔaṣó-ʔṣo-š	—	ʔəkwas

198

Voegelin and Hale reconstructed 171 Proto-Uto-Aztecan words, but only enough data are available from the California languages to use 116 words of their list. Considering the linguistic evidence quantitatively, we find that 48 percent of the available Gabrielino terms (43 of the 90 listed) are relatable to the Proto-Uto-Aztecan words; 53 percent of the Luiseño terms (60 of the 114 listed) are relatable. These figures must be considered as only approximate, since the data are not complete; but they suggest that in each language roughly one half of these basic vocabulary items are not directly derived from Proto-Uto-Aztecan. But of these words, a very low percentage can be explained as borrowings from the neighboring Hokan languages. Let us look at these.

The following are possible borrowings from a Hokan language into Shoshonean, either Gabrielino or Luiseño or both: 1, <u>Anus</u>, from Diegueño into Luiseño; 23, <u>Dog</u>, from Chumash into Gabrielino; 80, <u>One</u>, from Chumash into Gabrielino; 60, <u>Know</u>, possibly borrowed from Diegueño into Luiseño; [3] 83, <u>Put</u>, possibly from Diegueño into both Luiseño and Gabrielino. In addition, 26, <u>Eagle</u>, Gabrielino ?ašaw-t, Luiseño ?áṣwo-t shows some similarity with both Chumash and Diegueño forms. Also, possibly related are words for "bird" in Chumash, e.g. Barbareño čwiw, and in many other Hokan languages (McLendon 1964:129). The Gabrielino and Luiseño forms seem most likely to have been borrowed from Chumash.

The following words appear to be widespread in both the Hokan and Shoshonean languages, so that little can be said for the direction of borrowing: 43, <u>Grandfather</u> (mother's father): Proto-Uto-Aztecan *kwa?a, Gabrielino -kwáa?, Luiseño -kwá?; in Yuman, compare Diegueño nəkwaaw, Havasupai nakwáw, Walapai kwáw, Yavapai akwáw, Mohave nakwéw, Maricopa nakwówi, Cocopa nyikwáw, Tipai nakáw, Paipai nakwóo (Wares 1968). <u>Take</u>, 103: Luiseño yáw-, Hopi yáaw-, Comanche yaa-; in Yuman, compare Diegueño -yuuw, Havasupai kweyóhi, Yavapai yóo, Mohave kiɗáw, Maricopa aɗáw, Yuma aɗáw, Cocopa iyác. In 81, <u>Owl</u>, although likenesses are widespread, little can be said, due to the likelihood of onomatopoetic origin. Compare Gabrielino múuhot, Luiseño múu-ta, Southern Ute múpac (Goss 1961), Hopi moŋwɨ (Voegelin 1957), Mayo muu?u (Collard 1962), Yaqui múu?u (Johnson 1962); in Chumash, we have Island, Ventureño, and Barbareño muhu.

It seems that little can be gleaned from this meager evidence of borrowing. The question now arises as to where Gabrielino and Luiseño acquired their terms which are not derived directly from Proto-Uto-Aztecan. It is unlikely that they are all merely the products of change within the language group; and as we have seen, only a few appear to be borrowings from Chumash or Diegueño.

4. Turning again to the archaeology of the south coast area, we know that it was occupied at a relatively remote period; radiocarbon dates show occupation to be older than 6,000 B.C., and the common cultural substratum is dated at 5,000 B.C. It is possible that this substratum at 5,000 B.C. was not of Hokan speakers. Several considerations point to this possibility.

Transitional material between the San Dieguito hunting culture and the La Jollan millingstone culture has not been found. If these two cultures are genetically related and the San Dieguito people spoke a Hokan language, then the time depth for the existence of this language on the coast is great. This would account for the great diversity between the various Hokan languages. But it may be that another culture speaking a different language replaced the early hunters. In either case we cannot say what languages were spoken. As pointed out by Lamb 1964, it is extremely risky to even guess at what language may have been spoken more than a few millennia back, and here we are dealing with more than 8,000 years. We have noted above that the common cultural substratum may have been the uniform line of Hokan inhabitance of which Kroeber spoke, because it is the only uniformity that can be seen archaeologically. But it must be kept in mind how dangerous it is to name cultures from archaeological assemblages. The likenesses in the millingstone cultures could just as easily be attributed to a combination of ecological factors and technological development, which can override microcultural boundaries within a culture area or within linguistic boundaries.

The Santa Barbara area, where the highest cultural development on the south coast was reached, has been a controversial area for archaeologists for a long time. Referring to the development of this culture, Willey and Phillips (1958: 135) state: "The significant thing about these climactic food-gathering cultures is that they seem to have been the end products of extremely long and gradual internal development, without observable stimuli from outside. " Whether this occurred in the Santa Barbara Coastal area or not is an interesting question. Many sequences have been postulated for the area, but perhaps the best known of the early work is that of Rogers 1929: Oak Grove (milling-stone culture) — Hunting — Canalino (highly developed marine-oriented economy). He does not see the Canalino as a development out of the millingstone culture through a hunting stage, but as separate and as an entire replacement by new peoples.

Another archaeologist, William Harrison, has reported evidence (personal communication, 1964) that the people of the hunting culture did exist, and that they arrived with a fully developed marine economy based upon the hunting of large sea mammals. He feels that there was an exchange between the two groups, millingstone and hunting people, but that they remained as distinct ethnic groups, possibly up to contact. From this point of view the Canalino culture was a florescence of the hunting people but did not originate from the millingstone culture.

If one is inclined to agree with Rogers and Harrison, it is possible that the Hokan speakers came to the coast in what Rogers calls the hunting stage, and that the common cultural substratum is either the result of a universal ecological adaptation in the area, or that the substratum was composed of people speaking a common language other than Hokan.

From the linguistic side, relevant considerations are presented by Lamb in his paper on 'Linguistic diversification and extinction in North America'. He believes that the rate of extinction of languages is quite high, and that it is therefore impossible to tell what language was spoken in a culture known only from archaeological material. He estimates that less than one-sixth of the languages ever spoken in North America were represented at the time of contact; in this view, the rapid extinction of languages is an old phenomenon, not one which has taken place only in the last few centuries. Lamb summarizes his observations on linguistic extinction as follows (1964:463-4):

(1) linguistic diversification takes place because a language gets spread into a geographic area too large

for sufficient density of communication to maintain
unity; (2) linguistic diversification therefore usually implies an earlier territorial expansion of a
language; (3) such territorial expansion ordinarily
takes place at the expense of other languages; (4)
expansion, diversification and extinction are thus
all intimately related to one another.

He further adds that the type of culture determines the amount of diversification; i.e., a culture capable of maintaining a high population
density, such as an agricultural community, is less likely to diversi-
fy than people who spread out into an area to hunt and thus become
separated.

Since a large number of words in Gabrielino and Luiseño do
not derive from either Proto-Uto-Aztecan or from Hokan borrowings,
it seems likely that the Uto-Aztecan speakers encountered other Indians speaking a language (or languages) now presumably extinct, and
that they lived in the same area long enough to take over a lot of vocabulary. It seems most likely that the moving out to the coast by the
Shoshonean speakers was both gradual and peaceful. It is not likely
that these people, with their low-level desert economy, could ever
have had any military power. A glance at a physical map of the area
reveals that there is only one good pass out of the desert toward the
coastal area, and this probably acted as a funnel through which the
small groups of migrants moved and spread out.

It appears that no definite conclusions can be reached at this
time. Unfortunately, since native speakers of the California languages
are dying out, and important archaeological sites have long since been
destroyed by highway construction and population expansion, it is possible that many questions will never be answered. Returning to Kroeber's hypothesis, we can agree with him that the Shoshonean speakers
must have come out from the Great Basin, since a continuous line of
historical cultures exists from the Great Basin to the coast; but when
this occurred or what or who they encountered on arrival still remains
a mystery. Furthermore, Kroeber's assumption that the Shoshoneans
replaced a specifically Hokan population, thereby splitting off the Chumash from the Yumans, is clearly unwarranted.

NOTES

This article has been revised from its 1969 publication, principally in
that the Chumash forms have been replaced by fuller and more accu-
rate transcriptions, kindly provided by Richard Applegate. In addition,
the Diegueño data have been revised by reference to Couro and Hutcheson 1973. This improved data base allows the recognition of a few
more putative borrowings; it does not, however, change the general
conclusions of the paper.
[1] No archaeological data are available for the area south of
the border.
[2] Chumash data are from Ventureño, unless otherwise speci-
fied as Y (Ynezeño) or B (Barbareño). Ventureño and Ynezeño forms
are from the unpublished MSS of J. P. Harrington; Barbareño is from
Madison Beeler's field data.
[3] In this last case, the likeness in forms may be due to accident. Compare the Luiseño form ʔayále- with the following forms
from Yuman dialects (Wares 1968): Cocopa uyáx, ʔuʔyáa; Northern
Diegueño ʔuyáaw; Campo ʔnyáaw; Tipai uyáa.

REFERENCES

Bright, Marcia. 1965. California radiocarbon dates. UCLA Archaeo-
          logical Survey, Annual Report, 7.363-76.
Bright, William. 1968. A Luiseño dictionary. (University of Califor-
          nia publications in linguistics, 51.) Berkeley and Los Angeles.
Canonge, Eliot. 1958. Comanche texts. Norman, Oklahoma: Summer
          Institute of Linguistics.
Collard, Howard and Elizabeth. 1962. Vocabulario mayo. México:
          Instituto Lingüístico de Verano.
Couro, T., and C. Hutcheson. 1973. Dictionary of Mesa Grande Die-
          gueño. Banning, California: Malki Museum.
Goss, James. 1961. Short dictionary of the Ute language. Ignacio,
          Colorado: Southern Ute Tribe.
Heizer, R. F., and M. A. Whipple (eds). 1951. The California In-
          dians, a source book. Berkeley and Los Angeles: University
          of California Press.
Henshaw, H. W. 1955. California Indian linguistic records: the Mis-
          sion Indian vocabularies of H. W. Henshaw, ed. by R. F.

Heizer. (Anthropological Records, 15:2.) Berkeley and Los
        Angeles: University of California Press.
Johnson, Jean B. 1962. El idioma yaqui. México: I.N.A.H.
Kroeber, A. L. 1910. The Chumash and Costanoan languages.
        (UCPAAE 9.237-271.) Berkeley: University of California
        Press.
_____. 1923. The history of native culture in California. UCPAAE
        20.145-42. (Reprinted in Heizer and Whipple 1951, pp. 104-
        20.)
_____. 1925. Handbook of the Indians of California. (BAE-B 78.)
        Washington, D.C.: Government Printing Office.
Lamb, Sydney M. 1964. Linguistic diversification and extinction in
        North America. XXXV Congreso Internacional de American-
        istas, Actas y Memorias, 2.457-64. México.
McLendon, Sally. 1964. Northern Hokan (B) and (C): a comparison of
        Eastern Pomo and Yana. University of California Publications
        in Linguistics 34.126-44.
Pinart, Alphonse. 1952. California Indian linguistic records: the Mis-
        sion Indian vocabularies of Alphonse Pinart, ed. by R. F.
        Heizer. (Anthropological Records, 15:1.) Berkeley and Los
        Angeles: University of California Press.
Reinman, Fred M. 1964. Maritime adaptation on San Nicolas, Cali-
        fornia: a preliminary and speculative evaluation. UCLA Ar-
        chaeological Survey, Annual Report, 6.47-80.
_____, and Sam-Joe Townsend. 1960. Six burial sites on San
        Nicolas Island. UCLA Archaeological Survey, Annual Report,
        2.1-134.
Rogers, David Banks. 1929. Prehistoric man of the Santa Barbara
        coast. Santa Barbara: Museum of Natural History.
Rozaire, Charles E. 1959. Archaeological investigations at two sites
        on San Nicolas Island, California. Masterkey 34.129-52.
Voegelin, C. F. and F. M. 1957. Hopi domains. (IJAL Memoir 14.)
        Baltimore.
Voegelin, C. F. and F. M., and Kenneth L. Hale. 1962. Typological
        and comparative grammar of Uto-Aztecan: I (Phonology).
        (IJAL Memoir 17.) Baltimore.
Wallace, William James. 1954. The Little Sycamore site and the
        early milling stone cultures of Southern California. American
        Antiquity 20.112-23.
Wares, Alan C. 1968. A comparative study of Yuman consonantism.
        The Hague: Mouton.

Warren, Claude N.; D. L. True; and Ardith A. Eudey. 1961. Early
    gathering complexes of western San Diego County: results
    and interpretation of an archaeological survey. UCLA Archae-
    ological Survey, Annual Report, 3. 1–106.
Willey, Gordon R., and Philip Phillips. 1958. Method and theory in
    American archaeology. Chicago: University of Chicago Press.

16 | On Linguistic Unrelatedness

This is a belated reaction to an article in the International Journal of American Linguistics by Paul R. Turner, attempting to show that two languages of Mexico, Seri and Tequistlatec (Chontal de Oaxaca), which have widely been regarded since 1915 as related within the Hokan stock, are in fact unrelated.[1] I would like to claim, in rebuttal, (1) that it is impossible to prove the lack of relationship between any two languages, and (2) that the positive evidence for the relationship of Seri and Tequistlatec is in fact greater than admitted by Turner.

There are insurmountable difficulties in proving that languages are not related. Let us suppose that someone states that all languages of the world had a common origin at a time depth of two million years. If we assume that change has always been a fact of linguistic history, and at rates comparable to those observed in recent centuries, then we could hardly expect that any specific lexical items of 'Proto-Human' would have survived into modern times. Comparing the vocabularies of, let us say, English and Chinese, we could not expect to find any very convincing list of cognates. And yet we could not say that the alleged common origin was disproven by the lack of such data; we could only say that it is not demonstrable from the data available. The possibility of a single origin for all languages remains neither provable nor disprovable.

Ignoring these considerations, Turner attempts to disprove the relationship of Seri and Tequistlatec on several grounds. The most important are these: (1) In a hundred-word glottochronological list, he identified only 8% of apparent cognates, which might be attributable simply to accident. (2) When another 500 word pairs were

added, the percentage of apparent cognates dropped even lower. (3)
A comparison of kinship systems in the two languages reveals a lack
of cognates, and different semantic structures besides. (4) A comparison of numeral systems gives similar results. (5) Finally, "it
would be difficult to explain how two related languages could have different grammatical categories, and such is the case with Seri and
Chontal" (page 238). The examples show that Turner is not thinking
of grammatical differences in the usual sense, but of semantic differences — e.g., "Seri has separate words for the urine of men and women... Chontal does not have this feature" (page 239).

These arguments may be dealt with in turn:

(1) In the use of the glottochronological word list, the results depend a great deal on the criteria for recognizing cognates,
and there may in fact be more positive evidence than is recognized
by Turner. Turner has apparently relied on impressionistic judge-
ments in arriving at his estimate of 8% for a 100-word list. By contrast, in an earlier lexico-statistical study of these languages,[2] I
attempted to apply objective criteria, including the recognition of regular phonological correspondences. In the resulting comparison of 190
pairs (based on Swadesh's 200-word list), I counted 40 apparent cognates, or 21 percent. Nine apparent sound correspondences were
recognized, each exemplified by from three to six examples. Some
of the cognate pairs, and some of the sound-correspondences, are
probably spurious, but they were arrived at on a nonimpressionistic
basis, which produced contrastive results when applied to other language pairs; e.g., the comparison of Tequistlatec with Jicaque yield-
ed only 13% cognates and two sound correspondences. One may suspect that Turner's inability to identify cognates is based on a fundamental misunderstanding as to the nature of the task; thus he writes,
"Because of the lack of actual cognates, it seems unnecessary to even
attempt to describe systematic phonemic correspondences..." He
has the cart before the horse: true cognates can only be recognized
on the basis of sound correspondences. To cite a familiar example
from Bloomfield:[3] English day and Latin dies, in spite of their similarity, are not cognates, and precisely because they do not fit into
regular phonological patterns.

(2) The addition of another 500 word pairs to the comparison does not necessarily make the results more reliable, especially

if an objective means for counting cognates is still lacking. In addition, the question arises of how the additional 500 words were chosen. If they include much 'cultural' rather than 'basic' vocabulary, then of course they will only obscure whatever genetic link may exist.

(3) The use of kinship systems in studying the genetic relationships between languages is full of dangers. On the one hand, the near-universality of terms like 'papa, mama, tata, nana' may give a false impression of genetic closeness. On the other hand, and more importantly for the present discussion, kinship terms, as well as semantic characteristics of kinship systems, have especially close ties to specific cultures, and are frequently borrowed: note that English 'uncle, aunt, nephew, niece, cousin' are all loans from French. A comparison of two Indo-European languages like English and Hindi shows quite different semantic structures: unlike English, Hindi distinguishes sex of linking kin in the case of grand-relatives and collaterals; it distinguishes elder uncles and aunts from younger ones; and so on. The differences between Seri and Tequistlatec kinship systems are likely to reflect their association with different culture areas, rather than genetic affiliation.

(4) Numeral systems resemble kinship systems in being closely tied to cultural factors, and frequently borrowed, as has been emphasized by Emeneau.[4] Most of the languages of East and Southeast Asia have borrowed the majority of their numerals from Chinese; many Latin American Indian languages have now borrowed most of the Spanish numerals. The differences between Seri and Tequistlatec numerals simply prove nothing.

(5) Differences of semantic structure between languages have been referred to above, in connection with kinship systems. The general point is that semantic structures are highly culture-bound (some might say that they constitute cultures); they are subject to the well-known processes of cultural change, including borrowing. In this they contrast with purely phonological and grammatical aspects of language, which change in different and slower ways, and less often by borrowing. Many English-Hindi semantic differences could be cited, besides the Hindi kinship examples given above: e. g., Hindi /p̃āw/ foot (a cognate with the English) also includes leg — the semantic grouping probably being borrowed from Dravidian /kāl/ foot,

leg. Similarly, the semantic differences between Seri and Tequistlatec no doubt have a great deal to do with the very diverse culture
areas in which the two languages are spoken, but very little to do with
possible genetic relationship.

The relationship between Seri and Tequistlatec is certainly
not a close one, and I do not wish to claim that it has been firmly established; my 190-word lexicostatistic comparison is, I feel, inadequate for that purpose. But at least there is a reasonable hypothesis
of relationship, testable when a dictionary of Tequistlatec becomes
generally available, to compare with the Moser's dictionary of Seri.[5]

NOTES

[1]Paul L. Turner, Seri and Chontal (Tequistlateco), IJAL
33.235-39 (1967). The relation was posited in A. L. Kroeber,
Serian, Tequistlatecan, and Hokan, UCPAAE 11.279-90 (1915).
It would be welcome if the misleading term 'Chontal'
could be dropped. As was pointed out by D. G. Brinton (Chontales
and Popolucas, Proc. Int. Cong. of Americanists 8.556-64, Paris
1892), the term 'Chontal' has been applied to several linguistically
and ethnically diverse groups (including a Mayan group in Tabasco,
as well as the Tequistlatec), and confusion could be avoided if the
term were entirely eliminated.
[2]William Bright, Glottochronologic counts of Hokaltecan
material, Lg. 32.42-48 (1956).
[3]Leonard Bloomfield, Language (New York, 1933), pp. 346,
351-4.
[4]M. B. Emeneau, Numerals in comparative linguistics, Bull.
Inst. Hist. & Philol., Academia Sinica, vol. 29 (1967).
[5]Edward and Mary Moser, Vocabulario Seri (Mexico, 1961).
[Cf. now Paul & Shirley Turner, Dictionary: Chontal to Spanish-
English, Spanish to Chontal (Tucson, 1971).]

17 | North American Indian Language Contact

Scope

The proposed scope of this article includes the processes and effects of bilingualism and of linguistic acculturation involving the native languages of North American Indians in their contacts with each other and with European languages (specifically English, Spanish, French, and Russian). However, as will be seen below, there is relatively little work to report as regards ongoing processes of language contact; the bulk of published research deals with the post-facto results of such contact, especially as manifested in lexical borrowings. Geographically, the present survey covers mainly the area from the Arctic to the Rio Grande, with only a few incidental excursions into Mexico.

An important predecessor of this article is Haugen's monograph on Bilingualism in the Americas (1956), which provides bibliographical coverage and comment for both North and South America, and for colonial, immigrant, and creolized languages, as well as for the native languages. The successor to that work is Haugen's article, "Bilingualism, language contact, and immigrant languages in the United States", appearing in this volume,* but only dealing briefly with American Indian languages. Both of these works by Haugen provide important orientation into research on the theory of language contact. I have attempted to avoid unnecessary duplication of Haugen's work; thus, major emphasis in what follows is placed on data-oriented research reported since 1956.

---

*Current Trends in Linguistics: 10: North America, ed. by T. A. Sebeok (The Hague: Mouton, 1973).

1. Processes of Language Contact

    The recent popularity of sociolinguistics has brought in-
creasing attention to the dynamics and functions of language contact.
Wherever speakers of two or more languages are interacting with
each other, many questions can be asked: will speakers of A learn
language B, or will B speakers learn A, or both? Will a pidginized
language arise, instead of or in addition to other developments? In
what situations will a bilingual choose to use one or the other of his
languages? Given the existence of bilingualism, to what extent can
linguistic borrowing be expected, as contrasted with new uses of native linguistic materials? Where borrowing occurs, what will be its
effects on semantic, grammatical, and phonological structure? There
are still more basic questions: in the language contact situation, how
are the changes which occur related to speakers' attitudes toward
their own languages and toward the languages with which they are in
contact? What determines such attitudes toward languages? What
role is played by political and social relationships between the groups
in contact? What effect can deliberate language planning have? And,
following a historical process which is typical of language contact in
North America, we may ask: what factors bring about an end to bilingualism, when one language completely replaces another, as English
tends to replace the native languages? What are the psychological
and sociological circumstances of language obsolescence and extinction?

    These are questions which have, for the most part, not yet
been conclusively answered; the attempts to answer them constitute
an exciting branch of current research. Regarding the processes of
North American Indian language contact, however, our information
is relatively scanty. The study of sociolinguistic process has become
fashionable only in fairly recent years; but in the meantime, many
aboriginal languages have become extinct, and most others have become obsolescent. Thus we have lost many opportunities to study,
in vivo, the formative stages of bilingualism and of linguistic acculturation in native North America. Fortunately, however, a few languages are still in good health; Navajo, for instance, is spoken by a
large and increasing number of Indians, including both monolinguals
and bilinguals, and linguistic acculturation under the influence of English is an on-going process. Such present-day situations of language
contact offer attractive research possibilities.

Two types of language contact may be distinguished in our area: (1) that between one Indian language and another, which has clearly been important since pre-Columbian times, and retains importance in some areas; and (2) that between Indian languages and European languages, this being of course the dominant type of language contact in the more recent past. The distinction of these two types is founded not on differences of linguistic structure, but on the sociological differences in contact situations: only the European contact was accompanied by massive forcible conquest, exploitation, and genocide.

1.1 Contact between Native Languages

Extensive bilingualism and borrowing between Indian languages in prehistoric times is attested by the continuing existence of well-defined linguistic areas, where languages of evidently distinct genetic origins have, through processes of diffusion, come to share features of semantic, grammatical and phonological structure; such areas are characterized in Joel Sherzer's paper in the present volume.* However, we can at present only speculate as to the exact sociolinguistic processes which produced such areal phenomena. (Works focusing on the results of those processes are discussed in §2.1, below.) A very few studies have discussed the dynamics of recent bilingualism between American Indian languages: Olmsted (1954) for Achumawi and Atsugewi in northeastern California, Mierau (1963) for Yavapai and Apache in Arizona, and Voegelin and Schutz (1967) for the Southwest generally.

1.2 Contact with European Languages

Where Indian and European languages have come together, it has been rare for any significant number of Whites to learn the Indian languages. In some regions, for limited periods, Whites and Indians have communicated through pidgin languages: the one best known, used in the Pacific Northwest, was Chinook Jargon, with a largely Indian lexical base (see 2.1, below); in some other areas, varieties of American Indian Pidgin English were used, with a largely English lexical base (Hall and Leechman 1955). The tendency which has prevailed, however, has been that Indians have learned a Euro-

---

*Current Trends in Linguistics, op. cit.

pean language: Spanish in California and the Southwest, Russian in
Alaska, French in Quebec and Louisiana, and English elsewhere.
With the increasing dominance of Anglo society, Spanish, Russian,
and (in some areas) French have been supplemented or supplanted by
English as the Indians' language of contact with Whites. And from one
generation to the next, Indians have tended to use the European languages more, to introduce more European elements into their native
speech, and eventually to lose their native language entirely. A frequent result is that, although ethnically identifiable groups of Indians
remain, there may — as in the case of the Chumash in Southern California — be no individual who remembers more than a few words of
his ancestral language.

Glimpses of the processes of linguistic acculturation are provided by several of the contributors to the volume Perspectives in
American Indian culture change, edited by E. H. Spicer (1961). For
example, we may quote Dozier's article on the Rio Grande pueblos:

> The addition of the Spanish language to the Pueblo
> dialects must be considered an important acquisition.
> Undoubtedly not all Pueblo adults spoke Spanish, but
> the records reveal that during the revolt [of 1680] and
> after the reconquest [of 1693] communication between
> the Indians and Spaniards presented no difficulties.
> It is very probable that the Spanish language, even at
> this early date, had become a lingua franca among
> the Pueblos. By adopting Spanish as the language for
> communicating with the outside world, the individual
> Pueblo linguistic communities retained their own in-
> digenous languages as tools for retaining and perpet-
> uating their cherished and closely guarded customs
> and beliefs (141)...[In the contemporary period] Eng-
> lish is now an important second language, but the na-
> tive idioms continue to be dominant. Pueblo Indians
> are purists with regard to their language, a factor
> related to the phenomenon of compartmentalization.
> The native language is considered an area of cul-
> ture that must not be polluted by foreign loans...
> Pueblo speakers are keenly aware of borrowed terms
> and tend to delete or restrict their usage in the pres-
> ence of outsiders... The coinage of new words and the

extension of old meanings to cover new cultural acqui-
sitions are preferred to outright borrowing (Dozier 1961:
141, 174-5).

Other aspects of English-Indian bilingualism are touched upon by
Sasaki and Olmsted (1953), with reference to the Navajo; by Carroll
and Casagrande (1958), who note the tendency of bilingual Navajo to
operate more in terms of English semantic structures than monolingual Navajo; by Scott (1960), studying the Mescalero Apache; by
Polgar (1960), in connection with Mesquakie (Fox) biculturation; by
Ervin (1961), who comments further on Navajo bilingualism; by Fox
(1968), for the Keresan of New Mexico; and by Bodine (1968), discussing trends in personal names at Taos. Voegelin (1959) reports on
the 'expansion' of Hopi, through English loans, in the casual or non-
formal usage of bilinguals.

Recently, there has been new interest in the theoretical and
practical problems of teaching English to American Indians, in areas
such as the Southwest where non-standard English or Indian monolin-
gualism are still common; relevant publications include Shuy 1965,
Cook and Sharp 1966, Ohanessian 1967, and Bauer 1968.

Finally, regarding the obsolescence and extinction of American Indian languages in the contact situation, one may refer to the
pioneering article of Swadesh (1948). To end this section on a less
gloomy note, however, it may be observed that several obsolescent
languages are showing new signs of life; in southern California, for
instance, during 1969, classes in the Luiseño, Cupeño, and Diegueño
languages were being held by Indians, for Indians, and on Indian ini-
tiative, with some advice from White linguists. Such efforts may not
guarantee the survival of the languages in question, but they are an
encouraging sign of Indians' renewed interest and pride in their own
cultural and linguistic heritage.

2. Results of Language Contact

The majority of published studies of Amerindian language
contact are in a sense philological, in that they take as their data the
written records which reflect the results of the contact process; these

may be published texts or dictionaries, or unpublished fieldnotes.
Such data have been variously presented — either essentially unanalyzed, as of intrinsic interest; or interpreted in order to shed light on
specific histories of culture contact; or used to illustrate supposed
general principles of bilingualism and linguistic acculturation.

We may classify studies in the field by basically sociological
criteria, as was done in §1.0 above. Thus we have the following types:
(1) Contact occurs between two or more Indian groups; from the socio-
cultural point of view, this is essentially a meeting of equals, and the
linguistic results tend to show diffusion of semantic, grammatical,
and phonological features. (2) Contact occurs between Indian and
White, and the topic of interest involves features of the Indian's culture. As the White holds the dominant position, the areas of his interest in native culture are relatively limited: he wants to be able to
identify geographical features in the territory originally occupied by
the Indian; and he wants names for certain American flora and fauna
known to the Indian, as well as for some of the more conspicuous features of the Indian's material culture. The linguistic results consist,
then, of a large number of borrowed place names, from Massachu-
setts to Alaska, and of a much smaller number of common nouns such
as squash (the vegetable, from New England Algonkian), abalone (a
shellfish, from Costanoan of California), and kayak (from Eskimo).
(3) Contact occurs between Indian and White, and the topic of interest
involves features of the dominant white culture. In such cases the
force of acculturation, whether forced or spontaneous, has of course
generally tended to the replacement of the Indian culture and language;
the linguistic results usually include extensive new usages of Indian
lexical elements, plus varying amounts of lexical borrowing from
European sources — commonly consisting mainly of nouns which designate features of White culture, but occasionally also including other
parts of speech (see §2.3.2, below). It is of interest to note that, by
contrast with the situation of contact between Indian languages, the
Indian-White relationship in North America seems to result in little
phonological borrowing, and almost no grammatical borrowing. Rather, it appears that obsolescence and extinction have overtaken most
of the languages in our area before structural or deep-level borrowing could occur.

2.1 Effects among Native Languages

The results of past contact between Indian languages are reflected above all in the phenomenon of linguistic areas: see §1.1
above, and the article by Sherzer referred to above. Specific cases of
apparent borrowing are discussed in Kroeber 1959 (from Athabaskan
to Yuki, in central California), Bright 1959 (between Yurok and Karok,
northwestern California), Callaghan 1964 (by Lake Miwok, from its
neighbor languages in central California), Jacobsen 1966 (from Uto-
Aztecan to Washo, in Nevada), Pinnow 1968 (in the Na-Dené phylum),
and W. and M. Bright 1969 (between Hokan and Uto-Aztecan in southern California). Dozier (1955) reports the influence of Hopi on Arizona Tewa in the area of kinship, where borrowing has involved semantic structure rather than the forms of words (for other cases of
semantic acculturation, see §2.3.1).

Cases are known of American pidgin languages used between
different tribes in the contact situation. The Mobilian Jargon, used
in the Southeast, is little known; much more documentation is available for the Chinook Jargon of the Pacific Northwest, e.g. in Shaw
1909, Boas 1933, and Jacobs 1932, 1936. In the Great Plains, a system of communication by hand gestures served a similar function (cf.
Kroeber 1958; Voegelin 1958).

A few attempts have been made to generalize about results
of prehistoric language contact in North America; thus Sapir (1916)
discusses the detection of old loan words as evidence for culture-his-
torical reconstruction. Haudricourt (1961) hypothesizes that large
phoneme inventories, such as are found in languages of the Pacific
Northwest, are a reflection of extensive 'egalitarian' multilingualism
(the Lake Miwok case reported by Callaghan, 1964, is another plausible example). Lamb (1964) argues that pre-Columbian language contact must have already resulted in the extinction of many languages
and even whole language families, which are thus unrecoverable by
reconstruction; this hypothesis is questioned by C. F. and F. M.
Voegelin (1965).

2.2 Indian Words in European Languages

As noted above, the majority of these are place-names. The
etymological literature on the subject is extensive but not of very good

quality; the researchers involved have too often lacked sophistication either in general linguistics or in the structures of the relevant Indian languages. Typical examples are the place-name dictionaries for Arizona by Granger (1960), for California by Gudde (1960), and for New Mexico by Pearce (1965); these have been criticized in detail by Bright (1962a, 1962b, and 1967b, respectively). Specialists in American Indian linguistics have, however, produced some good place-name studies in recent years; excellent discussions of the general principles involved are provided by Beeler (1957) and by Lounsbury (1960); the latter work also gives exemplary etymological treatment for a number of Iroquois place-names. Other linguistically sophisticated treatments of particular place-names are those of Bright (1952b), Beeler (1954, 1955, and 1966), Oswalt (1960) (all the above relate to California), and Day (1961) (for New England). The name of Taos (New Mexico), for which a Spanish etymology was proposed by Jones (1960), has been shown by Trager (1960) to have an Indian source. And finally, Teeter (1958) has shown the name of Loleta, California, to be a classic put-on: it represents the Wiyot for 'Let's copulate!'

When place-names are set aside, the number of other loans from native North American languages is relatively small. Several important words for American plant foods are in fact borrowed, through Spanish, from Indian languages of the Caribbean, such as potato or maize, or from the Aztec (Nahuatl) of Mexico, such as tomato, avocado, chocolate, cocoa (cf. Watson 1938). The majority of words which have entered English from north of the Rio Grande are from the Algonkian languages encountered by the earliest English colonists; familiar examples are persimmon, pecan, raccoon, opossum, chipmunk, skunk, papoose, wigwam. A few such loans have undergone curious folk-etymologies — e.g., whiskey-jack 'Canada jay' from earlier Whiskey-john; c.f. Cree wiskitjân. As settlement moved westward, the number of borrowings seems to have become less.

The only cases known to me from Californian languages are the following: Spanish and English islay 'holly-leafed cherry' from Salinan; Sp. aulón, Eng. abalone from Costanoan; and Eng. chuckwalla 'lizard sp.' from Cahuilla čáxwal. The principal published reference for American Indian loans in European languages (other than place-names) is Friederici 1947.

2.3 Effects of European on Native Languages

        As has been noted, the effects of contact between Europeans
and Indians are more apparent in the Indian languages than in the European. We may distinguish three main types of development, which
reflect the typology of linguistic innovation provided by Haugen (1956:
101). (1) In certain types of culture contact, when bilingualism is
minimal, there may nevertheless be motivation to name new cultural
items. This can be done entirely with native lexical materials, by
two processes: (a) semantic extension, as when the word for 'arrow'
is extended to 'bullet', or 'dog' to 'horse' in many Indian languages;
(b) new combination — by whatever morphosyntactic devices a language may have — as when a hotel is called an 'eating-place'. As reported by Voegelin and Hymes 1953, such processes are well attested
in published dictionaries of American Indian languages. (2) Under
more favorable conditions of culture contact, bilingualism increases,
facilitating the admission of loanwords. (Note, however, that this
development may chronologically precede a period of type 1, as described in Herzog 1941.) The degree to which such loans are found
varies greatly from one Indian language to another: in areas of Spanish contact such as California, 'bullet' and 'horse' are frequently designated by native imitations of bala and caballo, but loans from English are in general less widely attested. Many languages have maintained European contacts for centuries and yet admitted very few loan
words. Thus Navajo has borrowed very little from Spanish, and this
may be correlated with a low degree of Navajo-Spanish bilingualism.
On the other hand, Pueblo languages such Santa Clara Tewa have
also been relatively conservative in their borrowing (Dozier 1956),
though Indian-Spanish bilingualism was common for many years.
(Possible explanations for such phenomena are discussed in §3, below.) Alongside loanwords, we also find occasional 'translation borrowings' ('loanshifts' or 'calques'): thus in Karok, a pear can be
called vírusur 'bear', because the Indians, lacking voiceless stops,
tended to equate the English bear and pear. Another possible type of
loan — the borrowing of linguistic structure — is, as noted above,
relatively rare in native North America. (3) In a third development,
bilingualism prevails to the extent that the native language takes on
secondary importance, becoming gradually obsolescent. In these circumstances, there is weakened motivation for new innovations in the
native language, since communication about elements of European

culture can simply be carried out in a European language. Some languages seem to have passed through the second type of development in contact with one European language, and then entered the third with another European language. Thus McLendon (1969) identifies about 150 Spanish loans in the Eastern Pomo language of California, but notes (page 39, fn. 2): 'Curiously enough, despite more than 100 years of contact, hardly a dozen English-derived forms are used by EP speakers. Presumably this reflects (in part) the increasing preference, in the frame of an English-speaking environment, for bilingualism in lieu of expansion of the indigenous lexicon.'

Published accounts of lexical innovations in native languages, encompassing use of both native and borrowed materials, include the following works: Bright 1952a (on Karok of northwestern California) and Bright 1960a (on terms for introduced domestic animals in California as a whole); Casagrande 1954-55 (for Comanche — discussed by Haugen 1956:16-19, 101, and by Troike 1956); Dozier 1956 and 1967 (for various languages of the Southwest); Garvin 1948 (for Kutenai of Idaho); Huot 1948 for Mohawk; Gross 1951 and Salzmann 1951 (for divergent reports on Arapaho); Herzog 1941 (for Pima in the Southwest); Johnson 1943 and Spicer 1943 (for Yaqui, originally spoken in northwestern Mexico, but now also in Arizona); Voegelin 1959 (for Hopi); and Lee 1943 (for Wintu of northern California).

2.3.1 Use of native elements

Some studies have focused particularly on innovation by use of native lexical resources, as being the dominant process reflected in the data for some languages. A particularly interesting approach to lexical innovation of this type is to view it as a partial restructuring of the native semantic system. Thus Basso (1967) shows that the Apache extension of body-part terms to automotive parts ('liver' to 'battery', etc.) is not a piecemeal process, but a well-motivated structural shift (cf. also the comment of Adams 1968). In Karok, a class of new coinages for colors not aboriginally distinguished ('smoke-like' for 'blue', 'grass-like' for 'green'), can be seen as exemplifying <u>semantic</u> borrowing, a process seldom reported (Bright 1952a:56; cf. the Hopi-Tewa case reported in Dozier 1955, and mentioned in §2.1 above). The recent revival of semantics among linguists has also produced an interesting study by Lindenfeld (1971) in which semantic structure is seen as impeding borrowing in a language (Yaqui) which has otherwise been relatively hospitable to Spanish elements.

2.3.2 Loanwords from European languages

A relatively large amount of attention has been given to words borrowed from European sources. The richest materials are on borrowings from Spanish in the Southwest: literature includes Hoijer (1939) on Chiricahua Apache; Trager (1944) on Taos, with the note of Hall (1947); Spencer (1947) on Keresan, with Miller (1959-60) for Acoma Keresan in particular; and Dockstader (1955) for Hopi. Some complex developments of Spanish loanwords for 'cat' in the Southwest and in Latin America are discussed in Landar 1959, Bright 1960b, Landar 1961, and Crowley 1962, with the fullest and most final word to date being provided by Kiddle (1964). Spanish loans in Californian languages have also been well documented; see W. and E. Bright 1959 for Patwin, Shipley 1962 for Central California in general, Sawyer 1964a, b for Wappo, and McLendon 1969 for Eastern Pomo and neighboring languages. Borrowings from Spanish in the Southeast United States are discussed by Sturtevant (1962), and a surprising Spanish loan in Eskimo by Taylor (1962).

Studies of loans from other sources are harder to find. French has furnished some loans to Tunica in the Southeast (Haas 1947), and to Algonkian (Geary 1945; Haas 1968), though few data on French loans in the northeast are available. Russian has been a major source for loans in Alaskan Eskimo (Hammerich 1954; Worth 1963), and — because of the brief Russian attempt to colonize Central California — in one California language, Southwestern Pomo (Oswalt 1958; see also the note of Worth 1960). English loans in a single Hopi text are reported by Kennard (1963). An instance of the English (actually Scottish) family name McKay being borrowed as an ethnonym, 'white man', in Northern California, is reported in Bright 1967a. Scattered data on other loanwords from all these European sources can be found among the references listed in §2.3.

3. Explanations

As reported above, there have been few studies of Amerindian language contact in vivo; the bulk of publications, as reported

in §2 above, simply present the lexical results of linguistic acculturation. An inspection of these results raises certain questions: why
do some Indian languages borrow much more than others? Why have
certain Indian languages, in contact with more than one European
model, borrowed much more from one than another? Given that borrowings are most likely to be nouns, plus occasional adjectives and
verbs, why do certain languages borrow significant numbers of 'function words' such as prepositions and conjunctions?

   The general question of differential degrees of borrowing has
been discussed most cogently by Dozier (1956), in a Southwestern context. His hypothesis is, essentially, that the amount of borrowing is
mainly determined by socio-cultural rather than purely linguistic
facts: it will be at a maximum where Europeans' policy toward the
Indians is benevolent, and at a minimum where that policy is repres-
sive. Support for this idea is provided from California languages in
Bright 1960a and, for an Aztec dialect in Mexico, in Bright and Thiel
1965.

   As to why certain types of words are borrowed, but not others, there has been very little discussion. Alongside nouns for artifacts, animals of acculturation, etc., we encounter items like Spanish trabajo 'work' as a loan into most languages of Central and Southern California (and, on phonological evidence, a very early loan). At
this point we might ask: didn't the Indians, in aboriginal times, live
by digging roots, carrying water, chopping wood, and other arduous
activities classifiable as 'work'? And if so, why did they need to
borrow a Spanish word for such activity? An answer is suggested by
McLuhan (1964:129): ' "Work"...does not exist in a nonliterate world.
The primitive hunter or fisherman did no work, any more than does
the poet, painter, or thinker of today. Where the whole man is involved there is no work.' We may say, then, that the Indian borrowing of the Spanish word was prompted not so much by introduction of
new modes of physical activity, but by a new semantic categorization
of such activity.

   Similar explanations may eventually be found for cases
where even more abstract terms have apparently been borrowed, as
when Cahuilla of Southern California uses Spanish más 'more'. A
real challenge is presented by Indian languages of Mexico which show

borrowing of many Spanish prepositions and conjunctions (e.g. , cf.
Hasler 1961; Bright and Thiel 1965). We must assume that the Indian
languages involved had their own native systems of indicating abstract
relationships; but we may speculate that those systems proved inadequate to the new world view which came in with Spanish civilization, and
that a motive for the borrowing of Spanish function words was thereby
provided. The testing of such speculations awaits new fieldwork, psy-
cholinguistically and sociolinguistically oriented, on the dynamics of
language contact in areas where — as among the Navajo — the process
is still in full swing.

REFERENCES

Adams, William Y. 1968. Navaho automotive terminology. AmA 70.
    1181.
Basso, Keith H. 1967. Semantic aspects of linguistic acculturation.
    AmA 69. 471-7.
Bauer, Evelyn. 1968. Teaching English to North American Indians in
    BIA schools. Linguistic Reporter 10: 4. 1-3. Washington,
    D. C. , CAL.
Beeler, M. S. 1954. Sonoma, Carquinez, Umunhum, Colma: Some
    disputed California names. WF 13. 268-77.
_____. 1955. Yosemite and Tamalpais. Names 3. 185-8.
_____. 1957. On etymologizing Indian place-names. Names 5. 236-
    40.
_____. 1966. Hueneme. Names 14. 36-40.
Boas, Franz. 1933. Note on the Chinook Jargon. Lg 9. 208-13.
Bodine, John J. 1968. Taos names: A clue to linguistic acculturation.
    AnL 10/5. 23-7.
Bright, William. 1952a. Linguistic innovations in Karok. IJAL 18.
    53-62. [In this volume, pp. 98-115.]
_____. 1952b. Some place names on the Klamath River. WF 11. 121-
    2.
_____. 1959. Review of The Yurok language, by R. H. Robins. Lg
    35. 100-4.
_____. 1960a. Animals of acculturation in the California Indian lan-
    guages. UCPL 4. 215-46. [In this volume, pp. 121-62.]
_____. 1960b. A note on the Southwestern words for cat. IJAL 26.
    167-8.

_____.1962a. Review of Arizona place names, ed. by B. H. Granger. JAF 75.77-8.

_____.1962b. Review of California place names, by E. G. Gudde. JAF 75.78-82.

_____.1967a. Karok mákkay < Scottish McKay. Names 15.79-80.

_____.1967b. Review of New Mexico place names, by T. M. Pearce. WF 26.140-3.

Bright, William and Elizabeth. 1959. Spanish words in Patwin. Rom Ph 13.161-4. [In this volume, pp. 116-20.]

Bright, William and Marcia. 1969. Archaeology and linguistics in prehistoric Southern California. UH WPL 10.1-26. [Revised version in this volume, pp. 189-205.]

Bright, William, and R. A. Thiel. 1965. Hispanisms in a modern Aztec dialect. RomPh 18.444-52.

Callaghan, Catherine. 1964. Phonemic borrowing in Lake Miwok. UCPL 34.46-53.

Carroll, John B., and Joseph B. Casagrande. 1958. The function of language classifications in behavior. Readings in social psychology, ed. by Eleanor Macoby et al., pp. 18-31. 3rd ed., New York, Holt.

Casagrande, Joseph B. 1954-55. Comanche linguistic acculturation. IJAL 20.140-51, 217-37; 21.8-25.

Cook, Mary Jane, and Margaret Amy Sharp. 1966. Problems of Navajo speakers in learning English. LL 16.21-9.

Crowley, Cornelius J. 1962. Some remarks on the etymology of the Southwestern words for cat. IJAL 28.149-51.

Day, Gordon M. 1961. The name Contoocook. IJAL 27.168.

Dockstader, Frederick J. 1955. Spanish loan words in Hopi: A preliminary checklist. IJAL 21.157-9.

Dozier, Edward P. 1955. Kinship and linguistic change among the Arizona Tewa. IJAL 21.242-57.

_____.1956. Two examples of linguistic acculturation: The Yaqui of Sonora and Arizona and the Tewa of New Mexico. Lg 32. 146-57.

_____.1961. Rio Grande pueblos. In Spicer 1961, pp. 94-186.

_____.1967. Linguistic acculturation studies in the Southwest. Studies in Southwestern ethnolinguistcs, ed. by Dell Hymes, pp. 389-402. Studies in general anthropology, 3. The Hague, Mouton.

Ervin, Susan M. 1961. Semantic shift in bilingualism. American Journal of Psychology 74.233-41. Urbana, Ill.

Fox, Robin. 1968. Multilingualism in two communities. Man (n. s.)
    3.456-64.
Friederici, Georg. 1947. Amerikanistisches Wörterbuch. Hamburg,
    Cram.
Garvin, Paul L. 1947. Christian names in Kutenai. IJAL 13.69-77.
_____.1948. Kutenai lexical innovations. Word 4.120-6.
Geary, James A. 1945. Algonquian nasaump and napŏpi: French loan-
    words? Lg 21.40-5.
Granger, Byrd H. , ed. 1960. Will C. Barnes' Arizona place names.
    2nd edition. Tucson, University of Arizona Press.
Gross, Feliks. 1951. Language and value changes among the Arapaho.
    IJAL 17.10-17.
Gudde, Erwin G. 1960. California place names. 2nd edition. Berkeley
    and Los Angeles, University of California Press.
Haas, Mary R. 1947. Some French loanwords in Tunica. RomPh 1.
    145-8.
_____.1968. The Menomini terms for playing cards. IJAL 34.217-
    19.
Hall, Robert A. ,Jr. 1947. A note on Taos k'owena horse. IJAL 13.
    117-8.
Hall, Robert A. ,Jr. , and Douglas Leechman. 1955. American Indian
    Pidgin English. AS 30.163-71.
Hammerich, Louis L. 1954. The Russian stratum in Alaskan Eskimo.
    Word 10.401-28.
Hasler, Juan. 1961. Juan del Oso en los Tuztlas. La Palabra y el
    Hombre 20.603-14. Xalapa, Universidad Veracruzana.
Haudricourt, André. 1961. Richesses en phonèmes et richesse en
    locuteurs. Homme 1.5-10.
Haugen, Einar. 1956. Bilingualism in the Americas: A bibliography
    and research guide. PADS 26. University, Ala. , University
    of Alabama Press.
Herzog, George. 1941. Culture change and language: Shifts in the
    Pima vocabulary. Language, culture, and personality, essays
    in memory of Edward Sapir, ed. by Leslie Spier et al. , pp.
    66-74. Menasha, Banta.
Hoijer, Harry. 1939. Chiricahua loanwords from Spanish. Lg 15.
    110-15.
_____.1948. Linguistic and cultural change. Lg 24.335-45.
Huot, Martha C. 1948. Some Mohawk words of acculturation. IJAL
    14.150-4.

Jacobs, Melville. 1932. Notes on the structure of Chinook Jargon.
    Lg 8. 27-50.
_____. 1936. Texts in Chinook Jargon. UWPA 7. 1-27.
Jacobsen, William H. , Jr. 1966. Washo linguistic studies. The cur-
    rent status of anthropological research in the Great Basin:
    1964, ed. by W. L. d'Azevedo et al. , pp. 113-36. Reno,
    University of Nevada.
Johnson, J. B. 1943. A clear case of linguistic acculturation. AmA
    45. 427-34.
Jones, William M. 1960. Origin of the place name Taos. AnL 2/3. 2-4.
Kennard, Edward. 1963. Linguistic acculturation in Hopi. IJAL 29.
    36-41.
Kiddle, Lawrence B. 1964. American Indian reflexes of two Spanish
    words for cat. IJAL 30. 299-305.
Kroeber, A. L. 1958. Sign language inquiry. IJAL 24. 1-19.
_____. 1959. Possible Athabascan influence on Yuki. IJAL 25. 59.
Lamb, Sydney M. 1964. Linguistic diversification and extinction in
    North America. PICAm 35/2. 457-64.
Landar, Herbert J. 1959. The diffusion of some Southwestern words
    for cat. IJAL 25. 273-4.
_____. 1961. The Southwestern words for cat. IJAL 27. 370-1.
Lee, Dorothy D. 1943. The linguistic aspect of Wintu acculturation.
    AmA 45. 435-40.
Lindenfeld, Jacqueline. 1971. Semantic categorization as a deterrent
    to grammatical borrowing: A Yaqui example. IJAL 37. 6-14.
Lounsbury, Floyd G. 1960. Iroquois place names in the Champlain
    Valley. Champlain Basin, past-present-future: Report of the
    New York-Vermont Interstate Commission on the Lake Cham-
    plain Basin, pp. 23-66. (New York State legislative docu-
    ment, 1960, no. 9.) Albany.
McLendon, Sally. 1969. Spanish words in Eastern Pomo. RomPh 23.
    39-53.
McLuhan, Marshall. 1964. Understanding media. New York, Signet.
Mierau, Eric. 1963. Concerning Yavapai-Apache bilingualism. IJAL
    29. 1-3.
Miller, Wick R. 1959-60. Spanish loanwords in Acoma. IJAL 25. 147-
    53, 26. 41-9.
Ohannessian, Sirarpi, ed. 1967. The study of the problems of teaching
    English to American Indians. Washington, D. C. , CAL.

Olmsted, D. L. 1954. Achumawi-Atsugewi non-reciprocal intelligi-
    bility. IJAL 20.181-4.
Oswalt, Robert L. 1958. Russian loanwords in Southwestern Pomo.
    IJAL 24.245-7.
_____.1960. Gualala. Names 8.57-8.
Pearce, T. M. 1965. New Mexico place names. Albuquerque, Univer-
    sity of New Mexico Press.
Pinnow, Heinz-Jürgen. 1968. Genetic relationship vs. borrowing in
    Na-Dene. IJAL 34.204-11.
Polgar, Steven. 1960. Biculturation of Mesquakie teenage boys. AmA
    62.217-35.
Salzmann, Zdeněk. 1951. Contrastive field experience with language
    and values of the Arapaho. IJAL 17.98-101.
Sapir, Edward. 1916. Time perspective in aboriginal American cul-
    ture. Canada Dept. of Mines, Geological Survey, memoir
    90, anthropological series 13. Ottawa. (Reprinted in SWES,
    pp. 389-462. 1949.)
Sasaki, Tom T. , and D. L. Olmsted. 1953. Navaho acculturation and
    English-language skills. AmA 55.89-99.
Sawyer, Jesse O. , Jr. 1964a. Wappo words from Spanish. UCPL 34.
    163-9.
_____.1964b. The implications of Spanish /r/ and /rr/ in Wappo
    history. RomPh 18.165-77.
Scott, Richard B. 1960. English language skills of the Mescalero
    Apache Indians. América Indígena 20.173-81. Mexico, D. F.,
    Mexico.
Shaw, George C. 1909. The Chinook Jargon and how to use it. Seattle.
Shipley, William. 1962. Spanish elements in the indigenous languages
    of central California. RomPh 16.1-21.
Shuy, Roger W. 1965. The problem of American Indian English. So-
    cial dialects and language learning, ed. by R. W. Shuy, pp.
    52-4. Champaign, Ill. , National Council of Teachers of
    English.
Spencer, Robert F. 1947. Spanish loanwords in Keresan. SJA 3.130-
    46.
Spicer, Edward H. 1943. Linguistic aspects of Yaqui acculturation.
    AmA 45.410-26.
_____, ed. 1961. Perspectives in American Indian culture change.
    Chicago, University of Chicago Press.

Sturtevant, William C. 1962. Spanish-Indian relations in southeastern
North America. Ethnohistory 9.41-94.

Swadesh, Morris. 1948. Sociologic notes on obsolescent languages.
IJAL 14.226-35.

Taylor, Allan R. 1962. Spanish manteca in Alaskan Eskimo. RomPh
16.30-2.

Teeter, Karl V. 1958. Notes on Humboldt County, California, place
names of Indian origin. Names 6.55-56.

Trager, George L. 1944. Spanish and English loanwords in Taos.
IJAL 10.144-60.

_____.1960. The name of Taos, New Mexico. AnL 2/3.5-6.

Troike, Rudolph C. 1956. Comanche linguistic acculturation: A critique. IJAL 22.213-15.

Voegelin, C. F. 1958. Sign language analysis, on one level or two?
IJAL 24.71-6.

_____.1959. An expanding language, Hopi. Plateau 32.33-9.

Voegelin, C. F. and D. H. Hymes. 1953. A sample of North American Indian dictionaries with reference to acculturation. PAPS
97.634-44.

Voegelin, C. F. and F. M. 1965. Extinction of American Indian languages before and after contact periods. CJL 10.135-46.

Voegelin, C. F. and F. M. , and Noel W. Schutz, Jr. 1967. The lan-
guage situation in Arizona as part of the Southwest Culture
Area. Studies in Southwestern ethnolinguistics, ed. by Dell
Hymes, pp. 403-51. Studies in general anthropology, 3.
The Hague, Mouton.

Watson, G. 1938. Nahuatl words in American English. AS 13.108-21.

Worth, Dean S. 1960. Russian kniga, Southwestern Pomo kalikak.
IJAL 26.62-5.

_____.1963. Russian and Alaskan Eskimo. IJSLP 7.72-9.

18 Areal Features in North American Indian Languages

In Collaboration with Joel Sherzer

1. Introduction

The term "linguistic area" generally refers to a geographical area in which, due to borrowing, languages of different genetic origins have come to share certain borrowed features — not only vocabulary items, which are known to be readily borrowed in most languages of the world, but also elements of phonological, grammatical, or syntactic structure, which are less liable to be diffused in this way. A classical instance of such a linguistic area is South Asia (i. e., the Indian subcontinent), as demonstrated by Emeneau 1956; and it is readily apparent that this linguistic area has come into existence as a result of a shared history and culture. So instances of areal diffusion might also be expected in aboriginal America — a region which, by general agreement, was characterized by a large number of languages, of many different genetic groupings — but which at the same time had, like South Asia, many elements of shared history and culture. Indeed, in reading the literature on American Indian linguistics, it is common to find statements like this from Sapir (1922: 282), referring to linguistic traits which crosscut genetic boundaries:

> Some of the more important of these typical or at any rate widespread American traits, that are found in Takelma, are: the incorporation of the pronominal (and nominal) object in the verb; the incorporation of the possessive pronouns in the noun; the closer association with the verb-form of the object than the subject; the inclusion of a considerable number of instrumental and local modifications in the verb-complex; the weak development of differences of tense in

the verb and noun; and the impossibility of drawing
a sharp line between mode and tense.

However, it does not seem possible to find linguistic features
which have spread through all American Indian languages — or even
all those of North America (north of Mexico), which will be the geographical focus of this article. Rather, we may see aboriginal North
America as a complex of linguistic areas, related by both genetic and
diffusional relationships which reflect the shared history of the native
peoples.

Understanding that similarities between any two or more languages may be caused either by common genetic origin or by diffusion,
a serious problem arises: given that a particular feature is shared
among languages, how can we know whether this fact is caused by common origin or by borrowing ? Are there any types of similarities
which are especially likely to be caused by borrowing, and so constitute poor evidence for genetic relationship ? The consensus among
historical linguists has been that similarities in "cultural" (i. e. non-
basic) vocabulary should be placed in such a category. But are there,
then, other types of similarities which are never borrowed, or only
rarely, and so constitute especially good evidence for genetic relationship ? It has sometimes been held that structural similarities, especially of grammar, should be placed in this category. But linguists
have disagreed on the importance which should be given to different
types of similarities.

In the history of American Indian linguistics, this disagree-
ment has become well known in the form of the "Boas–Sapir contro-
versy" (for a summary, see Sherzer 1973: 753-4). Basically, both
scholars recognized that grammatical structure could be borrowed,
and that structural similarities between languages could therefore be
evidence not of a genetic grouping, but rather of a linguistic area
within which diffusion had occurred. However, Sapir felt that one
could separate superficial elements of grammar, likely to undergo
diffusion, from more 'profound' elements which reveal genetic origins.
Boas, on the other hand, believed that at a certain time depth, one
could no longer distinguish similarities caused by borrowing from
those caused by common origin; this, he believed, was illustrated by
the numerous similarities between the Salish and Wakashan linguistic

families in the Pacific Northwestern culture area — which Sapir proposed to unite in a single, high-order genetic grouping.

In the subsequent development of American Indian linguistics, we can see a predominance of Sapir's approach: in the "Bloomfieldian" and "post-Bloomfieldian" era, historical studies of North American Indian languages concentrated mainly on the classification of languages within genetic groupings, from the level of the "family" to that of the "super-phylum". In most writings of this period, one gets the impression that neighboring languages were not believed to have serious influence on one another structurally.

During the 1960's and 70's, however, a return to areal interests has become apparent in work such as that of Haas (see especially chapter 5 of her book The prehistory of languages, 1969). In this context, an attempt has been made by Sherzer (1968, 1973) to develop a rigorous framework for the analysis of areal phenomena in aboriginal north America, and to use this framework for examining data from the entire continent. Some of the methods and findings are exemplified in §3, below. We believe that this work has validated the equal importance of genetic and areal groupings, as complementary findings in the pursuit of a single goal. To quote Boas (1920:369), "It should be borne in mind that the problem of the study of languages is not one of classification, but that our task is to trace the history of the development of human speech" — and, we might add, of human culture.

2. An excursus: Red Indians and East Indians

We have referred above to the crucial problem which lies between areal linguistics and genetic classification: if two languages share a particular feature, how does one know whether it is inherited or borrowed? Are certain types of linguistic features especially likely or unlikely to be borrowed? Everyone agrees that vocabulary is often borrowed, and some phonological features are known to be borrowed along with vocabulary; but what are the chances that borrowing will involve a morphophonemic rule, a morphological category, a syntactic pattern, or a semantic distinction?

It is hard to answer these questions on the basis of American
Indian data alone, simply because the languages lack historical documentation of significant time-depth. Salish and Wakashan, in the Pacific Northwest, share glottalized stops, perhaps because of common
origin, perhaps because of borrowing: only time-travel will enable
us to be certain. But what of other parts of the world, where written
records have been kept for centuries? There is at least one area in
which we have a long history of two-way interaction between genetically distinct families: namely, in India, where bilingualism and linguistic diffusion between Dravidian and Indo-Aryan (first Sanskrit, then
descendants such as Hindi) has continued for centuries. From the linguistic study of that area, we find the following (cf. Emeneau 1956,
1962):

(1) Borrowing of vocabulary in both directions has taken
place from the earliest time of contact.

(2) Phonemes have been borrowed in loan words, and then
have spread to non-borrowed vocabulary.

(3) In a few cases, morphological elements seem to have
been borrowed, in both shape and meaning; e.g., the Bengali plural
and dative suffixes show Dravidian resemblances.

(4) In many more cases, borrowing involves morphological
categories, along with the syntactic rules which pertain to them.
This has gone so far that morpheme-for-morpheme literal translation
between an Indo-Aryan and a Dravidian language will often produce
quite grammatical results—whereas the same kind of translation into
English will usually produce gibberish (cf. Gumperz 1967, Pandit
1972: 1-25).

(5) Semantic features are borrowed — not only as part of the
borrowing of vocabulary, but also as more abstract distinctions, manifested in syntax; thus the difference between two kinds of causative
is borrowed from Dravidian into Indo-Aryan.

(6) Borrowing of vocabulary may not only involve "cultural"
items, but may make serious inroads on the "basic" list; thus, in

Swadesh's 100-word "non-cultural" vocabulary, Kannada shows 13
items borrowed from Indo-Aryan (cf. Sjoberg 1956), presumably because of Sanskritic religious associations with such terms as "man",
"sun", and "heart". Even so, there remains a hard core of basic vocabulary which can be used diagnostically to distinguish Dravidian and
Indo-Aryan dialects, however similar their grammatical structures
may be.

To be sure, structural borrowing seems to have occurred in
India on a larger scale than in most parts of the world, presumably
because of special socio-cultural conditions. But an Americanist may
conclude that if structural features and basic vocabulary behave independently in the linguistic history of India, they may have done so
at some points in the prehistory of the New World. That is, the existence of glottalized stops in Salish and Wakashan cannot be taken as
conclusive proof of common origin: diffusion is just as good a hypothesis. This means that genetic classifications of North American
Indian languages can only be valid insofar as they are based on regular sound-correspondence in a substantial body of basic vocabulary.
Other observable similarities between languages, possibly due to diffusion, are then inadequate as proof of genetic origins — but they are
no less important as evidence for shared history. Indeed, one might
say that attempts at genetic pigeon-holing, in order to trace the most
remote possible origins of a given language, are of relatively little
help if we wish to understand the total cultural history of aboriginal
North America; in pursuing this goal, it is studies of areal diffusion
which become important.

3. Language areas and culture areas in North America

The reader is referred to Sherzer 1968, 1973 for details as
to general problems involved in areal linguistic studies — e.g., problems in the selection of appropriate linguistic traits for study, in the
comparability of diverse linguistic descriptions, and in the evaluation
of inadequate data. Definitive solutions may not be possible for any
of these problems; yet progress can be made in spite of them.

Much of the work by Sherzer has taken the culture area as a
point of departure, using Driver 1961 as a frame of reference for significant cultural groupings in North America. However, it should be
pointed out (cf. Sherzer 1973:759-60) that, in comparing culture areas

with language areas, we must recognize important differences between the two. A culture area has been traditionally defined as an
area in which many cultural traits cluster. In some cases, so many
traits cluster in a particular culture area that it becomes difficult if
not impossible to distinguish the cultures in question (or parts of
them) by this method. An example is the Hupa-Karok-Yurok region
in northern California (see Sapir 1921:214). But language, as has often been observed, is the most self-contained or conservative part of
culture. In spite of the great similarity of Hupa, Karok, and Yurok
cultures, the languages — all unrelated (or, at best, extremely distantly related) — are quite distinct from one another (for further discussion of this question, see Bright and Bright 1965, Haas 1967).
Linguistic traits, especially grammatical traits, do not spread with
the ease that many non-linguistic cultural traits seem to. This is
apparently due to two facts: on the one hand, linguistic phenomena
are usually less conscious than other cultural phenomena; on the other, their diffusion requires very intimate contact between groups, including bilingualism. We argue that agreement in a few linguistic
traits may often be more significant, as an indication of the nature of
relationships among groups in an area, than agreement in many nonlinguistic traits. Any definition of the language area, then, cannot
be strictly analogous to the above definition of culture area, since a
cluster of many linguistic traits occurs only in areas where all the
languages are related closely. To be sure, there are instances in
North America where the boundaries of a linguistic area (as defined
below) and a genetic area (all languages in the area are members of
one family) appear to coincide. Nonetheless, there is also a sense
in which it seems valuable to delimit linguistic areas which do not
coincide with genetic areas.

A language area, for our present purposes, is definable as
an area in which several linguistic traits are shared by the languages
of the area — and where, furthermore, there is evidence (linguistic
and non-linguistic) that contact between the speakers of the languages
contributed to the spread and/or retention of these traits and thereby
to a certain degree of linguistic uniformity within the area. It is important to remember that languages which are unrelated (or distantly
related) may disagree with regard to many traits, and yet be in the
same linguistic area according to the above definition, since they
share several of what one might want to call diagnostic traits. What

is significant, then, is that linguistic structure, usually resistant to influences coming from outside its own internal mechanism, has been massively affected by linguistic contact. The Northwest Coast is a good example of a linguistic area. Here are found languages belonging to eight families — Chemakuan, Hokan, Kutenaian, Na-Dené, Penutian, Ritwan, Salishan, and Wakashan; but the cultures of the speakers of these languages are in some cases markedly similar. In spite of the fact that the languages are quite distinct from one another from a genetic point of view, they share a complex of traits not found in any other area of North America, including a glottalized stop series, nominal and verbal reduplication, and numeral classifiers.

This fact clearly results from certain communicative characteristics of the Northwest Coast. In pre-Columbian times, the Northwest Coast had the second greatest population density of all North American culture areas (only California was more densely populated). This population consisted of seven linguistic families, each one consisting of several quite distinct languages. The great density of population in certain areas of the Northwest Coast, together with the genetic diversity of languages, enables us to imagine that most individuals came into intimate contact with languages other than their own (and perhaps quite distinct from their own). In addition, it has been reported by various authors that there was a great deal of trade and intermarriage among the groups of the Northwest Coast. Driver (1961: 230) notes that, at certain trading rendezvous near the coast, buyers and sellers spent days feasting, singing, and dancing: such events could only be successful if there was much multilingualism. Again, Boas 1896 reports much diffusion of folktales among the Northwest Coast groups. The areal spread of such a cultural trait also, of course, requires multilingualism. It is probable that, for a long period of time, bi- and multilingualism was the rule rather than the exception, and this no doubt led to the linguistic uniformity of the Northwest Coast. The uniformity results both from innovative developments in particular languages in the direction of others and from the retention of traits shared with neighboring languages.

By contrast, we may consider the Great Plains region of North America — which, although a recognized culture area, is by no means clearly characterizable as a language area. There are six language families represented in the Plains culture area: Athabaskan,

Algonkian, Siouan, Aztec-Tanoan, Caddoan, and Tonkawan. The
Plains is the most recently constituted of the culture areas of North
America (late eighteenth and nineteenth centuries). The linguistic
reflex of this fact is that languages share traits with <u>related</u> languages
(whether or not they are neighbors) rather than with unrelated neighbors. It is thus not possible to speak of the Plains as a linguistic
area in the same sense that we have spoken of the Northwest Coast.
And we find a correlation in the communicative characteristics of the
Plains, related to the recent development of this culture area. Its
constitution was partly the result of pressure from whites which
caused Indians to move west; the acquisition of the gun and the horse
led to the sudden and rapid development of 'classic' Plains culture.
We may also note the late southerly movement of the Athapaskans,
and the recent intrusion of the Uto-Aztecan Comanche. In sharp contrast to the Northwest Coast, then, we have here a case of diverse
groups of people who were not at all in intimate contact, and a contact which lasted a relatively short period of time. According to
Driver (1961:340), "The Plains tribes occupied fairly well-defined
territories which, although sometimes shared with friendly neighbors,
were at the same time defended against enemy tribes." Communication occurred thus mainly among members of the same tribe, speaking
the same language. Bilingualism must have been quite rare; note that
it is on the Plains that a manual sign language developed, enabling
individuals of diverse tongues to make themselves understood to one
another. It is not at all surprising, then, that languages of the Plains
cannot be seen as constituting a language area comparable to Northwest Coast.

Thus we find that the development of language areas depends
on communicative conditions — or, more broadly, on socio-cultural
factors in general. Areal studies can be seen as having important
ties to a theory of language change, and specifically to the question
of the relationship between synchronic and diachronic phenomena. We
agree with Weinreich, Labov and Herzog 1968 that we must assume
all speech communities to be heterogeneous, and must study the ways
in which this heterogeneity is projected in space and time. It seems
clear that one type of heterogeneity — namely bi- or multi-lingualism
— has played a major role in the linguistic history of aboriginal
North America.

4. Linguistic features and areal spread

In Sherzer 1968, 1973, culture areas as defined by ethnographers were taken as givens, and correlations were sought in terms
of complexes of linguistic traits. In the present work, we switch to a
different approach, taking the areal spread of linguistic features as
our basic data. Here we use culture areas only for convenience in
geographical orientation, and we use the term 'language area' in an
even narrower sense than above, as the area in which a single linguistic feature occurs. Our aim is to see to what extent such inde-
pendently-defined linguistic areas may be set up for aboriginal North
America, and to consider their implications as evidence for prehistoric contact of languages and cultures. We first examine selected
phonological features, then features of grammar.[1] In the "overview"
following each sub-section, we identify "family traits" characteristic
of genetic groupings found in more than one culture area, as well as
"areal traits" characteristic of genetically unrelated languages found
in a single culture area. (Features characterizing families such as
Eskimo, Salish, Wakashan, or Muskogean are not noted here, since
each of these families is located in a single culture area, making
"family traits" and "areal traits" difficult to distinguish.[2]

4.1 Phonology

(1) Voiceless vowels are not attested in the Arctic, Subarctic, Northwest, California, or Plateau areas. The areas where
they occur are as follows:

Southwest: voiceless vowels (as well as voiceless nasals and
semivowels) are found in (U.A.) Hopi, and in Zuni and Keresan.

Great Basin: voiceless vowels occur in all the Uto-Aztecan
languages, but not in Washo. It is interesting, however, that Washo
does have voiceless nasals and semivowels, like its Uto-Aztecan
neighbors.

Plains: voiceless vowels are attested for (Alg.) Cheyenne
and (Caddoan) Arikara. They also occur in (U.A.) Comanche, a recent arrival to the Plains from the Great Basin.

Southeast and Northeast: the Iroquoian languages tend to devoice vowels in certain predictable environments.

Overview: voiceless vowels are characteristic of Iroquoian in general; of a number of Uto-Aztecan languages — essentially the Numic group of the Great Basin, and Hopi in the nearby Southwest; and of Zuni and Keresan, also in the Southwest. We may conclude that voiceless vowels are basically a family trait in Iroquoian, but an areal trait of the Southwest-Great Basin complex.

(2) Nasalized vowels are not attested for the Arctic, California, Great Basin, or Plateau areas. The areas where they occur are as follows:

Subarctic: nasalized vowels are found in (Ath.) Beaver, Carrier, Chipewyan, Dogrib, Hare, Slave, and perhaps all of the Athabaskan languages of the Western Subarctic. They are found in eastern dialects of Ojibwa (in the last syllable of words), but not in other Algonkian languages of the area.

Northwest: nasalized vowels are found at the geographical extremes, and only in Na-Dené languages: in Eyak to the north, and in (Ath.) Galice and Tolowa to the south.

Southwest: nasalized vowels are found in all the (Na-Dené) Athabaskan languages, i. e. in Apachean; and in all Tanoan.

Plains: nasalized vowels are found in (Ath.) Kiowa Apache, in (Aztec-Tanoan) Kiowa, and in several Siouan languages: Dakota, Mandan, Winnebago, Iowa-Oto, and Dhegiha.

Southeast: nasalized vowels are found in all Siouan, Iroquoian and Muskogean languages of the area, and in Yuchi.

Northeast: nasalized vowels are found in all of the Iroquoian languages. Some of the neighboring Algonkian languages have nasalized a: Eastern and Western Abnaki, Mahican, Massachusett, Narragansett, and Pequot.

Overview: nasalized vowels are a trait of most Athabaskan languages — those of the Subarctic, the Apachean group, and some of

the Pacific Coast group. Nasalized vowels are characteristic of all
Iroquoian languages and of some Siouan. In Algonkian, vowel nasal-
ization is found mainly in languages with Iroquoian neighbors. We
may conclude that nasalized vowels are essentially a family trait in
Athabaskan, Iroquoian, and Siouan, with some spreading as an areal
feature in the Northeast.

(3) <u>Glottalized stops</u> are not attested in the Arctic or Northeast areas. The areas where they occur are as follows:

Subarctic: glottalized stops occur in all the (Na–Dené) Athabaskan languages which occupy the Western Subarctic.

Northwest: glottalized stops occur in all languages, including members of the Na–Dené, Penutian, Wakashan, Chemakuan, and
Salishan families. In (Pen.) Siuslaw, and perhaps some other languages, glottalization has primarily an expressive rather than a ref-
erential function.

Plateau: glottalized stops are found in all the Salishan and
Penutian languages which occupy most of the area; but not in Kutenai,
on the eastern periphery.

California: glottalized stops are found in all Athabaskan languages; in all Yukian; in (Algic) Yurok; in (Hokan) Chimariko, Shastan, Yana, some Pomoan, Salinan, and Barbareño Chumash; and in
(Pen.) Maidun, Wintun, some Miwokan, and Yokuts.

Southwest: glottalized stops are found in all (Ath.) Apachean;
in Zuni, Keresan, and all Tanoan; and in Coahuiltec.

Great Basin: glottalized stops are found in Washo, but in
none of the Uto–Aztecan languages.

Plains: glottalized stops occur in (Ath.) Sarsi and Kiowa-
Apache; in (Siouan) Dakota, Winnebago, Iowa–Oto, and Dhegiha; in
Caddo; and in (Aztec–Tanoan) Kiowa.

Southeast: glottalized stops are attested only in Yuchi and
Chitimacha.

Overview: glottalized stops are characteristic of all Na-Dené languages (including Athabaskan) and of all the Kiowa-Tanoan branch of Aztec-Tanoan. They are also found in many Penutian, Hokan, and Siouan languages, as well as in Zuni and Keresan. We may regard glottalized stops as a significant family trait of Na-Dené, Penutian, Hokan, and Kiowa-Tanoan. They are also a major areal trait of the Northwest, overriding genetic boundaries in that region; and they are areally significant for the Pueblo groups in the Southwest.

(4) <u>Labial stops</u> occur in almost all American Indian languages, as in most languages of the world; but a significant number of American languages have an incomplete series of labial stops — i.e. fewer stops in labial than in other ariculatory positions — and some lack labial stops entirely.

There are no restrictions on labial stops in the Arctic, Great Basin, and Plateau areas. In other areas, however, there are restrictions as follows:

Subarctic: most of the Athabaskan languages which occupy the Western portion of the area lack labial stops, though Tsetsaut clearly has them.

Northwest: labial sounds are rare in all the Na-Dené languages: Eyak, Tlingit, Haida, and (Ath.) Chasta Costa, Galice, Tolowa. It is interesting that Salishan Tillamook, a neighbor of now extinct Athabaskan languages for which we have no data, also lacks labial stops.

California: the Athabaskan languages have incomplete series of labial stops.

Southwest: (Ath.) Apachean has incomplete labial series.

Plains: (Ath.) Sarsi and Kiowa-Apache have incomplete labial series; in addition, (Caddoan) Kitsai and Wichita have no labial stops.

Southeast: (Iroq.) Cherokee and Tuscarora lack labial stops.

Northeast: all the Iroquoian languages lack labial stops.

Overview: We see that incomplete labial series constitute a
family trait of Na-Dené and (independently, we presume) of Iroquoian;
there are only slight indications of this trait becoming areal. The occurrence of the trait in some Caddoan languages is reminiscent of
the hypothesis that Caddoan is genetically related to Iroquoian.

(5) The k/q distinction is not attested in the Plains, Southeast,
or Northeast areas. The areas where it occurs are as follows:

Arctic: k̲ and q̲ contrast in all dialects of Eskimo.

Subarctic: k̲ and q̲ contrast in Ahtena, Ingalik, Koyukon,
Tanaina, and perhaps other Athabaskan languages in the northwestern
part of the area.

Northwest Coast: k̲ and q̲ contrast in most languages: in (Na-
Dené) Eyak, Tlingit, and Haida; in (Pen.) Tsimshian, Lower Chinook,
Alsea, Coos, Kalapuya, and Takelma; in Wakashan; in Chemakuan
(Quileute has k̲^{W}, q̲, q̲^{W}, but no k̲); and in Salishan.

Plateau: k̲ contrasts with q̲ in all languages except the Kathlamet dialect of Upper Chinook. However, (Salishan) Kalispel and
Coeur d'Alene have q̲, q̲^{W}, and k̲^{W}, but no k̲.

California: k̲ and q̲ contrast in (Ath.) Hupa and Wailaki; in
(Hokan) Chimariko, Achomawi, Atsugewi, most Pomoan, Chumashan,
and (Yuman) Northern Diegueno; in (Pen.) Wintu; and in (U.A.) Serrano, Luiseño, Cupeño, and Cahuilla.

Southwest: k̲ contrasts with q̲ in (U.A.) Hopi and in all (Hokan) Yuman.

Great Basin: k̲ and q̲ contrast in some Uto-Aztecan dialects.

Overview: the k/q distinction is clearly a family trait of Eskimo, with apparent areal spread into adjacent Athabaskan languages.
Its occurrence in California and the Southwest suggests that it may
have once been a family trait of Hokan, including Yuman, with areal

spread to Takic and Hopi. It is also an areal feature of the North-west–Plateau complex.

(6) The k/k^W distinction is represented in all culture areas except the Arctic, as follows:

Subarctic: k and k^W are distinguished in Chipewyan, Dogrib, Kutchin, and probably many other Athabaskan languages of the western region.

Northwest: k and k^W are distinguished in most languages: in (Na-Dené) Tlingit, Haida, and (Ath.) Chasta Costa, Galice, and To-lowa; in (Pen.) Tsimshian, Coos, Kalapuya, and Takelma; in Wa-kashan; in Chemukuan; and in all Salishan (except northern dialects of Tillamook.)

Plateau: k and k^W are distinguished in all Salishan and in (Pen.) Nez Perce (lower dialect only), Sahaptin, and Upper Chinook (but not Kathlamet).

California: k and k^W are distinguished in Algic; in (Ath.) Mattole and Kato; in (U.A.) all Takic; and in (Hokan) Yuman [Diegueño].

Southwest: k and k^W are distinguished in (U.A.) Hopi; in (Yu-man) Yuma, Mohave, and Yavapai; in (Ath.) Navajo; in Zuni; in all Tanoan; and in Coahuiltec.

Great Basin: k and k^W are distinguished in all the Uto-Aztecan languages, but not in (Hokan) Washo.

Plains: the k/k^W distinction is attested in contiguous Tonkawa and (Caddoan) Wichita, and in (U.A.) Comanche, a recent arrival from the Great Basin.

Southeast: k/k^W contrast only in Natchez.

Northeast: k and k^W contrast in Malecite-Passamaquoddy and perhaps other New England Algonkian languages.

Overview: the k/k^W distinction appears to be a family trait of Na-Dené, of Uto-Aztecan, and of (Hokan) Yuman. It has become an areal trait of the Northwest–Plateau complex, and in the Southwest; but its scattered occurrences elsewhere are hard to explain areally or genetically.

(7) <u>Voiceless labial fricatives</u> (f̱ or ɸ̱) are not attested in the Plains or Northeast areas. The areas where they occur are as follows:

Arctic: all dialects of Eskimo have a labial fricative, but without contrast between voiced and voiceless allophones.

Subarctic: f̱ or ɸ̱ occurs in a few Athabaskan languages: Hare, Dogrib, and Tsetsaut.

Northwest: a voiceless labial fricative is found in (Pen.) Kalapuya, on the borders of the Plateau area (where the contiguous Molala also has such a sound).

Plateau: voiceless labial fricatives occur in (Pen.) Cayuse and Molala.

California: voiceless labial fricatives are found in (Hokan) Karok, N.E. Pomo, and Esselen.

Southwest: f̱ occurs in (U.A.) Hopi and (Yuman) Havasupai. In Tanoan, Santa Clara Tewa has f̱ , Towa has ɸ̱.

Great Basin: ɸ̱ is found in all the (U.A.) Numic languages as a variant of p̱.

Southeast: f̱ or ɸ̱ occurs in (Iroq.) Tuscarora, in Yuchi; in all Muskogean; and in (Siouan) Ofo and Biloxi.

Overview: Voiceless bilabial fricatives are characteristic of Numic (Uto–Aztecan of the Great Basin), and therefore of the Great Basin as an area. They also are a family trait of Muskogean, and an areal trait of the Southeast.

(8) <u>Voiced labial fricatives</u> (v̱ or β̱) are not attested in the Northwest, Plateau, Plains, Southeast, or Northeast areas. The areas where they occur are as follows:

Arctic: see trait 7, above.

Subarctic: (Ath.) Kutchin has v̲.

California: voiced labial fricatives occur in (Hokan) Karok, in (Algic) Wiyot, and in (U.A.) all Takic.

Southwest: v̲ occurs in (U.A.) Hopi; in (Yuman) Yuma, Yavapai, Mohave, and Walapai; and (Tanoan) Tewa and Towa.

Great Basin: β̲ is found in all the (U.A.) Numic languages as a variant of p̲.

Overview: voiced labial fricatives are a family trait of Eskimo, of (U.A.) Takic and Numic, and of (Hokan) Yuman. They are an areal trait of the Southwest–Great Basin complex, extending (in Takic) into Southern California.

(9) A voiceless dental fricative (θ) is not attested in the Arctic or Plateau areas. The areas where it occurs are as follows:

Subarctic: θ̲ occurs in (Ath.) Kaska, Chipewyan, Slave, Koyukon, Tanana, Ingalik, Nabesna, Han, Tutchone, and Kutchin, as well as in some dialects of (Alg.) Western Cree.

Northwest: θ̲ is found only in (Ath.) Chasta Costa.

California: θ̲ is found in (Hokan) Karok and Atsugewi, and in (Pen.) Wintu.

Southwest: θ̲ occurs in all Yuman and in (Tanoan) Tewa of Santa Clara.

Great Basin: θ̲ is found in some dialects of Northern Paiute and Shoshoni, as a variant of t̲.

Plains: θ̲ occurs in (Alg.) Arapaho and (Siouan) Iowa–Oto and Dhegiha.

Southeast: θ̲ occurs only in (Iroq.) Tuscarora.

Northeast: ə occurs only in (Alg.) Shawnee.

Overview: ə is a family trait of the Athabaskan languages of the western Subarctic, and therefore of that area. It has no widespread distribution elsewhere. It may be noted that ə is accompanied by the contrasting voiced fricative ð only in the northern Athabaskan languages, in (Yuman) Mojave, and in Siouan. Voiced ð without ə occurs in scattered languages.

(10) The s/š distinction is found in all areas except the Arctic, as follows:

Subarctic: s and š are distinguished in almost all Athabaskan — though not in some Koyukon dialects, some Tanaina, or most Ahtena (the proximity of the languages to Eskimo may be significant). The s/š distinction is also found in some dialects of (Alg.) Western Cree.

Northwest: s and š are distinguished in most languages, as follows: (Na-Dené) Eyak, Tlingit, and (Ath.) Chasta Costa, Galice, Tolowa; (Wakashan) Nootka; (Chemakuan) Chemakum, Quileute; (Salishan) Comox, Squamish, Twana, Upper Chehalis, Snoqualmie, Snohomish, and Tillamook; (Pen.) Lower Chinook, Siuslaw, Coos.

Plateau: s and š are distinguished in (Salishan) Coeur d'Alene and Kalispel; and in (Pen.) Sahaptin and Upper Chinook (but not in Kathlamet).

California: s and š are distinguished in most languages, as follows: (Algic) Yurok, Wiyot; all Athabaskan; (Hokan) Chimariko, Achomawi, Atsugewi, Pomoan, Esselen, Salinan, Chumashan; (Pen.) Sierra Miwok, Lake Miwok, Costanoan, Yokuts; and (U.A.) all Takic.

Southwest: s and š are distinguished in the following languages: (U.A.) Papago; (Yuman) Yuma; (Ath.) all Apachean; Zuni; Keresan; (Tanoan) Tiwa (Isleta dialect), Tewa (Santa Clara), Towa; and Coahuiltec.

Great Basin: s and š are distinguished in Washo and in (U.A.) Southern Paiute.

Plains: s̲ and š̲ are distinguished in (Ath.) Sarsi and Kiowa-Apache; (Alg.) Cheyenne; (Siouan) Dakota, Crow, Mandan, Winnebago, and Dhegiha; and in (Caddoan) Arikara, Caddo.

Southeast: s̲ and š̲ are distinguished in Yuchi; in (Siouan) Ofo, Biloxi and Catawba; in (Musk.) Choctaw; in Tunica; and in Chitimacha.

Northeast: s̲ and š̲ are distinguished in (Alg.) Fox, Potawatomi, Miami, and Delaware; but not in any Iroquoian language.

Overview: the s̲/š̲ distinction is a family trait of Na-Dené, of Penutian, Hokan, Siouan, and Algonkian. It is an areal trait of the Northwest.

(11) <u>A voiceless velar fricative</u> (x̲) is found in all areas, as follows:

Arctic: x̲ occurs in all dialects of Eskimo.

Subarctic: x̲ occurs in all Athabaskan, but in no Algonkian.

Northwest: x̲ occurs in all languages except (Pen.) Kalapuya and (Ath.) Galice.

Plateau: x̲ occurs in Kutenai; in all Salishan; and in (Pen.) Nez Perce, Sahaptin, Upper Chinook, and Klamath.

California: x̲ occurs in most languages: in (Algic) Yurok, Wiyot; in all Athabaskan; in (Hokan) Karok, Chimariko, Shasta, Achomawi, Atsugewi, Yana, Pomo (N., E., and S. E. only), Esselen, Salinan, Chumashan, and Yuman [Diegueño]; in (Pen.) Wintu, Western Miwok, Costanoan, and Yokuts; and in (U.A.) all Takic.

Southwest: x̲ occurs in (Yuman) Yuma; in (Ath.) all Apachean; in (Tanoan) Tiwa (Taos, Picuris) and Tewa (Santa Clara); and in Coahuiltec.

Great Basin: x̲ occurs in all Uto-Aztecan languages, as a variant of k̲.

Plains: x̱ is found in (Ath.) Sarsi, Kiowa–Apache; in (Alg.) Blackfoot, Cheyenne, and Arapaho (except Atsina dialect); in Siouan (Dakota, Crow, Hidatsa, Mandan, Winnebago, Iowa–Oto, and Dhegiha; in (Caddoan) Arikara and Kitsai (as a variant of ẖ); and in Tonkawa.

Southeast: x̱ occurs in (Siouan) Biloxi and Tutelo, in (Iroq.) Tuscarora, and in Yuchi.

Northeast: x̱ occurs only in (Alg.) Delaware, a neighbor of (Siouan) Tutelo of the Southeast.

Overview: x̱ is a family trait of Algonkian, Penutian, Hokan, Uto–Aztecan, and Siouan. It is an areal trait of the Northwest, California, the Great Basin, the Plateau, and the Plains. Its limited distribution in the Southeast and Northeast may be due to spread from Siouan languages. (The corresponding voiced fricative ɣ̱ has a more scattered distribution; and languages with ɣ̱ but not x̱ are rare.)

(12) A voiced lateral (ḻ) is attested in all areas, as follows:

Arctic: ḻ occurs in all dialects of Eskimo.

Subarctic: ḻ occurs in all Athabaskan, and in some dialects of (Alg.) Cree.

Northwest: ḻ occurs in most languages: in (Na–Dené) Eyak, Haida, and (Ath.) Chasta Costa, Galice, Tolowa; in (Pen.) Tsimshian, Lower Chinook, Alsea, Siuslaw, Coos, Kalapuya, and Takelma; in ' (Wakashan) Kwakiutl; in Chemakuan; and in all Coast Salish.

Plateau: ḻ occurs in all languages.

California: ḻ occurs in most languages: in Algic, in all Athabaskan; in Yukian; in (Hokan) Chimariko, Achomawi, Atsugewi, Yana, most Pomoan, Esselen, Salinan, Chumashan, and Yuman [Diegueño]; in (Pen.) Maidun, Wintun, Miwokan, Costanoan, Yokuts [except the Tule–Kaweah dialect]; and in (U.A.) Tübatulabal, Luiseño, Cupeño, and Cahuilla.

Southwest: ḻ occurs in all languages except Keresan and (Tanoan) Tiwa (Isleta dialect), and Tewa (Santa Clara).

Great Basin: l is found only in Washo.

Plains: l occurs in (Ath.) Sarsi and Kiowa-Apache; in (Alg.) Arapaho [some dialects]; in (Siouan) Dakota [Teton dialect], Crow [in female speech], Iowa-Oto, and Dhegiha (Kansa and Osage, but not the Omaha dialect).

Southeast: l occurs in (Iroq.) Cherokee; in (Siouan) Ofo; in Yuchi; in all Muskogean; and in Natchez, Tunica, and Atakapa.

Northeast: l occurs in (Alg.) Eastern and Western Abnaki, Delaware, Malecite-Passamaquoddy, Miami, and Shawnee; and in (Iroq.) Oneida.

Overview: l is a family trait of Eskimo, Na-Dené, Penutian, Hokan, and Algonkian. It is an areal trait of the Arctic, the western Subarctic, the Northwest, California, the Southwest, the Plateau, and the Southeast. Its distribution in the Plains and the Northeast may be due to areal spread from Algonkian.

(13) A voiceless lateral fricative (ł) occurs in all areas, as follows:

Arctic: ł occurs in Alaskan dialects of Eskimo.

Subarctic: ł occurs in all Athabaskan languages, but not in any Algonkian.

Northwest: ł is found in all languages except (Salishan) Squamish and (Pen.) Lower Chinook.

Plateau: ł is found in all languages, except in the Kathlamet dialect of Upper Chinook.

California: ł is found in both Algic languages; in all Athabaskan; in (Hokan) E. Pomo, Ynezeño Chumash, and (Yuman) Diegueño; in (U.A.) Tübatulabal and (sub-phonemically) Cahuilla; and in (Pen.) Patwin and Western Miwok.

Southwest: ł is found in (Yuman) Yuma; (Ath.) all Apachean; in Zuni; and in (Tanoan) Tiwa.

Great Basin: ɬ is found only in Washo.

Plains: ɬ is found only in (Ath.) Sarsi and Kiowa-Apache.

Southeast: ɬ occurs in (Iroq.) Cherokee; in Yuchi; in all Muskogean; and in Natchez and Atakapa.

Northeast: ɬ is found only in (Iroq.) Oneida, as a variant of l.

Overview: ɬ is a family trait of Na-Dené and perhaps of Yuman. It is an areal trait of the western Arctic and western Subarctic, of the Northwest-Plateau complex, and of the Southeast.

(14) A voiceless lateral affricate (λ) does not occur in the Arctic, Great Basin, or Northeast. Elsewhere it occurs as follows:

Subarctic: all Athabaskan languages.

Northwest: (Na-Dené) Eyak, Tlingit, Haida and (Ath.) Chasta Costa, Galice; all Wakashan, Chemakuan, and Salishan; and (Pen.) Lower Chinook, Alsea, Siuslaw, and Coos.

Plateau: (Salishan) Kalispel; (Pen.) Sahaptin, Cayuse, Upper Chinook, and Molala.

California: (Pen.) Wintun.

Southwest: all Athabaskan.

Plains: (Ath.) Sarsi, Kiowa-Apache.

Southeast: (Iroq.) Cherokee.

Overview: The voiceless lateral affricate is a family trait of Na-Dené and an areal trait of the Northwest-Plateau complex. In many languages, e.g. Athabaskan, unaspirated and aspirated varieties contrast; voiced affricates, however, are very rare.

(15) A glottalized lateral affricate (λ') is not reported from the Arctic, Great Basin, Southeast or Northeast. The areas where it occurs are as follows:

Subarctic: all Athabaskan languages.

Northwest: (Na-Dené) Eyak, Tlingit, Haida, and (Ath.) Chasta Costa, Galice; all Waskashan, Chemakuan and Salishan; and (Pen.) Lower Chinook, Alsea, Siuslaw [expressively], and Coos.

Plateau: (Sal.) Kalispel, Columbian, Lillooet, Okanagon; and (Pen.) Sahaptin, Upper Chinook.

California: (Ath.) Hupa, Mattole, and Kato; (Pen.) Wintun and neighboring Lake Miwok. It is interesting that the Athabaskan languages and Lake Miwok have $\underline{\lambda}'$ but no $\underline{\lambda}$.

Southwest: (Ath.) Apachean.

Plains: (Ath.) Sarsi, Kiowa-Apache.

Overview: glottalized $\underline{\lambda}'$, like plain $\underline{\lambda}$, is a family trait of Na-Dené, and an areal trait of the Northwest-Plateau complex.

(16) <u>A palatal lateral</u> ($\underline{l}^y$) does not occur in any area except the following:

California: (U.A.) Cupeño, Cahuilla; (Hokan) Yuman [Diegueño].

Southwest: (Hokan) Yuman [Yuma, Mohave].

Overview: $\underline{l}^y$ appears to be a family trait of Yuman, in southern California and the Southwest, which has spread into some neighboring Uto-Aztecan languages of Southern California.

(17) <u>Glottalized nasals</u> are not found in the Arctic, Great Basin, Plains, or Northeast. The areas in which they occur are as follows:

Subarctic: (Ath.) Koyukon, Tuchone, and probably others.

Northwest: glottalized nasals (and semivowels) occur in a continuous area consisting of (Na-Dené) Haida, (Pen.) Tsimshian,

Wakashan, and (Salishan) Bella Coola. They are found elsewhere in (Salishan) Squamish, Twana, and (farther south) in (Ath.) Tolowa.

Plateau: glottalized nasals occur in a continuous area consisting of Salishan and (Pen.) Nez Perce. They are found elsewhere in (Pen.) Klamath, farther south.

California: (Yukian) Wappo; (Pen.) Yokuts; and (Hokan) Barbareño Chumash.

Southwest: (Keresan) Acoma and (Ath.) Navajo.

Southeast: glottalized nasals (as well as glottalized laterals and fricatives) occur here only in Yuchi. This is among other traits which suggests an earlier more westerly location for Yuchi.

Overview: glottalized nasals appear to be a family trait of Athabaskan, and an areal trait of the Northwest-Plateau complex.

(18) A palatal nasal (ñ) does not occur in the Arctic, Northwest, Great Basin, Plateau, Plains, Southeast, or Northeast. The areas where it occurs are the following:

Subarctic: (Ath.) Kaska, Slave, Carrier, and perhaps others.

California: ñ occurs in (Hokan) Pomo [N. E., S.], Yuman [Diegueño], and in (U. A.) Cupeño, Cahuilla.

Southwest: (U. A.) Papago, Hopi; (Hokan) Yuman [Yuma, Yavapai, Mohave, Walapai]; (Keresan) Acoma [as a variant of n]; and (Tanoan) Santa Clara Tewa.

Overview: ñ is a family trait of Yuman. It is also an areal trait of the Southwest plus southern California, perhaps with Yuman as its source of diffusion.

(19) A velar nasal (ŋ) does not occur in the Subarctic, Plains, or Northeast. It is found in the following areas:

Arctic: Eskimo.

Northwest: (Na-Dené) Haida; (Salish) Clallam.

Plateau: (Pen.) Cayuse, Molala.

California: all Athabaskan; (Hokan) Atsugewi; (Pen.) Sierra Miwok, Yokuts [Tule-Kaweah dialect only]; and (U. A.) Tübatulabal, Serrano, Luiseño, Cupeño, and Cahuilla.

Southwest: (U. A.) Hopi; (Hokan) Yuman [Yuma, Walapai]; and (Keresan) Acoma.

Great Basin: (Hokan) Washo; (U. A.) Southern Paiute, plus some dialects of Northern Paiute and Shoshoni.

Southeast: Atakapa.

Overview: ṇ appears to be a family trait of Uto-Aztecan, with limited areal spread into neighboring languages of California, the Southwest, and the Great Basin.

(20) An r-sound does not occur in the Northwest. It does oc-cur in the following areas:

Arctic: some Inupiaq dialects of Alaska.

Subarctic: (Ath.) Hare, Dogrib, Slave, Carrier, Koyukon, Tutchone, and perhaps others. Two dialects of (Alg.) Cree have r, Tête de Boule in the east and Île à la Crosse in the west.

Plateau: all Salishan.

California: (Algic) Yurok, Wiyot (a retroflex glide, not a vi-brant); (Hokan) Karok, Chimariko, Shasta, Achomawi, Atsugewi, Ya-na, E. Pomo, and Yuman [Diegueño]; (Pen.) Wintun, Costanoan; (U.A.) Serrano [and rarely in Luiseño, Cupeño, and Cahuilla].

Southwest: (U. A.) Hopi; (Hokan) all Yuman; (Keresan) Acoma; (Tanoan) Isleta Tiwa, Santa Clara Tewa.

Great Basin: (U. A.) Southern Paiute and some dialects of Shoshoni, as variants of t.

Plains: (Siouan) Crow, Hidatsa, Mandan, Winnebago; (Caddoan) Pawnee-Arikara, Kitsai, and Wichita.

Southeast: (Siouan) Catawba; (Iroq.) Tuscarora; and Tunica.

Northeast: (Iroq.) Huron, Mohawk.

Overview: r appears to be a family trait of Hokan and of Siouan, with some areal spread within California and the Plains respectively.

4.2 Grammar

(1) Reduplication to signify distribution or plurality is not found in the Arctic. Elsewhere it occurs widely, in nouns and verbs, as follows:

Subarctic: Reduplication is not used in the Athabaskan languages. In the Algonkian languages, reduplication of verbs indicates a distributive meaning.

Northwest: Reduplication is not used in (Na-Dené) Eyak, Tlingit, or Haida. It is used in (Pen.) Tsimshian, Lower Chinook [not productive], Siuslaw [verbs only], Coos [verbs] and Takelma [verbs]; and in all Wakashan, Chemakuan and Salishan. In (Wakashan) Kwakiutl and in Salishan, reduplication is also used to form the diminutive.

Plateau: Reduplication is used in (Pen.) Nez Perce, Sahaptin, Klamath, and to a lesser degree in Upper Chinook; and in all Salishan. In Nez Perce, Sahaptin, and Salishan, reduplication is also used to form the diminutive.

California: Reduplication is used in (Algic) Yurok; in (Hokan) Karok [verbs], Pomoan [verbs], Chumashan, and Yuman [Diegueño, verbs]; in (Pen.) Maidun [not very productive], Sierra Miwok, Yokuts [in verbs, rather marginal]; and in (U.A.) Tübatulabal, Luiseño, Cupeño, and Cahuilla.

Southwest: (U.A.) Papago, Hopi; (Hokan) Yuman [verbs]; Zuni; and (Tanoan) Taos.

Great Basin: (Hokan) Washo; all Uto-Aztecan.

Plains: Reduplication is used in (Alg.) Cheyenne [verbs]; in (Siouan) Dakota, Crow, Mandan, Winnebago, Iowa-Oto, and Dhegiha; and in Tonkawa.

Southeast: all Muskogean [verbs]; Tunica [auxiliary verbs]; Natchez [verbs]; Atakapa; and Yuchi. It probably occurs in the Siouan languages of the area, but not in the two Iroquoian languages.

Northeast: Reduplication of verbs is used in the Algonkian languages, indicating repetition and plurality, but in a derivational function; this is quite distinct from the reduplication found in western North America, which tends to be centrally involved in the aspectual system of verbs and the number system of nouns. None of the Iroquoian languages use reduplication.

Overview: Reduplication of nouns to indicate plurality, and of verbs in an aspectual function, is an areal feature spreading over all of western and southeast North America, with greatest development in the Northwest. It is strikingly absent, however, in Athabaskan and the other Na-Dené languages; this seems likely to be correlated with the relatively recent geographical spread of Athabaskan.

(2) Consonantal symbolism, i.e. meaningful alternations of consonants with diminutive/augmentative function, does not occur in the Arctic. The areas where it is used are the following:

Subarctic: traces in (Alg.) Cree. Consonantal symbolism is not reported in the Athabaskan languages of the area.

Northwest: (Wakashan) Nootka [traces]; (Salishan) Coast Salish [in varying degrees of productivity]; and traces in (Pen.) Lower Chinook and Coos.

Plateau: (Pen.) Nez Perce, Sahaptin, Upper Chinook, Klamath; and all Salishan.

California: Algic; (Ath.) Hupa; (Hokan) Karok, Yana, Yuman [Diegueño]; (Pen.) Sierra Miwok [traces], Yokuts; and (U.A.) Luiseño. The trait may well exist in other languages, but be unreported to date.

Southwest: (Hokan) Yuman.

Great Basin: traces in (U. A.) Northern Paiute.

Plains: (Siouan) Dakota, and probably traces in other Siouan languages.

Southeast: Siouan [traces].

Northeast: (Alg.) Delaware, traces in Fox and Ojibwa [information from Ives Goddard].

Overview: Consonantal symbolism may well be a family trait of Hokan, with areal spread in California; and of Salishan, with areal spread and greatest elaboration in the Northwest–Plateau complex (cf. Nichols 1971). Traces in Siouan and Algonkian suggest a wider areal spread in the past.

(3) Pronominal dual is found in some languages of all areas, as follows:

Arctic: Eskimo.

Subarctic: (Ath.) Chipewyan, Carrier, Dogrib, and perhaps others.

Northwest: (Pen.) Lower Chinook, Alsea, Siuslaw, Coos, Takelma.

Plateau: (Pen.) Sahaptin, Upper Chinook.

California: (Algic) Yurok [in a few verbs]; (Ath.) Mattole; (Yukian) Wappo [3rd person only]; (Hokan) Chimariko, Achomawi, Atsugewi, Chumashan; (Pen.) Maidun, Wintun, Miwokan, Costanoan, Yokuts.

Southwest: (Ath.) all Apachean; Zuni; Keresan; and (Tanoan) Taos.

Great Basin: (Hokan) Washo; all Uto–Aztecan.

Plains: (Siouan) Winnebago, Iowa-Oto, Dhegiha; (Caddoan) Pawnee; (Kio-Tanoan) Kiowa; (Ath.) Kiowa-Apache; and Tonkawa.

Southeast: Siouan [perhaps all]; Iroquoian; Muskogean; Tunica; and Natchez.

Northeast: Iroquoian; (Alg.) inflectional in Micmac, Malecite-Passamaquoddy, and Eastern Abenaki [information from Ives Goddard].

Overview: A pronominal dual is clearly a family trait of Penutian and Iroquoian; probably also of Athabaskan; and perhaps of Hokan and Siouan. It has a moderate areal spread in California, the Great Basin, the Southwest, the Plains, and the Southeast. However, the fact that it is found in all parts of the continent, though with a rather discontinuous distribution, suggests greater geographical unity at an earlier period.

It is interesting to note that the pronominal dual occurs in almost all the Penutian languages of the Northwest-Plateau complex, but in no other languages of that area. This suggests either that the Penutians had not been in the area very long — a hypothesis supported by little other evidence — or that the Penutians have not, for sociocultural reasons, been an important source for grammatical loans in the area.

(4) An inclusive/exclusive contrast in 1st person plural pronominal reference is absent in the Arctic and the Southwest. Elsewhere it occurs as follows:

Subarctic: (Alg.) Cree, Ojibwa.

Northwest: (Wakashan) Kwakiutl; (Pen.) Lower Chinook, Siuslaw. (Pen.) Coos and Alsea contrast inclusive and exclusive in the dual, though not in the plural; we have not noted this characteristic anywhere else in North America.

Plateau: (Salishan) Shuswap; (Pen.) Sahaptin, Upper Chinook.

California: (Hokan) Achomawi, Atsugewi, Yuki; (Pen.) Wintun, Sierra Miwok, Yokuts; (U.A.) Tübatulabal.

Great Basin: (Hokan) Washo; all Uto-Aztecan.

Plains: (Alg.) Blackfoot, Cheyenne, Arapaho; (Siouan) Dakota, Winnebago, Iowa-Oto, Dhegiha; (Caddoan) Pawnee; and Kiowa.

Southeast: Iroquoian; Yuchi (Siouan data are doubtful); (Musk.) Choctaw (some dialects).

Northeast: all Algonkian and Iroquoian.

Overview: The inclusive/exclusive contrast is clearly a family trait of Algonkian, Iroquoian, and Siouan, and perhaps also of Penutian. It is an areal trait of the Great Basin, the Plains, and the Northeast.

(5) Prefixation of person markers to nouns and verbs is absent in the Arctic. Elsewhere it occurs as follows:

Subarctic: all Athabaskan and Algonkian.

Northwest: (Pen.) Lower Chinook, Alsea, Siuslaw, Coos, Takelma; and perhaps in Coast Salishan.

Plateau: Kutenai; all Salishan; (Pen.) Nez Perce, Sahaptin [proclitics loosely connected to almost any word], Upper Chinook.

California: (Algic) Wiyot [nouns only], Yurok; all Athabaskan; (Yukian) Yuki [inalienable nouns only], Wappo; (Hokan) Karok, Chimariko [inalienable nouns and active verbs], Achomawi and Atsugewi [verbs], Yana, Pomoan [inalienable nouns], Salinan, Chumashan, Yuman [Dieguéño]; (Pen.) Maidun [nouns]; (U.A.) Luiseño, Cupeño, Cahuilla.

Southwest: (U.A.) Hopi [nouns], Papago; (Yuman) Walapai [verbs], Yuma; (Ath.) all Apachean; (Keresan) Acoma; (Tanoan) Taos; and Coahuiltec.

Great Basin: (Hokan) Washo. The Uto-Aztecan languages, apart from marking person by independent pronouns (trait 7, below), also have shortened, clitic pronoun forms — loosely prefixed in Northern Paiute and Shoshoni, loosely suffixed in Southern Paiute.

Plains: Athabaskan; all Algonkian; all Siouan; and Kiowa. In Pawnee (and perhaps other Caddoan), person markers are prefixed at least to verbs. In Tonkawa they are prefixed to some kin terms.

Southeast: Iroquoian; Yuchi; Muskogean [verbs]; Tunica [nouns and static verbs]; Natchez [verbs]; and Siouan (most comprehensively in Tutelo).

Northeast: all Iroquoian and Algonkian.

Overview: Prefixation of person markers is a family trait of Athabaskan, Penutian, Hokan, Uto-Aztecan, Siouan, Iroquoian, and Algonkian. It is an areal feature of North America in general, except for its absence in the Arctic and its limited distribution in the Northwest. It is interesting to note the apparent spread of the feature from Penutian to other languages in the Plateau, as compared with its restriction to Penutian in the Northwest; this suggests different historical roles of the Penutians in the two areas.

(6) <u>Suffixation of person markers</u> to nouns and verbs is found in all areas, as follows:

Arctic: Eskimo.

Subarctic: Algonkian [verbs].

Northwest: (Pen.) Tsimshian [nouns, static verbs], Alsea, Siuslaw, Coos [verbs], Takelma; all Wakashan, Chemakuan and Salishan.

Plateau: Kutenai [nouns in 2nd and 3rd persons]; Salishan; (Pen.) Sahaptin [enclitics], Nez Perce [suffixation to particles].

California: (Algic) Yurok [verbs], Wiyot [verbs]; (Hokan) Karok [verbs], Chimariko [alienable nouns, static verbs], Atsugewi [verbs], Yana, Salinan, Chumashan [verbs]; (Pen.) Northern Maidu [verbs], Wintun [verbs], Sierra Miwok; (U.A.) Tübatulabal.

Southwest: (U.A.) Hopi [verbs], Papago [3sg. marker on nouns]; (Yuman) Walapai [nouns].

Great Basin: (U. A.) Southern Paiute, in the form of enclitics (cf. trait 5, above).

Plains: Algonkian; Tonkawa [verbs].

Southeast: (Siouan) Biloxi, Catawba, and Ofo [suffixes on inalienable nouns]; Muskogean [verbs]; Tunica [active verbs]; Natchez [nouns]; Chitimacha [verbs]; and Atakapa [verbs].

Northeast: Algonkian [verbs].

Overview: Suffixation of person markers is a family trait of Salishan, Algonkian (in verbs), probably of Hokan, and perhaps of Penutian. It is an areal trait of the Northwest-Plateau complex, of California, and of the Southeast.

(7) Marking of person by independent pronouns, as opposed to affixes, is absent in the Arctic, Subarctic, and Northeast. Elsewhere it occurs as follows:

Northwest: (Chemakuan) Quileute [for some modes of verbs].

Plateau: (Pen.) Nez Perce [nouns], Sahaptin [nouns], Klamath.

California: Yuki (verbs and alienable nouns); (Hokan) Achomawi [nouns], Pomoan (verbs and alienable nouns), Esselen: (Pen.) Southern Maidu [verbs], Wintun [nouns], Western Miwok, Costanoan, Yokuts; (U. A.) Tübatulabal [verbs], Luiseño [enclitics, referring to verbs, are attached to the first word in the sentence].

Southwest: Zuni.

Great Basin: Uto-Aztecan (but see also traits 5-6, above).

Plains: Tonkawa.

Southeast: Muskogean, Natchez, Chitimacha, and Atakapa [for nouns, in all these languages].

Overview: Marking of person by independent pronouns is perhaps a family trait of Penutian (in the Plateau and California, but mysteriously missing in Penutian languages of the Northwest). The areal distribution in the Southeast may be ascribed either to diffusion or to the putative "Gulf" genetic unity.

(8) An overtly marked case system for nouns is absent in the Subarctic and Northeast. It occurs in the following areas:

Arctic: Eskimo.

Northwest: (Pen.) Siuslaw, Coos.

Plateau: (Pen.) Nez Perce, Sahaptin, Klamath.

California: Yukian; (Hokan) Achomawi, Esselen, Yuman [Diegueño]; (Pen.) Maidun, Wintun, Miwokan, Costanoan, Yokuts; (U. A.) Tübatulabal, Luiseño, Cupeño, Cahuilla.

Southwest: (U. A.) Hopi; (Hokan) Yumàn; and Coahuiltec.

Great Basin: all Uto-Aztecan.

Plains: (Siouan) Ponca dialect of Dhegiha [nominative vs. accusative]; Tonkawa (a 7-case system).

Southeast: Tunica; (Siouan) Biloxi.

Overview: Nominal case is a family trait of Penutian, Yuman, and Uto-Aztecan. It seems to show some areal spread in California.

(9) Distinction of alienable vs. inalienable possession — sometimes by the rule that inalienably possessed nouns can only occur in possessed form, sometimes by different morphological treatment of the two types of possession — occurs in all areas, as follows:

Arctic: Eskimo requires inalienable nouns to occur in possessed form only.

Subarctic: Athabaskan and Algonkian also have inalienable nouns in possessed form only.

Northwest: (Na-Dené) Eyak, Tlingit, Haida, all Athabaskan; (Pen.) Tsimshian, Lower Chinook, Siuslaw, Coos, Takelma; all Wakashan, Chemukuan, and Salishan.

Plateau: Kutenai; (Pen.) Upper Chinook, Sahaptin, Nez Perce. The trait has not been reported for Salishan languages of the Plateau.

California: Algic; Yukian; (Hokan) Chimariko, Pomoan, Chumashan, Yuman [Dieguaño]; (Pen.) Maidun, Sierra Miwok, Costanoan; (U. A.) Tübatulabal, Luiseño.

Southwest: (U. A.) Papago, Hopi; (Hokan) Yuman; (Ath.) Apachean; Zuni; and Keresan.

Great Basin: (Hokan) Washo; all Uto-Aztecan.

Plains: Athabaskan; Algonkian; Siouan; Tonkawa.

Southeast: (Iroq.) Cherokee; Siouan; Yuchi; Muskogean; Tunica; Chitimacha.

Northeast: all Algonkian and Iroquoian.

Overview: The alienable/inalienable distinction is a family trait of Athabaskan, Penutian, Uto-Aztecan, Algonkian, Siouan, Iroquoian, and perhaps of Hokan. It is an areal trait of the Subarctic, the Northwest, the Southwest, the Plains, the Southeast, and the Northeast. Its wide, though scattered, distribution suggests a greater degree of geographical consolidation at an earlier date.

(10) Instrumental prefixes in the verb system, expressing the instrument by which an action is performed, do not occur in the Arctic, Subarctic, Southwest, or Northeast. They are found in the following areas:

Northwest: (Na-Dené) Tlingit, Haida; (Pen.) Takelma.

Plateau: (Pen.) Sahaptin and Klamath [in remnant form].

California: (Yukian) Wappo; (Hokan) Karok [remnants], Chimariko, Shastan, Pomoan, Yuman [Diegueño]; (Pen.) Maidun, Miwokan
[traces].

Great Basin: (Hokan) Washo; all Uto-Aztecan.

Plains: Siouan; Tonkawa [in remnant form].

Southeast: Siouan (except Catawba).

Overview: Instrumental prefixes are a family trait of Siouan,
and, in a less pronounced way, of Hokan; they are an areal trait of
the Great Basin. Since this trait is apparently an unusual one in languages of the world, its scattered distribution in North America suggests greater geographical concentration at an earlier period.

(11) Locative-directional markers in the verb system, indicating place or direction of action, are not reported for the Arctic,
but occur in other areas as follows:

Subarctic: all Athabaskan. The Algonkian languages of the
area indicate location and direction by preverbal particles.

Northwest: (Na-Dené) Tlingit, Haida, all Athabaskan; (Pen.)
Tsimshian, Lower Chinook, Alsea, Takelma; all Wakashan and Salishan.

Plateau: all Salishan; (Pen.) Nez Perce, Sahaptin, Upper
Chinook, Klamath.

California: Athabaskan; Yukian; (Hokan) Karok, Chimariko,
Shasta, Achomawi, Yana, Pomoan, Chumashan, Yuman [Diegueño];
(Pen.) Maidu; (U.A.) Tübatulabal.

Southwest: (U.A.) Papago; (Hokan) Yuman; and (Ath.) Apachean.

Great Basin: (Hokan) Washo; Uto-Aztecan.

Plains: all Algonkian and Siouan; (Caddoan) Pawnee; (Ath.) Kiowa-Apache; Tonkawa.

Southeast: (Siouan) Catawba; (Iroq.) Cherokee; Yuchi; Muskogean; Tunica; Natchez; Chitimacha; Atakapa.

Northeast: Iroquoian [translocative and cislocative prefixes].

Overview: Locative-directional marking in the verb is a family trait of Na-Dené (including Athabaskan), Salishan, Hokan, Siouan, Iroquoian, and perhaps of Uto-Aztecan. It is an areal trait of the Northwest-Plateau complex, the Plains, and the Southeast. The fact that it is reported for only one California Penutian language suggests that its presence in Northwest and Plateau Penutian is due to diffusional spread in those areas.

(12) Numeral classifiers, used to count nouns in different ways according to their form and shape, are not reported for the Arctic, Southwest, Great Basin, or Southeast. The areas in which they do occur are:

Subarctic: (Alg.) Ojibwa has a fairly complex numeral classifier system.

Northwest: (Na-Dené) Tlingit; (Pen.) Tsimshian, Lower Chinook [counting humans]; all Wakashan, Chemakuan, and Salishan.

Plateau: Salishan. In (Pen.) Nez Perce, Sahaptin, and Upper Chinook, humans and non-humans are distinguished in counting.

California: Algic; (Hokan) Karok [only for counting humans]. In nearby (Ath.) Hupa, numerals for counting humans and non-humans are distinct.

Plains: (Alg.) Plains Ojibwa, like the Subarctic dialects, has a complex system.

Northeast: (Alg.) Menomini and Potawatomi have rather simple systems of numeral classifiers.

Overview: Numeral classifiers are a family trait of Salishan, and perhaps of Algic (more widespread in earlier times?).
They are an areal trait of the Northwest-Plateau complex, with an
apparent extension into northwestern California. But scattered languages elsewhere have separate ways of counting humans vs. non-
humans (e.g. Washo, Blackfoot), which should perhaps be considered
a separate trait.

4.3 Discussion

It is apparent that the geographical distribution of many linguistic features cuts across genetic boundaries; insofar as these features are relatively rare or highly marked, they provide evidence for
prehistoric diffusion. In some cases, the areal spread of linguistic
features also cuts across the boundaries of culture areas; such data
suggest shared linguistic history at a time before the culture areas
had their present constitution, and provide evidence for prehistoric
migrations between culture areas. Let us review some of the relevant materials:

(1) In the Southwest-Great Basin complex, voiceless vowels
occur in all the Uto-Aztecan languages, and in some other languages,
Zuni and Keresan, which are not now immediate neighbors to the Uto-
Aztecans. It seems unlikely that vowel devoicing is to be reconstructed
for Proto-Uto-Aztecan (Pima-Papago has it, but close relatives in
northwestern Mexico do not); rather, voiceless vowels seem to have
spread as a strictly areal feature. A plausible hypothesis is that the
direction of spread was between particular Uto-Aztecan languages and
Zuni and Keresan, at a time when they still formed part of a continuous linguistic area. A considerable time depth seems indicated for
this contact.

(2) The existence of incomplete labial series shows little
areal spread, being mainly a family trait of Na-Dené and of Iroquoian.
However, the absence of labial stops in two Caddoan languages of the
southern Plains suggest two possibilities: (a) this feature may be a
family trait of a Caddoan-Iroquoian genetic grouping which some
writers have proposed; or (b) Caddoan and Iroquoian may have been
areally linked at some period, and later separated by migration.

(3) Among areal traits of the Northwest, several are family traits of Na-Dené: e.g., glottalized stops; the k/kᵂ distinction; the s/š distinction; the presence of ḻ, ɫ, λ, and λ'; the distinction of alienable vs. inalienable possession; and locative-directional markers. These facts suggest that Na-Dené languages, specifically Tlingit and Haida, may have once been an important center of diffusion in the Northwest culture area.

(4) The striking absence of reduplication in Athabaskan, though most other languages of western North America have the feature, may be correlated with the relatively recent geographical spread of Athabaskan, as suggested in 4.2(1). The same absence in the other Na-Dené languages, Tlingit and Haida, which are not thought to be recent arrivals in the Northwest, perhaps indicates that these languages were primarily centers from which diffusion took place (see preceding paragraph), rather than receivers of diffused features.

(5) As noted in 4.2(3), the pronominal dual exists in most Penutian languages of the Northwest-Plateau complex, but not in other languages of that area; on the other hand, prefixation of person markers (4.2(5)) has apparently spread from Penutian to other languages in the Plateau, while remaining limited to Penutian in the Northwest. These data suggest that the Penutian speakers were primarily receivers, rather than spreaders, of diffused features, but that their role was less passive in the Plateau than in the Northwest.

(6) Several linguistic features which are rather highly marked have a wide-spread but discontinuous distribution in North America; examples are consonantal symbolism, the pronominal dual, the distinction of alienable versus inalienable possession, and the presence of instrumental prefixes in the verb system. Such facts suggest an earlier shared history, whether genetic or diffusional, of the languages concerned; e.g., the presence of instrumental prefixes in Siouan and in Hokan may derive from a Hokan-Siouan genetic unity, as Sapir thought, or it may reflect the participation of Hokan and Siouan in some prehistoric linguistic area, though we can say little about the location.

As these examples show, the study of areal-linguistic phenomena in aboriginal North America can be a means of formulating reasonable hypotheses about the linguistic prehistory of the continent.

Of course, no single hypothesis so arrived at can be ascribed any strong degree of validity. But the juxtaposition of such hypotheses with each other, and with hypotheses derived from other sources such as archaeology and oral literature, will be an important method in the reconstruction of American Indian history.

5. Conclusions

To summarize what has been said above:

(1) North American Indian languages, taken as a group, are as diverse as any such large number of languages might be expected to be. Yet similarities are found, spanning large numbers of languages and great distances. Many of these can be explained as due to common descent within genetic families; but other such similarities can only be explained as due to diffusion, i.e. borrowing.

(2) In the attempt to trace American Indian linguistic prehistory, many scholars have concentrated on genetic relationship. But as Boas emphasized in his time, and as is now being increasingly realized, diffusion is as important a part of language change as common descent. The linguistic area, defined by the distribution of linguistic features — either in complexes, or individually — thus becomes a concept as important as the linguistic family.

(3) It has been shown that similarities in phonological or grammatical structure, which some writers have held to reflect common descent rather than borrowing, have clearly been borrowed in many parts of the world. We must conclude that structural borrowing also occurred in North American linguistic prehistory, and that features of shared structure properly define linguistic areas.

(4) If we take culturally defined areas of North America as our point of departure, e.g. the Pacific Northwest and the Plains, we find that some — notably the Northwest — display many similar features of linguistic structure which crosscut genetic lines; a close-knit linguistic area, defined in terms of this complex of features, may be recognized. By contrast, the Plains shows little such linguistic diffusion, and thus does not constitute a well-defined linguistic area. These facts correlate well with the differing communicative characteristics of these culture areas.

(5) Taking a different viewpoint, and using the distribution of the single linguistic feature as our point of departure, we may map the linguistic area (usually discontinuous) defined by it. Such areas correlate only in part with culture areas; where they do not, they suggest genetic and diffusional relationships on more remote historical levels.

(6) The light which is shed by areal studies on linguistic prehistory is also useful for the study of cultural history. In several cases, e.g., the apparent direction of linguistic borrowing permits inferences about the nature of the contact between societies.

For further research, we need more descriptive data, more historical reconstructions, and more sociolinguistic study of North American Indian languages. The areal groupings which we seek to identify, however, are not to be regarded as ends in themselves, nor as units opposed to those of genetic classification. Rather than simply classifying languages or linguistic features, our aim is to learn what happened in aboriginal American history.

NOTES

Bright's work on this article was made possible by a fellowship from the Guggenheim Foundation, which is gratefully acknowledged. We are grateful for the help of Geraldine Anderson, Richard Bauman, Lawrence Foley, Ives Goddard, Mary R. Haas, Dell Hymes, William H. Jacobsen Jr., Michael Krauss, Pamela Munro, Bruce Rigsby, Michael Silverstein, and Rudolph C. Troike.
[1] Data are drawn mainly from the sources cited in Sherzer 1968. Features have been chosen, on the one hand, to point up cases of apparent diffusional history, and on the other hand, to correlate with general concerns for language typology. Our features are more 'surface' than 'deep', which reflects the nature of our data sources; however, it seems clear that the 'surface' nature of a feature is no hindrance to its diffusion.
      The geographical distribution of the features discussed, and of the languages and genetic groupings mentioned, can be best appreciated if this section is read with a linguistic map of aboriginal North America before one. That of Voegelin & Voegelin 1966 is suggested.

[2] The following abbreviations are used for language families:
Alg[onkian], Ath[abaskan], Iroq[uoian], Musk[ogean], Pen[utian], and
U[to-]A[ztecan].

REFERENCES

Boas, Franz
  1896. The growth of Indian mythologies. Journal of American
    Folklore 9.1-11.
  1920. The classification of American languages. American
    Anthropologist 22.367-376.
Bright, Jane O., and William Bright
  1965. Semantic structures in Northwestern California and
    the Sapir-Whorf Hypothesis. Pp. 249-258 in Formal
    semantic analysis, ed. by Eugene Hammel. American
    Anthropologist Special Publication, 67 (5) Pt. 2. [In
    this volume, pp. 74-88.]
Driver, Harold E.
  1961. Indians of North America. Chicago: University of
    Chicago Press.
Emeneau, Murray B.
  1956. India as a linguistic area. Language 32.3-16.
  1962. Bilingualism and structural borrowing. Proceedings
    of the American Philosophical Society 106.430-432.
Gumperz, John J.
  1967. On the linguistic markers of bilingual communication.
    Journal of Social Issues 23.48-57.
Haas, Mary R.
  1967. Language and taxonomy in Northwestern California.
    American Anthropologist 69.358-392.
  1969. The prehistory of languages. The Hague: Mouton.
Pandit, P. B.
  1972. India as a sociolinguistic area. Poona: University of
    Poona.
Sapir, Edward
  1921. Language. New York: Harcourt Brace.
Sherzer, Joel
  1965. An areal-typological study of the American Indian
    languages north of Mexico. Philadelphia: University of
    Pennsylvania dissertation. (Now published by North-
    Holland Publ. Co., Amsterdam, 1976.)

1973. Areal linguistics in North America. Pp. 749–795 in
        Current trends in linguistics, vol. 10: Linguistics in
        North America, ed. by Thomas A. Sebeok et al. The
        Hague: Mouton.

Sjoberg, Andrée, and Gideon Sjoberg
        1956. Culture as a significant variable in linguistic change.
        American Anthropologist 58.296–300.

Voegelin, C. F., and F. M. Voegelin
        1966. Map of North American languages. Seattle, Washing-
        ton: American Ethnological Society.

Weinreich, Uriel; William Labov; and Marvin L. Herzog
        1968. Empirical foundations for a theory of language change.
        Pp. 95–188 in Directions for historical linguistics, ed.
        by W. P. Lehmann and Yakov Malkiel. Austin: Univer-
        sity of Texas Press.

Author's Postscript

I am grateful to Anwar Dil for the keen judgment and sympathetic understanding which he has brought to the preparation of the present volume, and for giving me the opportunity to add this postscript. I would like to use the space to expand in certain ways on Dr. Dil's Introduction—to focus on certain themes which have been important for my work, to thank some people who have been especially helpful to me, and to entertain some speculations about the future. I will not attempt to be especially objective or impersonal; for me, scholarship is interesting to just the extent that it derives from the richness of individual experience, and permits us to renew connection with that experience in an even richer way.

I never had much formal training in anthropology, but I had the good fortune to be trained by two students of Edward Sapir's — Murray Emeneau and Mary Haas. I later had the further good fortune to work as a junior colleague of still another student of Sapir's — Harry Hoijer, whose death we are still mourning as I write this. In fact, I think of Hoijer as the scholar who, more than anyone else, preserved the spirit of Sapir's work through four decades of change in linguistic fashion. That spirit will, I believe, be as relevant in linguistics of the future as it has been in the past, and the full debt that we owe to Hoijer will become more obvious as time goes on.

What do I mean by "the spirit of Sapir's work"? Essentially, it is the spirit which inspires the best in linguistic anthropology and anthropological linguistics. It embraces, on one hand, the most basic kind of field work—sitting on the ground in the summer heat of a desert Indian reservation, equipped only with pencil, notebook and human

empathy —and, on the other hand, the generation of the most imagina-
tive hypotheses —intuitively based, but explicity stated —about the
nature of human communication. It is a spirit which recognizes no
arbitrary limitations on the study of language —which seeks out links
in ethnology, sociology, psychology, or any other human science, and
pursues them as far as they may go. It is a spirit which recognizes
language as having multiple functions: not only to convey information,
but to express social attitudes and affiliations, emotional states, and
aesthetic impulses. It is, perhaps most importantly, a spirit which
finds endless fascination in the attempt to understand exactly what is
happening when one individual communicates with another, and which
recognizes MAN as the measure of linguistic research.

In the late 1940's and early 1950's, when I was a student, it
was of course the anti-mentalist, neo-Bloomfieldian school which dominated American linguistics; but at Berkeley, fortunately for me, the
loaf was leavened by what I have called the spirit of Sapir. In subsequent years, linguistic and anthropological fashions took strange turns.
In linguistics, the generative-transformational revolution embraced
the concept of mentalism, but tended to view human speakers as ab-
stractions, devoid of cultural or social characteristics, and for years
it allowed semantics only a subordinate place. At the same time,
anthropologists of the 1960's began to apply linguistic methods to the
analysis of culture as a semantic system —but, unfortunately, their
methods were often ones which had already become discredited among
linguists, and they fell far short of revolutionary ethnography. Most
recently, however, there are encouraging developments in both fields.
In linguistics, semantics is fully established at last; pragmatics is
increasingly acknolwedged as a crucial area of study; and empirical
linguistcs is moving from the phonetics laboratory into all areas. In
anthropology, more and more interesting work is being done in what
Dell Hymes has inspired us to call the ethnography of communication —
an area which can be seen as a kind of empirical, field-work-based,
cross-cultural pragmatics. One may even begin to hope that increasing
coöperation between linguists and anthropologists will bring the two
fields as close together again as they were in the work of Sapir.

Another aspect of my training was that Mary Haas was my
teacher both for American Indian linguistics and for Thai, while Murray

Emeneau introduced me to Sanskrit and Dravidian; thus I began a career divided between American and Asian languages, like that of Haas herself (and other distinguished names such as Leonard Bloomfield, Fang-Kuei Li, and Charles Hockett). After my dissertation research on a native American language, I worked for two years in India; but on returning to California, resumed my Americanist interests —and so it has gone ever since. I feel this has been a lucky combination for me in two ways. The first of these is largely personal: I find things in Asian and native American philosophies which seem especially compatible with each other, and especially valuable for my life. I am grateful to my friend Gary Snyder, the poet, who has helped me to realize this.

The second way in which the American-Asian connection has been important for me is reflected in my recent views on language history, as reflected in the article co-authored with Joel Sherzer in this volume. My first work in American Indian historical linguistics was on comparative Hokan —a search for rather remote genetic relationships, with no historical documents to aid one's exploration of the past. Moving then to the South Asian area, I met with a sharp contrast: in both the Indo-Aryan and Dravidian families, the historical relationships were clear, and evidenced by centuries of documentation. But more than that: South Asia was an area where the phenomena of language contact and linguistic area were impossible to ignore, as demonstrated in Emeneau's classic paper on "India as a linguistic area" (1956). And it was also an area where the sociolinguistic phenomena of language variation were impossible to ignore. One day in 1956, in Poona, a conversation with John Gumperz inspired me to explore the role of these sociolinguistic phenomena in language history. At that time, it did not occur to me that similar phenomena might have operated in the history of native American languages; but now I believe that language variation and language contact are crucial for all historical linguistics.

The South Asian data are especially valuable because they give us a long record of interaction between two linguistic families, Indo-Aryan and Dravidian, which were quite distinct at the outset, but have progressively grown more alike through two-way processes of borrowing, affecting every part of linguistic structure. The lesson seems clear to me: in languages of native America or anywhere else, we cannot successfully explain structural resemblances solely in terms of common genetic origin. Structural diffusion must be recognized as an equally important factor in language history.

In his Introduction, Anwar Dil hints at another kind of relationship between my Asian and American studies, which I would now like to make more explicit. Anyone who studies the linguistic history of South Asia will be struck by the tremendous extent of lexical and structural borrowing between Indo-Aryan and Dravidian. Why should borrowing have gone so much further here than in many other parts of the world? I believe the answer can only be found in the socio-cultural context—specifically in what I will call the ACCOMMODATIVE spirit of South Asian culture, often commented on by scholars, in which many different religious and social systems have been subsumed over the course of history. In native North America, the same accommodative spirit facilitated the relatively large amount of borrowing from Spanish in the languages of Southern California, as well as the formation of a linguistic area in the Pacific Northwest. The opposite type of socio-cultural influence, which we might call the SEPARATIST spirit, is illustrated in the contact between English and the native languages of Northern California (and, indeed, most American Indian languages): the usual result is that the language of the socially subordinate group is simply replaced. There is, then, an implication for language planning: languages survive better in a setting where linguistic and cultural diversity is encouraged.

I want finally to say a few words about the editorial work which, in the past ten years, has occupied so much of my attention. I enjoy this job: it puts me in touch with linguists of every type, in every part of the world; it keep me abreast with the most stimulating new developments in linguistic thought; it gives me the satisfaction of helping my colleagues to disseminate their ideas in widely readable form; and it lets me have the great fun of dealing with types and printing and publishing. I want to give thanks to a number of people who helped me reach this position: to Verna Bloom, who gave me my first editing experience, on high-school publications; to the U.S. Army, which gave me a job editing intelligence reports; to Mary Haas, who taught me how to work with linguistic manuscripts; to Harry Hoijer, who recommended me to succeed him as Review Editor of <u>IJAL</u>; to Robert Stockwell, who proposed me for the editorship of <u>Language</u> and has backed me up in many ways ever since; and to Vicki Fromkin, who has successively been my student, my colleague, and now my boss, and has given me the help I needed most, when I needed it most. Whatever contributions I may have made to linguistics through teaching and research, I take a special pleasure in what I am able to contribute as an editor, and hope that the history of our field will show my efforts to have been useful.

Bibliography of William Bright's Works

Compiled by Anwar S. Dil

List of Abbreviations:

AA	American Anthropologist
DCMS	Deccan College Monograph Series
IJAL	International Journal of American Linguistics
IL	Indian Linguistics
ILMS	Indian Linguistics Monograph Series
JAF	Journal of American Folklore
JAOS	Journal of American Oriental Society
Lg	Language
RPh	Romance Philology
UCPL	University of California Publications in Linguistics

1952 a. Linguistic innovations in Karok. IJAL 18.53-62. [In this volume, pp. 99-116]
     b. Some place names on the Klamath River. Western Folklore 11.121-22.

1954 a. Some Northern Hokan relationships. UCPL 10.63-67.
     b. The travels of Coyote, a Karok myth. Kroeber Anthropological Society Papers 11.1-16. [Reprinted as 'Karok Coyote stories' in The American Indian reader: Literature, ed. by J. Henry, pp. 79-91. San Francisco: Indian Historian Press, 1973.]

1955   A bibliography of the Hokan-Coahuiltecan languages. IJAL 21.276-85.

1956 a. Glottochronologic counts of Hokaltecan material. Lg 32.
          42–48.
      b. Review of Kolami, by M. B. Emeneau. Lg 32.390–95.

1957 a. The Karok language. UCPL 13. 458 p.
      b. Singing in Lushai. IL 17.24–28.
      c. Alternations in Lushai. IL 18.101–10.

1958 a. An outline of colloquial Kannada. DCMS 22; ILMS 1. Poona,
          India: Deccan College. 75 p.
      b. (With S. A. Khan). The Urdu writing system. New York:
          American Council on Learned Societies. 48 p.
      c. Karok names. Names 6.172–79.
      d. A note on visarga. Bulletin of Deccan College 18.271–73.
      e. Review of Proto-Mixtecan, by R. E. Longacre. Lg 34.
          164–67.

1959 a. Spelling for foreign students of English. Berkeley: Califor-
          nia Book Co. 86 p.
      b. (With D. L. Olmsted). A Shasta vocabulary. Kroeber Anthro-
          pological Society Papers 20.1–55.
      c. (With E. Bright). Spanish words in Patwin. RPh 13.161–64.
          [In this volume, pp. 117–21.]
      d. Review of The Yurok language, by R. H. Robins. Lg 35.
          100–04.

1960 a. (With S. Rau and M. Narvekar). Spoken Kannada. Berkeley:
          Center for South Asian Studies, University of California.
          184 p.
      b. Animals of acculturation in the California Indian languages.
          UCPL 4:4. 25 p. [In this volume, pp. 122–63.]
      c. Linguistic change in some Indian caste dialects. Linguistic
          diversity in South Asia, ed. by C. A. Ferguson and J. J.
          Gumperz, 19–26. IJAL 26:3, Part 3 [= Publication 13 of
          the Indiana University Research Center in Anthropology,
          Folklore and Linguistics.] [Kannada version: Maisūru kan-
          naḍada sāmājika bhāṣaprahēdagaḷu, in Prabuddha Karṇāṭaka
          (India), 1963, pp. 17–26.] [In this volume, pp. 39–46.]
      d. Post-basic training in South Asian languages. Resources for
          South Asian language studies in the United States, ed. by

W. Norman Brown, 26-31. Philadelphia: University of
Pennsylvania Press.

e. Bhāratīya bhāṣāõ mẽ mahāprāṇ vyanjan ("Aspirated consonants in the languages of India.") Hindī Anuśīlan (Allahabad)
[Dhirendra Varma commemoration volume] 13.16-20.

f. Social dialect and language history. Current Anthropology 1.
424-25. [Reprinted in Language in culture and society, ed.
by Dell Hymes, pp. 469-72. New York: Harper and Row,
1964.] [Portuguese version: Dialeto social e história da lin-
guagem, in Sociolingüística, ed. by M. S. V. Fonseca and
M. F. Neves, pp. 41-47. Rio de Janeiro: Eldorado, 1974.]
[In this volume, pp. 32-38.]

g. A study of caste and dialect in Mysore. IL 21.45-50.
[Almost = 1960c]

h. 'Accent' in classical Aztec. IJAL 26.66-68.

i. A note on the Southwestern words for cat. IJAL 26.167-68.

j. Review of Les Khyang des Collines de Chittagong, by D. and
L. Bernot. Lg 36.184-86.

k. Review of Turner jubilee volume, I-II. IJAL 26.354-56.

1961 a. Diversity and basic forms. Te. Po. Mī. Maṇiviṟā Malar
(Coimbatore, India) [T. P. Meenakshisundaram commemoration volume], 389-95.

b. Review of Diccionario histórico de la lengua Española, fasc.
1. IJAL 27.74-76.

c. Review of Crow texts and Crow word lists, by R. Lowie.
IJAL 27.268-70.

d. Review of Versuch einer historischen Lautlehre der Kharia-
Sprache, by H. J. Pinnow. AA 63.451-52.

e. Abstracts and translations: Latin American publications.
IJAL 27.156-60.

f. Abstracts and translations: Latin American, Anglo-American, and European publications. IJAL 27.251-55, 258-59.

1962 a. (With A. K. Ramanujan). Tamil phonemics. Chicago, Illinois: Committee on Southern Asian Studies, University of
Chicago. 27 p. (Mimeographed)

b. (With A. K. Ramanujan). A study of Tamil dialects. Chicago, Illinois: Committee on Southern Asian Studies, University of Chicago. 65 p. (Mimeographed)

    c. Review of <u>Arizona place names</u>, by Will Barnes, 2nd ed.
       <u>JAF</u> 75.77-78.

    d. Review of <u>California place names</u>, by E. G. Gudde, 2nd ed.
       <u>JAF</u> 75.78-82.

    e. Abstracts and translations: Latin American publications.
       <u>IJAL</u> 28.119-21.

    f. Abstracts and translations: Latin American publications.
       <u>IJAL</u> 28.199-205.

1963 a. Language. <u>Biennial review of anthropology 1963</u>, ed. by
       Bernard J. Siegel, 1-29. Stanford, California: Stanford
       University Press.

    b. Language and music: areas of cooperation. <u>Ethnomusicol-
       ogy</u> 7.26-32. [French version: Points de contact entre lan-
       gage et musique, in <u>Musique en Jeu</u> 5.67-74 (Paris, 1971).]

    c. Review of <u>Publicações do Museu Nacional, Série lingüística
       especial</u>, No. 1. <u>IJAL</u> 29.79-81.

    d. Review of <u>Catálogo de las lenguas de América del Sur</u>, by
       Antonio Tovar. <u>Lg</u> 39.143-46.

    e. Abstracts and translations: Latin American publications.
       <u>IJAL</u> 39.143-46.

    f. Abstracts and translations: Latin American publications.
       <u>IJAL</u> 29.372-77.

1964 a. (Ed.). <u>Studies in Californian linguistics</u>. <u>UCPL</u> 34. ix, 238 p.

    b. (With A. K. Ramanujan). Sociolinguistic variation and lan-
       guage change. <u>Proceedings of the Ninth International Con-
       gress of Linguists</u>, ed. by H. Lunt, 1107-13. The Hague:
       Mouton. [In this volume, pp. 47-58.]

    c. A bibliography of the publications of Harry Hoijer through
       1963. <u>IJAL</u> 30.169-74.

    d. Review of <u>A functional view of language</u>, by André Martinet.
       <u>AA</u> 66.203-05.

    e. Abstracts and translations: Latin American publications.
       <u>IJAL</u> 30.83-87.

    f. Abstracts and translations: Publications on anthropological
       linguistics. <u>IJAL</u> 30.178-84.

    g. Abstracts and translations: Publications of the Summer
       Institute of Linguistics. <u>IJAL</u> 30.291-97.

h. Abstracts and translations: Publications on Latin American languages. IJAL 30.397-404.

i. Dravidian languages. Encyclopaedia International 6.109.

1965 a. (With R. A. Thiel). Hispanisms in a modern Aztec dialect. RPh 18.444-52.

b. The history of the Cahuilla sound system. IJAL 31.241-44.

c. Luiseño phonemics. IJAL 31.342-45.

d. (With J. O. Bright). Semantic structures in Northwestern California and the Sapir-Whorf Hypothesis. Formal semantic analysis, ed. by Eugene Hammel, AA (Special Publication) 67:5, Part 2.249-58. [Reprinted in Cognitive anthropology, ed. by S. A. Tyler (New York, Holt, 1969), pp. 66-78.] [In this volume, pp. 74-88.]

e. A field guide to Southern California Indian languages. UCLA Archaeological Survey, Annual Report, 7.393-407.

f. Linguistics. Handbook of Latin American studies 27.152-62. Gainesville: University of Florida Press.

g. (With H. Hoijer and E. P. Hamp). Contributions to a bibliography of comparative Amerindian. IJAL 31.346-53.

h. Review of Louisiana-French, by W. A. Read, revised edition. RPh 18.352-54.

i. Review of A history of Palaihnihan phonology, by D. L. Olmsted. Lg 41.175-78.

j. Review of Proceedings of the Ninth International Congress of Linguists, ed. by H. Lunt. IJAL 21.259-63.

k. Abstracts and translations: From U.S. publications; Books briefly noted. IJAL 31.247-49.

1966 a. (Ed.) Sociolinguistics; Proceedings of the UCLA Sociolinguistics Conference, 1964. The Hague: Mouton. [Introducduction: The dimensions of sociolinguistics, pp. 11-15.] [Spanish version: Las dimensiones de la sociolingüística, in Antología de Etnolingüística y Sociolingüística, ed. by P. L. Garvin and Y. Lastra de Suárez, pp. 147-202. México: UNAM, 1974. Portuguese version: As dimensões da sociolingüística, in Sociolingüística, ed. by M. S. V. Fonseca and M. F. Neves, pp. 17-23. Rio de Janeiro: Eldorado, 1974.] [In this volume, pp. 24-31.]

b. Dravidian metaphony. Lg 42.311–22.
c. Language, social stratification, and cognitive orientation. Explorations in sociolinguistics, ed. by Stanley Lieberson (Sociological Inquiry 36:2), pp. 313–8. [= Publication 44 of the Indiana University Research Center in Anthropology, Folklore, and Linguistics, 1967.] [Spanish version: Lengua, estratificación social y cognoscitiva, in Antología de Estudios de Etnolingüística y Sociolingüística, ed. by P. L. Garvin and Y. Lastra de Suárez, pp. 217–23. México: UNAM, 1974.] [In this volume pp. 59–66.]
d. Research on two American Indian languages of Northwestern California. Yearbook of the American Philosophical Society, 1965, pp. 487–8.
e. Review of Enciclopédia Bororo, vol. 1, by C. Albisetti and A. J. Venturelli. IJAL 32.81–2.
f. Review of Louisiana French grammar, by M. Conwell and A. Juilland. RPh 19.490–5.
g. Review of Kharia-Texte, by H. J. Pinnow. AA 68.806–7.
h. (With J. Minnick). Reduction rules in Fox kinship. Southwestern Journal of Anthropology 22.381–8. [In this volume, pp. 90–98.]

1967 a. (With Jane Hill). The linguistic history of the Cupeño. Studies in Southwestern ethnolinguistics, ed. by D. Hymes, pp. 351–71. The Hague: Mouton. [In this volume, pp. 164–88.]
b. The Cahuilla language. The ethnobotany of the Cahuilla Indians of Southern California (new edition), by D. P. Barrows, pp. xxi–xxix. Banning, California: Malki Museum.
c. Linguistics. Handbook of Latin American studies, 29.213–24. Gainesville: University of Florida Press.
d. Un vocabulario nahuatl del Estado de Tlaxcala. Estudios de Cultura Nahuatl 7.233–53.
e. Karok makkay < Scottish McKay. Names 15.79–80.
f. Nominalizations as verbal complements in English syntax. Bulletin of the Central Institute of English (Hyderabad, India) 6.1–12.
g. Review of New Mexico place names, by T. M. Pearce. Western Folklore 26.140–3.
h. Review of Boas, Powell, Pilling, Freeman. Lg 43.584–6.

1968 a. A Luiseño dictionary. UCPL 51. 88p.

   b. Language and culture. International Encyclopaedia of Social Sciences 9.18-22. New York: Crowell-Macmillan. [In this volume, pp. 1-11.]

   c. (With J. Lindenfeld). Complex verb forms in colloquial Tamil. Studies in Indian linguistics [Prof. M. B. Emeneau Saṣṭipūrti volume], ed. by Bh. Krishnamurti, pp. 30-45. Poona: Linguistic Society of India.

   d. Social dialect and semantic structure in South Asia. Structure and change in Indian society, ed. by B. Cohn and M. Singer [Viking Fund publication in anthropology 47], pp. 455-60. Chicago: Aldine Press. (Almost = 1966c.)

   e. Inventory of descriptive materials. Handbook of Middle American Indians, Vol. 5, Linguistics, ed. by N. A. McQuown, pp. 9-62. Austin: University of Texas Press.

   f. Language and culture in India. Milieu (Hyderabad, India) 2.154-8.

   g. Questions on the information problem in linguistics. Information in the language sciences, ed. by R. R. Freeman et al., pp. 53-5. New York: American Elsevier.

   h. Review of Uto-Aztecan cognate sets, by W. R. Miller. IJAL 34.56-9.

   i. Review of Census of India 1961, Language tables, by A. Mitra. Lg 44.684-7.

1969 a. Diversity and unity in languages of India. Language and society in India, ed. by A. Poddar, pp. 159-64. [Transactions of the Indian Institute of Advanced Study, Simla, Vol. 8.]

   b. (With Marcia Bright). Archaeology and linguistics in prehistoric Southern California. University of Hawaii Working Papers in Linguistics 1:10.1-26. [Revised version in this volume, pp. 189-205.]

   c. Review of Reader in the sociology of language, ed. by J. A. Fishman. AA 71.719-20.

   d. Review of Dravidian etymological dictionary, Supplement, by T. Burrow and M. B. Emeneau. Lg 45.680-3.

   e. Index to Language 41-45. Baltimore: Linguistic Society of America. 59 p.

1970 a. Phonological rules in literary and colloquial Kannada. JAOS
        90.140-4. [In this volume, pp. 67-75.]
     b. Toward a cultural grammar. IL 29.20-29. [In this volume,
        pp. 12-23.]
     c. On linguistic unrelatedness. IJAL 36.288-90. [In this vol-
        ume, pp. 206-9.]

1971 a. Language. Anthropology today: an introduction, pp. 409-19.
        Del Mar, California: CRM Books.
     b. Discussion of papers by Sjoberg and Emeneau. Symposium
        on Dravidian civilization, ed. by Andrée F. Sjoberg, pp.
        27-29, 69-71. Austin, Texas: Jenkins.
     c. Review of An introduction to Luiseño, by V. Hyde et al.
        The Indian Historian 4:2.22. [Reprinted in The American
        Indian reader: Education, ed. by J. Henry, pp. 197-8.
        San Francisco: Indian Historian Press, 1972.]

1972 a. The enunciative vowel. International Journal of Dravidian
        Linguistics 1.26-55.
     b. Hindi numerals. Studies in linguistics in honor of George L.
        Trager, ed. by M. E. Smith, pp. 222-30. The Hague:
        Mouton.
     c. Review of Man's many voices, by R. Burling. Language in
        Society 1.297-302.

1973 a. North American Indian language contact. Current trends in
        linguistics, 10: North America, ed. by T. A. Sebeok, pp.
        713-26. The Hague: Mouton. [In this volume, pp. 210-27.]
     b. Replies to comments on 'The enunciative vowel'. Interna-
        tional Journal of Dravidian Linguistics 2.55-63.
     c. Review of Barkur Kannada, by A. S. Acharya. Indo-Iranian
        Journal 15.236-73.

1974 a. North American Indian languages. Encyclopaedia Britannica,
        15th ed., 13.208-13.
     b. Index to Language 1-50 (1925-74). Baltimore: Linguistic
        Society of America. 215 p.
     c. Three extinct American Indian languages of Southern Cali-
        fornia. American Philosophical Society Year Book, pp. 573-
        4. Philadelphia: American Philosophical Society.

d. Review of <u>Newe natekwinappeh: Shoshoni stories and dic-</u><u>tionary</u>, by W. R. Miller. <u>AA</u> 76.167-8.

1975 a. The Alliklik mystery. <u>Journal of California Anthropology</u> 2.228-30.
b. The Dravidian enunciative vowel. <u>Dravidian phonological</u> <u>systems</u>, ed. by H. F. Schiffman and C. M. Eastman, 11-46. Seattle: South Asian Studies Program, University of Washington. (Revision of 1972a.)
c. Review of <u>CIIL phonetic reader series</u>, 1-4, ed. by H. S. Biligiri. <u>Indo-Iranian Journal</u> 16.232-8.

1976 a. (With Joel Sherzer). Areal features in North American Indian languages. [In this volume, pp. 228-68.]
b. Comments on Pattanayak's "Caste and language". <u>Inter-</u><u>national Journal of Dravidian Linguistics</u> 5.65-8.
c. Author's [William Bright's] postscript. In this volume, pp. 269-72.

Bright, William   1928-
        Variation and change in language:
essays by William Bright. Selected and
Introduced by Anwar S. Dil. Stanford, California:
Stanford University Press [1976]
        xvi, 282 p. 24cm.
(Language science and national development series,
Linguistic Research Group of Pakistan)
        Includes bibliography.
I. Dil, Anwar S. , 1928-   ed.
II. (Series) III. Linguistic Research Group of Pakistan